Palgrave Macmillan Memory Studies
Series Editors: **Andrew Hoskins** and **John** ⸻

The nascent field of Memory Studies e⸻
include a shift from concern with hist⸻
memory, from 'what we know' to 'how w⸻
memory; the rapid advance of technolc⸻
powers of memory, which mirror our fasc⸻
enhancement; and the development of tr⸻

These factors have contributed to an intensification of public discourses on our past over the last thirty years. Technological, political, interpersonal, social and cultural shifts affect what, how and why people and societies remember and forget. This groundbreaking series tackles questions such as: What is 'memory' under these conditions? What are its prospects, and also the prospects for its interdisciplinary and systematic study? What are the conceptual, theoretical and methodological tools for its investigation and illumination?

Evelyn B. Tribble and Nicholas Keene
COGNITIVE ECOLOGIES AND THE HISTORY OF REMEMBERING
Religion, Education and Memory in Early Modern England

Forthcoming titles:

Anne Fuchs
ICON DRESDEN
A Cultural Impact Study from 1945 to the Present

Owain Jones and Joanne Garde-Hansen (*editors*)
GEOGRAPHY AND MEMORY
Exploring Identity, Place and Becoming

Emily Keightley and Michael Pickering
CREATIVE MEMORY

J.Olaf Kleist and Irial Glynn (*editors*)
HISTORY, MEMORY AND MIGRATION
Perceptions of the Past and the Politics of Incorporation

Palgrave Macmillan Memory Studies
Series Standing Order ISBN 978–0–230–23851–0 (hardback)
978–0–230–23852–7 (paperback)
(*outside North America only*)

You can receive future titles in this series as they are published by placing a standing order. Please contact your bookseller or, in case of difficulty, write to us at the address below with your name and address, the title of the series and the ISBN quoted above.

Customer Services Department, Macmillan Distribution Ltd, Houndmills, Basingstoke, Hampshire RG21 6XS, England

Memory in Culture

Astrid Erll

Translated by Sara B. Young

Original German language edition: **Astrid Erll: Kollektives Gedächtnis und Erinnerungskulturen. Eine Einführung.** (ISBN: 978-3-476-01893-9) published by J.B Metzlersche Verlagsbuchhandlung und Carl Ernst Poeschel Verlag GmbH Stuttgart, Germany. Copyright © 2005

First published 2011 by
PALGRAVE MACMILLAN

Palgrave Macmillan in the UK is an imprint of Macmillan Publishers Limited, registered in England, company number 785998, of Houndmills, Basingstoke, Hampshire RG21 6XS.

Palgrave Macmillan in the US is a division of St Martin's Press LLC, 175 Fifth Avenue, New York, NY 10010.

Palgrave Macmillan is the global academic imprint of the above companies and has companies and representatives throughout the world.

Palgrave® and Macmillan® are registered trademarks in the United States, the United Kingdom, Europe and other countries.

ISBN 978–0–230–29744–9   hardback
ISBN 978–0–230–29745–6   paperback

This book is printed on paper suitable for recycling and made from fully managed and sustained forest sources. Logging, pulping and manufacturing processes are expected to conform to the environmental regulations of the country of origin.

A catalogue record for this book is available from the British Library.

Library of Congress Cataloging-in-Publication Data
Erll, Astrid.
[Kollektives Gedächtnis und Erinnerungskulturen. English]
Memory in culture/Astrid Erll; translated by Sara B. Young.
p. cm.
Includes bibliographical references and index.
ISBN 978–0–230–29745–6 (alk. paper)
1. Collective memory.   2. Culture.   3. Memory—Social aspects.   I. Title.
HM621.E7413 2011
306.01—dc23   2011016888

10   9   8   7   6   5   4   3   2   1
20   19   18   17   16   15   14   13   12   11

Printed and bound in Great Britain by
CPI Antony Rowe, Chippenham and Eastbourne

Contents

List of Tables and Figures

Tables

Figures

Acknowledgements

This book is the outcome of more than a decade of engagement with memory studies. It has emerged from my work on literary and media memories of the First World War, the Spanish Civil War, the Holocaust, Vietnam and the Gulf War, on the 'Indian Mutiny' and the mnemonic legacies of British colonialism, and, most recently, on the permutations of the Odysseus myth. The study of such diverse constellations of memory propelled me into very different academic quarters. Holocaust studies 'does' memory differently than colonial discourse studies, or gender studies. Literary theory has developed concepts of memory which may prove difficult to translate into sociology. Yet all these approaches feed into the reservoir of contemporary memory studies – a vast, heterogeneous, and constantly evolving research field, which has taken on a markedly international and interdisciplinary shape. This book was born out of the desire to record this richness and, by charting the concepts developed in disciplines as far apart as cultural history and the neurosciences, enable dialogue among memory researchers and provide access for those who are new to the field.

A first version of this book appeared in Germany in 2005. In the ensuing years, the field has already changed swiftly and profoundly. This English version, *Memory in Culture*, therefore not only represents the history of memory studies, with its main threads winding through the work of Maurice Halbwachs, Aby Warburg, Frances Yates, Endel Tulving, Pierre Nora, and many others, but it also considers the field's most recent developments, such as the growing interest in globalized remembrance and mediatized memories.

This book has benefited from a long-standing and fruitful exchange with many scholars, who will find their work acknowledged in the following chapters. I am particularly grateful to the colleagues who established and for 12 years fostered the 'Memory Cultures' research centre at Giessen University. My special thanks go to Ansgar Nünning, who was a trailblazer for literary studies' opening up towards cultural history and who supported me for many years with the greatest possible engagement and enthusiasm. In Stephanie Wodianka I found a most congenial colleague and enjoyable collaborator in many projects.

Memory in Culture could not have been translated without the financial support of Giessen University and its Research Prize in 2005.

Moreover, I am very grateful to the gender equality office at Wuppertal University which, with a generous endowment in 2009, facilitated a year of research leave.

The Netherlands Institute for Advanced Study (NIAS) gave me, as a Fellow-in-Residence in the academic year 2009/10, the possibility to thoroughly update and rewrite this book. It was also home to the 'Memory Studies Group', and I would like to thank all its members and guests for inspiring discussions. I am especially grateful to Anna-Maria Brandstetter, Julia Noordegraaf, Michael North, Pamela Pattynama, Judith Pollmann, and, above all, to Ann Rigney, whose sophisticated work on the dynamics of cultural memory I greatly admire and whose ongoing support I cannot overrate. I would also like to acknowledge my debt to Jeffrey Olick, whose publications are of vital importance for the shaping of contemporary memory studies and who tirelessly endorsed the adventure of translating my work into English.

I am glad that this book appears in the Palgrave Macmillan Memory Studies Series. This is doubtless the merit of Andrew Hoskins and his open-mindedness, indefatigable support and belief in this project. I am also grateful to Felicity Plester and Catherine Mitchell for a very pleasant collaboration.

The greatest debt I clearly owe to Sara B. Young, who put a tremendous amount of work and all her unmatched linguistic sophistication into this English translation of what was once in many ways a German book. In a complex process of translating and rewriting we have both begun to understand what it means to transcribe memory studies from one language and academic context into another. It is tremendously hard work. But it is the only way to begin a dialogue.

Frankfurt am Main, April 2011

I
Introduction: Why 'Memory'?

I.1 Why 'memory'?

Why indeed 'memory' – some people might ask themselves, wondering about the popularity of the term in current discourse. Why and how would one do research on memory in culture, as a literary scholar, historian, or sociologist? And what can we gain when we add to the existing repertoire of terms for the study of culture – mentalities, identities, ideology, symbols, texts, performance – yet another word in order to examine social formations, historical processes, literature, art, and media from this new perspective of memory?

'Memory' is a topic that integrates disparate elements like no other. An impressively diverse array of public discourses, media, and academic fields are currently examining the question of memory *together*. Both the practice of remembering and reflection on that practice have become an all-encompassing sociocultural, interdisciplinary, and international phenomenon.

As an all-encompassing sociocultural phenomenon, memory plays an important role in various areas of social practice. The calendar of commemorations – national, religious, ethnic – seems to be ever-increasing. Remembering and forgetting are major themes in contemporary literature and art. Memory enjoys practically top billing in daily and weekly newspapers. It has become a controversial topic in politics and the public sphere (in the context of phrases such as 'national tradition', 'Holocaust memory', or 'truth and reconciliation'). And memory even occupies us in our free time, in the form of a thriving heritage industry.

Over the course of the last two decades, memory as an interdisciplinary phenomenon has become a key concept of academic discourse across established fields. However, 'memory' is not owned by any one single discipline. Instead, sociology, philosophy and history, archaeology and religious studies, literary and art history, media studies, psychology and the neurosciences are all involved in exploring the connection between culture and memory.

This preoccupation with memory is by no means restricted to any one country, but is an international phenomenon. Pierre Nora's influential concept of sites of memory (*Les Lieux de Mémoire*, 1984–92) came into being in France and was soon emulated in other countries. A 'memory boom' (Huyssen 1995) in society and academia is evident in the United States as well as in Israel, the Netherlands, Italy, Germany, Great Britain, and elsewhere. Transnational sites of memory such as '9/11' demonstrate that we can no longer think solely in terms of national memory. Instead, religion, ideology, ethnicity, and gender are increasingly the central coordinates of cultural remembering. As a theoretical notion and in practice, 'memory' touches upon many different areas.

The connection between culture and memory cannot be approached solely within the purview of one single discipline. On the contrary, memory is a transdisciplinary problem. What is nowadays called 'memory studies', or 'cultural memory studies', has therefore emerged as a multidisciplinary field. And it is essentially an interdisciplinary project: 'memory' both renders possible and requires dialogue. This project may still be in its infancy – but what is clear even at this point is that the burgeoning field of memory studies has made possible, in a virtually unprecedented way, collaboration among the otherwise widely divergent areas of social science, humanities, and natural sciences.

Organs of this interdisciplinary and international dialogue include the journals *History and Theory* (since 1960), *Memory & History* (founded in 1989 and edited by Saul Friedländer), and *Rethinking History* (since 1997); the series *Studies in Memory and Narrative*, established in 1998 with Routledge and now moved to Transaction Press; the Stanford University Press series *Cultural Memory in the Present*, which started in 1998; the series *Media and Cultural Memory*, established at de Gruyter in 2004; the journal *Memory Studies*, begun in 2008; and the book series of the same name, appearing with Palgrave Macmillan (since 2009). An ever-increasing number of centers for memory studies have been established virtually all across the globe. Bachelor's and Master's degree programmes in memory studies have been founded. Edited volumes represent the diverse strands of memory research (see Fara and Patterson 1998; Radstone 2000; Agazzi and Fortunati 2007; Erll and Nünning 2008; Radstone and Schwarz 2010), and anthologies collect the fundamental theoretical texts of the field (see Rossington et al. 2007; Olick et al. 2010).

For students and scholars, the emergence of memory studies has been in many ways a windfall, 'a rare combination of social relevance and intellectual challenge' (Kansteiner 2002, 180). Part of the intellectual challenge is that in working on the topic of memory, individual disciplinary approaches flow together with general theories of human cognition, culture, and media as well as with findings of neighboring disciplines. In addition, concepts of cultural remembering also make possible a preoccupation with constellations and artifacts that are historically and spatially as far apart as the pyramids of Egypt and the AIDS epidemic in the United States (on the former, see J. Assmann 1992; on the latter, Sturken 1997). At the same time, the social relevance of memory has propelled scholarly work from the ivory tower into the public sphere. Consider, for example, the host of controversies about remembrance in recent years. Discussions such as those surrounding the 'Memorial to the Murdered Jews of Europe' in Berlin, 'District Six' in Cape Town, or 'Ground Zero' in New York City illustrate how the topic of memory provokes a close interplay among politics, public media, art, and academic research.

I.2 Why now?

What is the reason for this extraordinary fascination with memory? The abundance of explanations for the current omnipresence of 'memory' is surpassed only by the flood of commemorative ceremonies, memory controversies, and writings on memory. Michael Kammen (1995, 247–51), for example, has identified no fewer than nine reasons for the widespread interest in the memory discourse in the USA, including the many anniversaries celebrated in the country since the 1980s, multiculturalism, Holocaust denial, memory of the Vietnam War, the emergence of a 'memory industry', and the end of the Cold War. His list makes clear that memory's ubiquity can hardly be explained monocausally. Kammen himself advocates an 'explanatory pluralism' (ibid., 251). However, it is striking that of the reasons Kammen put forward in the mid-1990s to explain the causes of what seemed a singular proliferation of memory discourses, only about one-third were, for example, relevant to the German context (where 'memory work' showed an even greater diffusion in society and elaboration in academia) – and less than half are still applicable to the situation of present-day America (where memory is ever-present). Obviously, every era and every society can list its own specific reasons for a perceived 'memory boom'.

What seems qualitatively new today is perhaps not so much a heightened frequency and depth of cultural remembering (which may be claimed for other historical periods, too), but the fact that memory discourses and practices are increasingly linked across the globe. 'Memory' has become a truly transnational phenomenon. And this appears to be by and large attributable to a convergence of three factors over the past twenty years:

1. *Historical transformations*: Of international importance is the loss of the generation that had first-hand experience of the Holocaust and the Second World War. For the cultural memory of the Shoah, this represents a significant turning point, since death puts an end to the oral passing on of lived experience within the framework of what Jan and Aleida Assmann have called 'communicative memory'. Without eyewitnesses to history, societies are dependent on media-supported forms of remembrance (such as historiography, monuments, or movies). This marks the transition to 'Cultural Memory', in the Assmanns' terminology (see chapter II.4). In addition, with the end of the Cold War, the binary structure of eastern and western memory cultures has collapsed. Following the dissolution of the Soviet Union, a multitude of national and ethnic memories came to the fore. With the transition from authoritarianism to democratization in many societies (such as South Africa, Argentina or Chile) truth and reconciliation has emerged as a major form of societies' memory work. Moreover, as a result of decolonization and migration, the increasingly multi(-memory-)cultural nature of modern societies comes into focus. A diversity of ethnic groups and religious affiliations in a society brings with it a diversity of traditions and views of history; recognizing minorities includes giving voice to their versions of the past. And finally, 9/11 and the War on Terror have also had a deep memorial impact. In all these areas, memory proves to be a fundamentally political phenomenon with strong ethical implications. (For more on these topics, see chapter III.1.)

2. *Changes in media technology and the role of popular media*: Another oft-cited reason for the strong presence of 'memory' in current discourse is changing media technology. Today's computers offer possibilities for data storage that were unimaginable in the recent past. The Internet has rapidly become a kind of global mega-archive. Yet at the same time the digital revolution confronts us with the paradoxical connection of unprecedented medial storage capabilities and the looming danger of cultural amnesia, since information that merely rests on hard drives is 'dead knowledge'. Choosing and appropriating

that which is worth remembering, however, becomes ever more difficult in the face of the sheer mass of digital information.

Second, global media cultures and popular representations of the past play an important role as both expression and driving force of the current 'memory boom'. Semi-fictional feature films about the Shoah (most famously, perhaps, Steven Spielberg's *Schindler's List*, 1994), period pictures, war movies and cinematic retellings of ancient myths, television documentaries and interviews with witnesses of recent history as well as, lastly – as an example of that time-tested medium of memory, the book – the 'Wilkomirski case', a worldwide scandal about an alleged Holocaust autobiography (*Fragments*, 1995), can be considered typical instances of the contemporary landscape of media and memory. What these examples share is that they raise questions about the role the arts and other media play in shaping the way people around the world think about the past. (For more on this topic, see chapters V and VI.)

3. *Developments within academia*: The impact of the notion of memory appears to belong to the somewhat unexpected results of poststructuralism in the 1980s and postmodern philosophies of history (see also Klein 2000). Insights into the constructed nature and narrativity of historiography and talk of the 'end of history' (Francis Fukuyama), or at least of the 'end of the grand narratives' (Jean-François Lyotard), have undermined concepts of history as a monolithic 'collective singular' (Reinhart Koselleck), as a given fact, or as a process of teleological progression. It is under the memory paradigm that the study of the past can be combined with these insights of postmodern theory, because the focus of memory studies rests, precisely, not on the 'past as it really was', but on the 'past as a human construct'.

At the same time, the memory paradigm has endowed the humanities, written off by many as irrelevant, with a new legitimacy within society. The humanities have always functioned as institutions which administer cultural heritage. Their methods, such as historical source criticism or textual analysis, make a scholarly preoccupation with tradition possible in the first place. More recently, it has become obvious that the humanities can also apply their theoretical and terminological instruments to reflect critically on practices of cultural remembering (be they scholarly, political, or aesthetic), compare different memory cultures, and contribute to current public debates. To quote Aleida Assmann (2002, 45): 'The academic memory discourse is increasingly important in its role of reflexive observation and therapeutic accompaniment of social and political processes.'

I.3   What is meant by 'memory'?

Terminology is one of the most intricate issues in memory studies. The proliferation of memory discourses has resulted in a multitude of terms and concepts, whose commonalities and differences are by no means clear. In roughly chronological order from the 1920s to today, the most influential of these terms are: *mémoire collective*, Mnemosyne, *storia e memoria*, *lieux de mémoire*/sites, or realms, of memory, Cultural Memory vs communicative memory, social memory, memory cultures, cultural remembrance, social forgetting, the cultural brain, memory in the global age, and transcultural memory. (For more on these concepts, see chapter II and III.) As Jeffrey Olick and Joyce Robbins (1998, 106) have observed, memory research is a 'nonparadigmatic, transdisciplinary, centerless enterprise'. It is also an 'outstanding example of how far apart methods and research interests in the individual disciplines can be despite the close relationship of the objects of study' (Pethes and Ruchatz 2001, 5).

The heterogeneity of the concepts and disciplinary approaches to possibly identical objects of research represents one of the most important challenges of contemporary memory studies. Another provocation the field must face is the widespread criticism of the very idea that it is occupied with identical phenomena. For many skeptics, the term 'memory' in fact refers to the opposite: an unacceptable homogenization of vastly different objects. Can we really take individual mental processes, myths, memorials, debates about the past, autobiographies, and families looking at snapshots and bring them all together under the umbrella of 'memory'? Or is this an unacceptable over-extension of the term? Is 'memory' in danger of becoming a 'catch-all category' (see Zelizer 1995, 235)?

Of course, the very existence of this book is itself proof that the reader will here encounter a more optimistic view. Despite the centrifugal forces of the field and the danger of blurring boundaries, considering the intersections between culture and memory is a worthwhile undertaking. It is an excellent strategy to 'make visible new connections where previously only disparate elements could be seen' (A. Assmann 2002, 40). First and foremost, however, we need to see memory as a 'discursive construct' (Pethes and Ruchatz 2001, 13). 'Memory' is constituted differently in different contexts – be they linguistic (Amberber 2007), historical, social, national or disciplinary. Thus, one important goal of this book is to point out the development, differences, and connections between various concepts of memory and to bring them together in a theoretical model of memory in culture (see chapters II–IV).

The underlying idea of this book is to promote a broad understanding of memory, one which unites under one roof such heterogeneous phenomena as neuronal connections, everyday conversations, and tradition. Seen in this way, 'memory' (to give a preliminary definition) is an umbrella term for all those processes of a biological, medial, or social nature which relate past and present (and future) in sociocultural contexts.

This expansive understanding of the term can, in fact, be traced back to the founding father of cultural memory studies, Maurice Halbwachs; and it is also justified by the field's desire for precision. It is namely only by locating them in the overarching complex of 'memory' that the connections between many single, seemingly disparate cultural phenomena become evident. To take as an example the present constellation of memory in Germany: Phenomena such as grandparents' autobiographical memories of the Nazi period and images of Nazism circulating among today's grandchildren, academic historiography of the years 1933–45 and the shape of curricula for German history classes, commemorative ceremonies and heated discussions about how to address the history of genocide (*Historikerstreit*), architectural memorials such as Peter Eisenman's field of pillars near the Berlin Reichstag and the impact of literary works such as Imre Kertész's *Fateless* (1992/1975) or popular movies about Hitler like *Downfall* (2004) – all these cannot be considered each in a vacuum, independently of one another. Attempts to separate 'individual memory', 'tradition', 'history' or 'fiction' from 'memory' (in favour of other terms, out of dislike for any universal 'super theory', or out of fear for the legitimacy of one's own discipline) prevent us from seeing the threads that connect such phenomena.

There has been considerable confusion about the nature of the relationship between 'memory' and 'history'. Cultural memory is not the Other of history. Nor is it the opposite of individual remembering. Rather, it is the totality of the context within which such varied cultural phenomena originate. Precisely in order to guard against misunderstandings, confusions, and the tendency of critics to shadowbox, the concept of memory must be very broad to begin with. In a second step, once the expanse of the field is acknowledged, terminological and conceptual differentiation is of course necessary. But this project is – particularly when we consider the international dialogue – still in a fledgling state. This book aims to contribute to this undertaking by distinguishing among uses of the term 'memory', demarcating various systems and modes of collective remembering, as well as drawing attention to different cultural dimensions and symbolic forms of memory (see chapter IV).

I.4 Memory, remembering or forgetting?

This, of course, is the wrong question to pose: The study of memory cannot do without any one of these three terms. There are, however, academic contexts in which one of the terms is privileged over the others. Some researchers write predominantly about cultural *memory* and the archive (see A. Assmann 2008), others accentuate amnesia, oblivion and social *forgetting* (see Huyssen 1995; Esposito 2008); and still others highlight dynamic, performative acts of cultural *remembering* (see Irwin-Zarecka 1994; Bal, Crewe, and Spitzer 1999; Rigney 2005).

Memory, remembering and forgetting are closely intertwined on both an individual and a collective level (for more on the possible pitfalls of the metaphorical application of these terms to the collective level, see chapter IV.1). Across the disciplines there is a general agreement that 'remembering' is a process, of which 'memories' are the result, and that 'memory' should be conceived of as an ability. Memory itself is, however, not observable. Only through the observation of concrete acts of remembering situated in specific sociocultural contexts can we hypothesize about memory's nature and functioning.

Despite the unavoidable heterogeneity of the terminology, there are two generally agreed-upon central characteristics of (conscious) remembering: its relationship to the present and its constructed nature. Memories are not objective images of past perceptions, even less of a past reality. They are subjective, highly selective reconstructions, dependent on the situation in which they are recalled. *Re*-membering is an act of assembling available data that takes place in the present. Versions of the past change with every recall, in accordance with the changed present situation. Individual and collective memories are never a mirror image of the past, but rather an expressive indication of the needs and interests of the person or group doing the remembering in the present. As a result, memory studies directs its interest not toward the shape of the remembered pasts, but rather toward the particular presents of the remembering.

Remembering and forgetting are two sides – or different processes – of the same coin, that is, memory. Forgetting is the very condition for remembering. Total recall, after all, the complete memory of every single event in the past, would amount to total forgetting, for the individual as well as for the group or society. Friedrich Nietzsche had emphasized this as long ago as his 1874 critique of historicism, *On the Use and Abuse of History*. Forgetting is necessary for memory to operate economically, for it to be able to recognize patterns. In this sense, scholars of systems theory postulate the 'priority of forgetting' and maintain that 'the main function of memory lies in forgetting, which prevents the system from blocking itself with the accumulation of the results of former operations, and frees processing capabilities' (Esposito 2008, 182). Even in ancient discussions of *ars memoriae* (see chapter III.2.1), the relevance of forgetting was highlighted. Themistocles called for a 'lethotechnics' instead of 'mnemotechnics'. However, in a playful reflection upon this idea, the semiotician Umberto Eco (1988) showed that an *ars obliviona-lis*, willful forgetting, would be paradoxical, in fact both an adynaton and oxymoron.

It is true that memories are small islands in a sea of forgetting. In processing our experience of reality, forgetting is the rule and remembering the exception. Indeed, the functions of forgetting within cognitive and social systems are at least as important as those of remembering. Memory studies has reconstructed the intellectual history of forgetting – for Harald Weinrich, in his rich study *Lethe: The Art and Critique of Forgetting* (2004), it has its origin in Greco-Roman mythology with the image of the underworld river Lethe – and emphasized the social, historical, and ethical significance of forgetting and related aspects, such as amnesia, oblivion, silence, and forgiving (see Augé 2004; Ricoeur 2004; Passerini 2005; Connerton 2009; Ben-Ze'ev et al. 2010). However, in the end, the phenomenon of forgetting is every bit as unobservable as is memory. As an object of research it only comes into view via the observation of remembering – by considering its peculiarities, mistakes and changes, by focussing, for instance, on what Sigmund Freud described as condensation, displacement and screen memories.

I.5   Goals and structure of this book

The subject of this book is the connection between culture and memory. This connection has an impact on both an individual and a collective level: The individual person always remembers within sociocultural contexts. And cultural formations are based on a 'collective memory', to apply Maurice Halbwachs's concept (see chapter II.1); in other words, on symbols, media, institutions, and social practice which convey versions of a shared past. The following chapters will deal with both levels and their multiple overlappings, and guide interested students and researchers through what has become a veritable labyrinth.

This book does not attempt either to be a history of cultural remembering or to recapitulate a history of the general, and until 1900 predominantly philosophical, reflection on memory – although both of these elements are present to a degree. The history of cultural remembering is over 5,000 years old, as has been shown by Jan Assmann (1992). The history of the reflection on memory is also far-reaching, going back in western culture as far as Plato and Aristotle (Yates 1966; Gross 2000). The long list of memory philosophers and proto-psychological thinkers who have made key contributions to the question of the location and functioning of memory include Aurelius Augustinus, Giordano Bruno, Michel de Montaigne, John Locke, David Hume, Immanuel Kant, G.W.F. Hegel, Friedrich Nietzsche, Henri Bergson, Sigmund Freud and Edmund Husserl. Highly recommended collections of texts and histories of thinking about memory have already been published (see Harth 1991; Draaisma 2000; Byatt and Wood 2008; Whitehead 2009).

This book addresses the question of how to theorize and work with 'cultural memory'. It presents concepts and methods for the study of memory in culture. Since the field has long since overcome disciplinary and territorial borders, the book necessarily also focuses on the transdisciplinary and international dimension of memory research. It introduces, among others, German, American, British, French, Italian, and Dutch concepts of memory. Research done in history and the social sciences is considered alongside literary, media and art studies, as well as psychology and the neurosciences.

The present heterogeneity of the field of memory studies has historical and disciplinary, but also linguistic and cultural causes. Taken together, these factors have impeded the exchange of concepts, led to simultaneous but unrelated academic activity, and to a tendency to 'reinvent the wheel' in different places. To the barriers posed by language belongs the fact that much of Halbwachs's fundamental work on *mémoire collective* has not yet been fully translated into English. But there are also very different ways of doing memory studies, which are the result of distinct national academic cultures and traditions. This can be shown by a quick look at the different national histories of memory studies: In France, Maurice Halbwachs's homeland, the discourse about cultural memory has been dominated, since the 1980s, by Pierre Nora's concept of the *lieux de mémoire* (see chapter II.2). The problematic distinction between 'history' and 'memory' (see chapter III.1.1) is discussed heatedly in public, and historians engage in debates about who may or should represent the past, which have turned into veritable *guerres de mémoires* (Blanchard and Veyrat-Masson 2008). This notion of 'memory wars' is then, significantly, also used by French scholars to describe cultural memory in *other* countries (Blanchard, Ferro and Veyrat-Masson 2008).

In the United States, on the other hand, a significant strand of academic memory research has its origin in Holocaust studies, trauma studies, and in poststructuralist critiques of representation (see chapter III.1.2). Looking at memory with Derrida will, of course, shape the field differently than looking at memory with Halbwachs. In Great Britain we encounter yet another scene: Memory studies there has developed from Gramscian cultural studies, as practiced at the Birmingham Centre for Contemporary Cultural Studies (Raphael Samuel being the major founding protagonist). It is informed by radical Marxism and characterized by its decided interest in ideology. Much of its methodology is based on a politically informed psychoanalysis. It is against this backdrop that Susannah Radstone (2008, 36) argues for a nuanced and critical view of memory studies and emphasizes 'the attempt to understand culture – including ... memory culture – as ambiguous, as struggle, as a grey area'. British memory studies is moreover closely bound up with the work of oral historians, as it is best represented in the journal *History Workshop* (see also Thompson and Samuel 1990, which also includes fundamental work from Italian oral history). In Germany, to give one last example, the difficult task of remembering the Holocaust, national guilt and the public discussions connected with these issues were of great importance for the emergence of a widespread memory discourse in the 1980s; a more general turn in German humanities towards social and cultural anthropology (in the framework of *Kulturwissenschaften*) taking place at roughly the same time has lent the field its specific conceptual shape (see chapter II.3).

Coming from the German research context, perhaps, makes me therefore want to emphasize that memory studies, as I see it, has at its basis a general anthropological question: How do people refer to temporal processes? How do they construct images and narratives of the past in different social, cultural and historical contexts? Such a view of memory studies is justified when we look at the fundamental theories of collective memory that have been developed since the 1920s. Maurice Halbwachs and Aby Warburg (see ch II.1 and 2) proposed concepts which recognize and problematize the constructed and collective nature of memory and which focus on the influence of signs, media and social contexts on remembering. The development of a modern understanding of culture as a shared sign system with a social, a material and a mental dimension (see chapter IV.2) and the formation of theories of collective memory were in fact closely related. Both culture and memory can be understood as 'webs of significance spun by human beings' (Clifford Geertz), as the products of man, the 'animal symbolicum'

(Ernst Cassirer). Remembering is a constitutive component of what the Tartu–Moscow group of semioticians around Jurij Lotman and Boris Uspenskij have called the 'semiotic mechanism of culture'. Thus, what the various approaches of cultural memory studies all have in common is that they analyse memory as prerequisite for, component and product of culture.

This book addresses first the historical and then the systematic dimension of memory studies. In a further step, attention is directed to the medial construction of memory. A final, yet central concern is to shed light on literature as a powerful medium of cultural memory.

- Chapter II introduces the fundamental and most sophisticated concepts of cultural memory developed in the twentieth century – from Maurice Halbwachs's *mémoire collective* and Aby Warburg's Mnemosyne project to Pierre Nora's *lieux de mémoire* and to Aleida and Jan Assmann's theory of the Cultural Memory (*das kulturelle Gedächtnis*), thereby outlining the intellectual history of memory studies.
- Chapter III offers, in light of the highly specialized research landscape, an overview of discipline-specific concepts of memory (from history, social sciences, literature and art studies, and psychology). Even with the chapter's disciplinary focus, possibilities for interdisciplinary cross-fertilization are kept in mind.
- Chapter IV outlines a semiotic model of memory in culture, in an attempt to build a framework for transdisciplinary research. It clarifies the distinction between literal and metaphorical uses of the term 'memory'; and then differentiates between remembering on the individual and the collective level (*'collected* and *collective* memory'); between social, material and mental dimensions; and between explicit and implicit systems of cultural memory.
- Chapter V takes into account the important role of the media in cultural remembering. It shows how memory is constructed through media, what components constitute a medium of memory, and what different functions media may fulfil in memory culture.
- Chapter VI sketches the foundation for literary studies as part of memory studies and introduces concepts and methods for the study of literature as a medium of cultural memory.
- Chapter VII offers some concluding remarks.

II
The Invention of Cultural Memory: A Short History of Memory Studies

Titling this chapter the 'invention' of cultural memory is intended to emphasize that this is not a history of the phenomenon of memory itself, but rather a history of memory studies. Acts of cultural remembering seem to be an element of humans' fundamental anthropological make-up, and the history of creating a shared heritage and thinking about memory can be traced all the way back to antiquity, for example to Homer, Plato, and Aristotle. However, it was not until the beginning of the twentieth century that there developed a scientific interest in the phenomenon. Forms of collective reference to the past were observed methodically and made the focus of research in the humanities and the social sciences. The field's fundamental assumption about the constructedness of cultural memory, however, is also valid for the level of theory: Every theoretical idea about the contents or functions of cultural memory is itself a construct and more of an academic 'invention' than a discovery of cultural givens.

Today's research on cultural memory takes its origin from two strands of tradition in particular, both of which have their roots in the 1920s: Maurice Halbwachs's sociological studies on *mémoire collective* and Aby Warburg's art-historical interest in a European memory of images (*Bildgedächtnis*). Halbwachs and Warburg were the first to give the phenomenon of cultural memory a name ('collective' and 'social' memory, respectively), and to study it systematically within the framework of a modern theory of culture.

Yet it was not until the 1980s that the topic of memory again elicited interest in the humanities and social sciences, in the context of what may be called the 'new cultural memory studies'. Pierre Nora's *lieux de mémoire* have proven to be the most influential notion internationally. Roughly at the same time, Aleida and Jan Assmann, with their idea of a 'Cultural Memory', advanced a theory which is the most authoritative in the German-speaking world and, in international comparison, also the most elaborate.

II.1 Maurice Halbwachs: *Mémoire collective*

The French sociologist Maurice Halbwachs (1877–1945), a student of Henri Bergson and Emile Durkheim, wrote three texts in which he developed his concept of *mémoire collective* and which today occupy a central place in the study of cultural memory. In 1925 he published his study *Les cadres sociaux de la mémoire* (1994; 'The Social Frameworks of Memory', partially translated in *On Collective Memory*, 1992) in which he attempted to establish that memory is dependent on social structures. In this he opposed the theories of memory of his contemporaries such as Henri Bergson and Sigmund Freud, who emphasized the individual dimension of memory. Halbwachs's theory, which sees even the most personal memory as a *mémoire collective*, a collective phenomenon, provoked significant protest, not least from his colleagues at the University of Strasbourg, Charles Blondel and Marc Bloch. The latter accused Halbwachs, and the Durkheim School in general, of an unacceptable collectivization of individual psychological phenomena (see Bloch 1925).

Stirred by this criticism, Halbwachs began elaborating his concept of collective memory in a second book. For more than 15 years he worked on the text *La mémoire collective* (1997; *The Collective Memory*, 1980), but it did not appear until 1950, posthumously and incomplete. Before that, Halbwachs did publish a third book, in which he illustrated the forms and functions of memory sites using a specific example: *La Topographie légendaire des Évangiles en Terre Sainte* (1941; 'The Legendary Topography of the Gospels in the Holy Land'; partially translated in *On Collective Memory*, 1992). In August 1944 the Nazis deported Halbwachs, whose wife was Jewish, to Buchenwald, where he was killed on 16 March 1945. (See also Vromen 1975; Namer 2000; Becker 2003; Marcel and Mucchielli 2008.)

Halbwachs's writings on collective memory in particular, and also the interest in the cultural dimension of remembering in general, were largely forgotten in the postwar period. Today, however, virtually no theoretical model of cultural memory exists without recourse to the sociologist. It is possible to distinguish three main areas of analysis in Halbwachs's studies on *mémoire collective*, which point to three prominent directions of research on cultural memory:

- first, Halbwachs's theory of the dependence of individual memory on social structures;

- second, his studies of the forms of intergenerational memory; and
- third, his expansion of the term *mémoire collective* to include cultural transmission and the creation of tradition.

Thus, Halbwachs unites – albeit not explicitly – two fundamental, and fundamentally different, concepts of collective memory (see chapter IV.1):

1. Collective memory as the organic memory of the individual, which operates within the framework of a sociocultural environment (see chapter II.1.1).
2. Collective memory as the creation of shared versions of the past, which results through interaction, communication, media, and institutions within small social groups as well as large cultural communities (see chapter II.1.2).

II.1.1   *Cadres sociaux*: the social frameworks of individual memory

The starting point of Halbwachs's theory of collective memory is his concept of *cadres sociaux*. In the first part of *Les cadres sociaux de la mémoire*, using his reflections on dreams and language, Halbwachs gives a detailed illustration of the collective elements of individual memory. He comes to the conclusion that the recourse to *cadres sociaux*, social frameworks, is an indispensable prerequisite for every act of remembering. Social frameworks are, for Halbwachs, first of all simply the people around us. Humans are social creatures: Without other humans, an individual is denied access not only to such obviously collective phenomena as language and customs, but also, according to Halbwachs, to his or her own memory. This is partly because we generally experience things in the company of other people, who can also later help us to remember the events.

Much more fundamental for Halbwachs, however, is the fact that it is through interaction and communication with our fellow humans that we acquire knowledge about dates and facts, collective concepts of time and space, and ways of thinking and experiencing. Because we participate in a collective symbolic order, we can discern, interpret and remember past events. From *cadres sociaux* in the literal sense, our social environment, derive 'social frameworks' in the metaphorical sense: Metaphorically speaking, *cadres sociaux* are thought patterns, cognitive schemata, that guide our perception and memory in particular directions. Social frameworks, thus, form the all-encompassing horizon in which our perception and memory is embedded. They are constituted from social, material, and mental phenomena of culture. Hence Halbwachs would probably have said Kaspar Hauser (a young man in nineteenth-century Germany who allegedly grew up without any human contact) had no collective memory, while the lonely Robinson Crusoe most certainly did, since in his thoughts he could fall back on the social frameworks of his homeland, the English middle-class ways of thinking he had learned in his youth. For Halbwachs the sociologist, however, it is the *cadres sociaux* in the literal sense, the social group, which is of central importance, since without social interaction worlds of meaning can neither come into being nor be passed on.

Social frameworks convey and interpret the contents of collective memory – the supply of shared knowledge and experiences relevant to the group. 'It is in this sense that there exists a collective memory and social frameworks for memory; it is to the degree that our individual thought places itself in these frameworks and participates in this memory that it is capable of the act of recollection' (Halbwachs 1992, 38). Our perception is group-specific, our individual memories are socially formed, and both are unthinkable without the existence of a collective memory. However, the collective memory is not a supraindividual entity separate from the individual's organic memories. Collective and individual memory are instead mutually dependent: 'One may say that the individual remembers by placing himself in the perspective of the group, but one may also affirm that the memory of the group realizes and manifests itself in individual memories' (Halbwachs 1992, 40).

It is only through individual acts of memory that the collective memory can be observed, since 'each memory is a viewpoint on the collective memory' (Halbwachs 1980, 48). This 'viewpoint' (Halbwachs's French term is *point de vue*) can be understood as a position people assume based on their socialization and cultural influences. Every individual belongs to several social groups: family, religious community, colleagues, and so on. Each person thus has at his or her disposal a supply of different, group-specific experiences and thought systems. Thus, what Halbwachs seems to suggest is that while memory is no purely individual phenomenon, but must be seen in its fundamentally collective dimension, it is the combination of various group allegiances and the resultant frameworks for remembering that are the actual individual element which distinguishes one person from another.

II.1.2 Intergenerational memory and religious topography

In the second part of *Les cadres sociaux de la mémoire*, Halbwachs distinguishes between various forms of collective memories and provides sociological case studies, addressing family, religious community, and social class. Family memory is a typical intergenerational memory. This type of collective memory is constituted through social interaction and communication. Through the repeated recall of the family's past (usually via oral stories which are told at family get-togethers), those who did not experience the past firsthand can also share in the memory. In this way an exchange of living memory takes place between eyewitnesses and descendants. The collective intergenerational memory thus goes back as far as the oldest members of the social group can remember.

Halbwachs makes a sharp distinction between history and memory, which he sees as two mutually exclusive forms of reference to the past. Right at the beginning of his comparison of 'lived' memory and 'written' history in *La mémoire collective*, Halbwachs emphasizes that 'general history starts only when tradition ends and the social memory is fading or breaking up' (1980, 78). History and memory are irreconcilable: Halbwachs sees history as universal; it is characterized by a neutral coordination of all past events. Central to history are contradictions and ruptures. Collective memory, in contrast, is particular; its carriers are groups which are restricted both chronologically and spatially, whose memory is strongly evaluative and hierarchical. A central function of remembering the past within the framework of collective memory is identity formation. Things are remembered which correspond to the self-image and the interests of the group. Particularly emphasized are those similarities and continuities which demonstrate that the group has remained the same. Participation in the collective memory indicates that the rememberer belongs to the group.

For Halbwachs, history deals with the past. Collective memory, in contrast, is oriented towards the needs and interests of the group in the present, and thus proceeds in an extremely selective and reconstructive manner. Along the way, what is remembered can become distorted and shifted to such an extent that the result is closer to fiction than to a past reality. Memory thus does not provide a faithful reproduction of the past – indeed, quite the opposite is true: 'A remembrance is in very large measure a reconstruction of the past achieved with data borrowed from the present, a reconstruction prepared, furthermore, by reconstructions of earlier periods wherein past images had already been altered' (ibid., 68). This already points to what half a century later, within poststructuralist discussions, will be called 'the construction of reality.'

Already in his work *Les cadres sociaux de la mémoire* (in the chapters on aristocracy and the memories of religious communities), and even more so in his later study on the Christian mnemonic topography of Palestine, Halbwachs breaks through the constrictions that had limited his studies to intergenerational memories, whose medium is everyday communication and whose contents are for the most part autobiographical memories. In 'The Legendary Topography' he turns his attention to collective memories, whose temporal horizons reach back thousands of years, thus transcend the horizon of living memory, and therefore need objects and topographical sites of memory to provide structure. Material phenomena, such as architecture, pilgrimage routes, or graves, take on a primary meaning. At this point, Halbwachs leaves the area of socially shared memories of recent events and enters the area of culturally constructed knowledge about a distant past and its transmission through the creation of traditions.

Halbwachs's theory of collective memory has been applied by a broad spectrum of disciplines to a wide variety of research objects. But his writings have not been able to serve as the basis of a single, coherent theory of cultural memory; this might be because his broad concept of *mémoire collective* is insufficiently differentiated. However, specific elements of Halbwachs's writings have been adapted in various disciplines. Halbwachs thus became the forefather of a variety of memory theories (see Table II.1): In the field of psychology the focus is on Halbwachs's idea of the collective nature of individual memory, and the *cadres sociaux* are understood as culturally specific schemata (see chapter III.3.1). Oral history refers to his studies of intergenerational, communicative and everyday forms of remembrance (see chapter III.1.4). And Halbwachs's interest in mnemonic space and objects, as, for example, in his studies of the religious topography of Palestine, broke the ground for later historical and cultural studies approaches which deal with the transmission of cultural knowledge and national sites of memory (see chapters II.3 and II.4 on Jan and Aleida Assmann and Pierre Nora).

Table II.1   Three dimensions of Halbwachs's concept of *mémoire collective* and fields in which they have been applied

Halbwachs's *mémoire collective*	1. Dependence of individual memory on social frameworks	→ Social psychology
	2. Intergenerational memory	→ Oral history
	3. Transmission of cultural knowledge	→ Theory of the 'Cultural Memory' (A. and J. Assmann), *Lieux de mémoire* (Nora)

II.2 Aby Warburg: Mnemosyne – pathos formulas and a European memory of images

The second fundamental concept of cultural memory is likewise the work of a scholar of the 1920s. The art and cultural historian Aby Warburg (1866–1929) is today considered an important forefather of the modern, interdisciplinary study of culture, and the Warburg Library (*Kulturwissenschaftliche Bibliothek Warburg*), once situated in Hamburg, its icon. Its original arrangement was characterized by Warburg's dislike of the 'policing of disciplinary boundaries'. He organized his extensive collection according to cultural-historical themes, thus encouraging an approach that transcends borders between different epochs, media, and genres. A circle of significant researchers, including Ernst Cassirer, Erwin Panofsky, and Hellmut Ritter, were associated with the Warburg Library. After Warburg's death, the library was transferred to London in 1933, rescuing it from the Nazi takeover in Germany. Since 1944, the Warburg Institute has been part of the University of London. The Warburg Foundation in Hamburg, in cooperation with the publishing house Akademie Verlag of Berlin, has edited Aby Warburg's collected works.

Aby Warburg's interest was in a memory of art, in the readoption of vivid images and symbols in different epochs and cultures (see Gombrich 1986; Ginzburg 1989; Woodfield 2001). Warburg observed a return of artistic forms – for example, motifs of classical frescos in Renaissance paintings by Botticelli and Ghirlandaio or on stamps in the 1920s – and instead of interpreting the re-use of these forms as the result of a conscious appropriation of the ancient world by artists of later periods, attributed it to the power of cultural symbols to trigger memories.

Warburg placed particular importance on the so-called pathos formulas (*Pathosformeln*), a kind of *imagines agentes*: in their attempts to represent the 'superlatives' of human expression – passionate excitement in gesture or physiognomy – Renaissance artists returned to the symbols of ancient models. Because, according to Warburg, ancient pathos, pagan emotional intensity, is reflected in these symbols, he termed them 'pathos formulas'. In order to explain why the affective properties of these symbols had such an unusual staying power across the centuries, he used a model suggested by the memory psychologist Richard Semon and conceived of pathos formulas as cultural 'engrams' or 'dynamograms', which store 'mnemic energy' and are able to release it under other historical circumstances or at far distant locations.

According to Warburg, the symbol is a cultural 'energy store'. Culture rests upon the memory of symbols. In this way, Warburg developed the concept of a cultural memory of images which he called, among other terms, 'social memory' (see also Kany 1987; Ferretti 1989; Michaud 2004).

Warburg felt that the 'social memory' was tied to deeply moral questions, since the pathos of antiquity is a memory which artists can succumb to but which they can also master. The re-use of pathos formulas is connected to two fundamental aspects of culture, 'expression' and 'orientation'. The affective content of symbolic gestures offers the 'civilized' artist who comes into contact with them the chance to create an intensive and incisive vivid expression, but on the other hand also represents a threat as it stems from 'primitive' levels of culture. Art always moves within the dangerous zone between magic and logic, between 'primitive' ecstasy and 'civilized' self-control. The decisive factor is whether the artist is able to take up the traditional symbolism and simultaneously maintain a safe distance from it in order to create clarity and beauty through this balancing act. Warburg is interested in 'artistic sophrosyne', the restraint and moral self-assertion of modern humans in the face of the memory of the deep layers of their culture. Artistic techniques of sophrosyne can include an emphasis on the purely metaphorical character of the symbols, for example through grisaille painting techniques, or on modern re-interpretations, such as new, Christian understandings of pagan symbols. 'Warburg describes the reserves of transmitted cultural possessions as "humanity's treasure of suffering" (*Leidschatz*) which is waiting to be transformed into human property. "Humanity's stores of suffering become the possessions of the humane"' (Diers 1995, 68).

Warburg emphasizes the changes and actualizations of social memory typical for every place and time. As a result of this constant renewal, studying the specific interplay between continuity and re-interpretation of cultural symbols in artworks allows one to draw conclusions regarding the mental dimension of culture. 'The variations in rendering, seen in the mirror of the period, reveal the conscious or unconscious selective tendencies of the age and thus bring to light the collective psyche that creates these wishes and postulates these ideals' (quoted in Gombrich 1986, 270–1).

How central the concept of memory and the idea of administering an artistic inheritance was to Warburg's thought becomes evident in his last exhibition project, which was entitled 'Mnemosyne' (1924–29; see Warburg 2000), after the muse who personifies memory and is also the mother of all the other Muses. The exhibit was an atlas and was meant to illustrate the transcultural memory of images, which crosses the chronological and spatial borders of epochs and countries. By bringing together apparently heterogeneous panels, the atlas presents an outline of an overlapping community of memory which connects Europe and Asia.

Warburg referred to his concept of memory not only as 'social memory' but also as a 'European collective memory' (quoted in Gombrich 1986, 270), pointing to a significant expansion of its scope. This is possible since Warburg assumed as the central medium of cultural memory not oral speech but rather works of art, which can potentially survive for long periods of time and traverse great spaces. Warburg's concept of memory thus accommodates the historical variations and local imprints of cultural memory, while at the same time not losing sight of its embeddedness in the European-Asian community of memory.

Halbwachs's and Warburg's concepts of cultural memory are fundamentally different. While Halbwachs's writings are an example of the elaborate development of a theory, Warburg did not leave behind any general theory or system. Warburg proceeded inductively, starting with the material – following his famous dictum: 'God is in the details'. His approach shifts the material dimension of culture to the centre of focus. Warburg studied the ability of objects and symbols to evoke memory and create cultural continuity. His primary interest was the highly expressive visual culture, which he saw as closely related to unconscious, mental processes, albeit in such a broad understanding that he also enlisted for his analysis objects of everyday culture, festivals, and literary sources. In contrast, Halbwachs's argument begins with the social dimension of culture (for more on this difference, see also chapter IV.2). He was primarily interested in social groups' creation of a past related to their identity, which he saw as an active, constructive process, one attuned to the needs of the present.

What the two concepts have in common, however, is the perception that culture and its transmission are products of human activity. At the beginning of the twentieth century this assumption was by no means a matter of course. Inspired by Darwin and the evolutionism and biological determinism of the turn of the century, many scientists tried to explain the phenomenon of cultures' survival with concepts of 'racial memory'. Halbwachs and Warburg deserve credit for showing that the key to the continuation of ephemeral culture lies not in any kind of genetic memory but rather in its transmission through social interaction and its codification in material objectivations. At the same time, the two scholars demonstrated through their approaches that getting to the root of the phenomenon of cultural memory necessitates an interdisciplinary methodology.

Halbwachs's and Warburg's studies were part of a very animated discussion about cultural memory in the first decades of the twentieth century. Friedrich Nietzsche (*Vom Nutzen und Nachteil der Historie für das Leben*, 1874), Henry Bergson (*Matière et mémoire*, 1896), and Sigmund Freud (*Die Traumdeutung*, 1900) had brought the theme of memory to center stage. Arnold Zweig, in his essay *Caliban* (1927), developed an idea inspired by Sigmund Freud's psychoanalysis: a concept of collective 'group affects', on the basis of which he attempted to explain the anti-Semitism of the time. Siegfried Kracauer, in an essay entitled 'Photography' (1927), considered the differences between photographic and memory images. Frederic Bartlett, at the end of the decade, began his experiments on culture-specific schemata and constructive processes of memory (*Remembering*, 1932). Wilhelm Pinder (*Das Problem der Generation in der Kunstgeschichte Europas*, 1926) and Karl Mannheim (*The Problem of the Generations*, 1928/29) addressed concepts of identity, the perception of time, and the memory of generations. Walter Benjamin doubted that, in the modern era and in particular after the shock of mechanized warfare in the First World War, direct experience and meaning-creating memory were still possible (see 'The Storyteller', 1936). In his essay 'On the Concept of History' (1940), he criticizes the historicist tradition of the nineteenth century, whose selection criteria invariably yielded solely a 'history of victors'. Using a term borrowed from Jewish tradition – remembrance (*Eingedenken*) –, Benjamin pleads instead for reading history 'against the grain', and for keeping alive the memory of the victims and the nameless.

II.3   Pierre Nora's *lieux de mémoire* – and beyond

Whereas today Halbwachs's and Warburg's concepts are acknowledged as having laid the foundations for theories of cultural memory, at the time of their writing they found only a limited audience. Ideas of memory as a collective phenomenon which constitutes and maintains culture were not taken up again on a broad basis until the 1980s. One of the most influential concepts of the interdisciplinary 'new cultural memory studies' emerging in the late twentieth century was developed within the field of French cultural history, namely Pierre Nora's *lieux de mémoire*, a notion which revolves around memory, history and nation. As early as 1978 Pierre Nora had drawn on the idea of collective memory, in order to describe the numerous popular and political forms of addressing the past, which he – and this is Halbwachs's legacy – strictly separated from history.

Between 1984 and 1992 Nora edited his monumental, seven-part work *Les lieux de mémoire* (for English translations see Nora 1996–98 and Nora 2001–10). The collection is introduced by an essay entitled 'Entre mémoire et histoire' ('Between Memory and History', 1989, 8) in which Nora, closely following Halbwachs, emphasizes that 'memory and history, far from being synonymous, appear now to be in fundamental opposition'. Yet unlike Halbwachs, who starts from the premise of the existence of collective memories, Nora summarizes our current time by saying: 'We speak so much of memory because there is so little of it left' (ibid., 7). Thus, the focus of his attention shifts to *lieux de mémoire*, sites of memory. In the tradition of ancient mnemotechnics, they can be understood as *loci* in the broadest sense of the term, which call up *imagines*, the memory images of the French nation. Such sites can therefore include geographical locations, buildings, monuments and works of art as well as historical persons, memorial days, philosophical and scientific texts, or symbolic actions. Thus, Paris, Versailles, and the Eiffel Tower are sites of memory, but so are Joan of Arc, the French flag, 14 July, the *Marseillaise*, and Descartes's *Discours de la méthode*.

However, sites of memory cannot constitute a collective memory as defined by Halbwachs. Quite the contrary, as Nora explains: 'There are *lieux de mémoire*, sites of memory, because there are no longer *milieux de mémoire*, real environments of memory' (ibid.). The French sites of memory have their origin in the nineteenth century, during the time of the Third Republic. At that point, the national memory was still capable of fostering a collective identity, but this function has disintegrated during the twentieth century. According to Nora, today's society is in a transitional stage, during which there is a breakdown of the connection to a lived, group- and nation-specific, identity-forming past. Thus, sites of memory function as a sort of artificial placeholder for the no longer existent, natural collective memory.

Les lieux de mémoire, edited by Nora, is a collection of essays about different elements of French culture. And while they each stand for aspects of a common past, they do not, in their variety, amount to a binding comprehensive memory, but instead leave the reader with a fragmented image of the French past. Each individual will make his or her own selection from the many sites of memory offered. Their pluralization does not allow for any hierarchization, any configuration into a coherent narrative or structured meaning. In addition, the rupture which separates the past from the present is too great for sites of memory to elicit reactions in a contemporary observer that are anything but nostalgic. Sites of memory are thus signs which not only refer to aspects of the French past which should be remembered, but at the same time always point to the absence of living memory (see Carrier 2000).

In his theoretical preface to the first volume of *Les lieux de mémoire*, Nora explains the conditions which an event or an object must fulfil in order to be identified as a site of memory. According to him, three dimensions of memory sites can be distinguished: material, functional, and symbolic (1989, 19).

- Material dimension: Sites of memory are cultural objectivations in the broadest sense of the term. They include not only 'graspable' objects, such as paintings or books; past events, too, and even commemorative minutes of silence exhibit a material dimension, since they, as Nora explains, 'literally (break) a temporal continuity' (ibid.).
- Functional dimension: Such objectivations must fulfil a function in society. Famous books, such as the *Histoire de France* by Ernest Lavisse (Nora 1997, 151–86), are first – before being turned into memory sites – created for a particular purpose. The *Histoire de France* served as a textbook and structured history teaching in schools. The aforementioned minute of silence has the function of periodically evoking a memory.
- Symbolic dimension: Finally, the objectivation must, in addition to its function, also have a symbolic meaning. This is the case, for example, when actions become rituals or places are shrouded with a 'symbolic aura' (Nora 1989, 19). It is this intentional symbolic signification – whether ascribed to the objectivation already at the point of its creation or not until later – that first makes a cultural object a site of memory.

These last two characteristics, symbolic dimension and intentionality, distinguish sites of memory from other cultural objectivations: 'To begin with, there must be a will to remember. If we were to abandon this criterion, we would quickly drift into admitting virtually everything as worthy of remembrance' (Nora 1989, 19).

This actually quite clear definition of a site of memory, however, is, in the course of the three volumes – *La République*, *La Nation*, and *Les Frances* – with their 130 contributions, deconstructed bit by bit: Popular phrases ('dying for the fatherland'), ways of thinking and arguing ('Gaullists and Communists'), and social manners ('gallantry') are promoted to the status of *lieux de mémoire* and become objects of mnemo-historical research. Thus, many critics pose the question of just what exactly can become a site of memory (see for example, den Boer and Frijhoff 1993). The answer is likely: any cultural phenomenon, whether material, social or mental, which a society associates with its past and with national identity. Aleida Assmann (1996a) has blazed a trail in the thicket of sites of memory with her distinction between *lieux de mémoire* as media and topoi of cultural memory.

Nora's strict separation of history and memory is also not entirely unproblematic. While Halbwachs's polemic needs to be understood against the backdrop of nineteenth-century historicism, blocking out the memorial function of historiography appears strange in light of the discussions among historians – beginning as early as the 1970s – regarding the constructed nature, subjectivity, and perspectivity of all history writing.

In addition, it is hard to understand Nora's civilization-critical, strongly judgemental construction of a history of the deterioration and decline of collective memory. According to Nora, contemporary memory cultures are confronted with 'globalization, democratization, and the advent of mass culture', the end of 'societies based on memory', and the end of 'ideologies based on memory' (1996, 1f.). Nora contrasts this with a romanticized version of original, natural and authentic *milieux de mémoire*, such as 'peasant culture, that quintessential repository of collective memory' (ibid.). What we are faced with today, in Nora's diction, is a 'terror' or 'tyranny' of memory. Accordingly, he ends his *Lieux*-project with the words 'The tyranny of memory will reign for only a certain time – but this time will have been ours' (Nora 1984–92, III.1012).

Nora's *lieux de mémoire* are the most prominent example of a mnemohistorical approach, in which an (admittedly discontinuous) theoretical conception of cultural memory is borne out by a rich variety of case studies illuminating the dynamics of cultural remembrance. The concept of *lieux de mémoire* is restricted neither to the discipline of history nor to the study of French memories; on the contrary, it has inspired scholars of the most varied of disciplines to undertake memory research. Nora's project of charting national sites of memory has been favourably received and imitated in many other countries. There are publications on Italian *luoghi della memoria* (Isnenghi 1987ff.), American sites of memory (Hebel 2003), sites of memory in Quebec (Kolboom and Grzonka 2002), as well as Dutch *Plaatsen van Herinnering*

(Wesseling 2005–06), which, however, concentrates only on literal, physical places of memory.

Arguably, one of the greatest problems of the *lieux de mémoire*-approach is its nation-centredness. Hue-Tam Ho Tai (2001a) has convincingly criticized Nora's construct of a *nation-mémoire*, a French national memory, which ignores, despite its striving for polyphony, 'la *France d'outre-mer*' (the French colonies) as well as the memory cultures of immigrants (see also Judt 1998; Taithe 1999). More and more scholars are trying to address these shortcomings and focus on sites of memory under postcolonial, multicultural, diasporic, transcultural, and transnational perspectives, on what Andreas Huyssen (2003, 95) has called 'memory sites in an expanded field'.

Building on Nora's work, Etienne François and Hagen Schulze initiated the project *Deutsche Erinnerungsorte* (2001, 'German Sites of Memory'), which is, in contrast to the French model, strongly oriented towards Europe as a whole: International authors, a combination of insider and outsider perspectives, as well as the inclusion of sites of memory which are also significant for Germany's neighbors (for example, 'Versailles' and 'Charlemagne') all serve to reflect the more general process of an opening up of Germany towards Europe. More recent publications show an even greater sensitivity towards the complex inter-, multi- and transcultural constellations of memory sites. With *België, een parcours van herinnering* (Tollebeek and Buelens et al. 2008) and *Lieux de mémoire au Luxembourg/Erinnerungsorte in Luxembourg* (Kmec et al. 2008) this pertains, perhaps unsurprisingly, to volumes which address the memory sites of nation-states that are characterized by bilingualism and diglossia. Finally, projects dedicated to European memory sites are increasingly coming to the fore, for example on the transnational *lieux de mémoire* in Central Europe (Le Rider, Czàky and Sommer 2002; Le Rider 2008) or on European realms of memory (Buchinger et al. 2009).

One notable attempt to rethink the conception of the *lieu de mémoire* and provide a more solid theoretical fundament is Ann Rigney's work on the emergence and 'life' of memory sites. She emphasizes that:

> Although it has proven useful as a conceptual tool, the metaphor of 'memory site' can become misleading if it is interpreted to mean that collective remembrance becomes permanently tied down to particular figures, icons, or monuments. As the performative aspect of the term 'remembrance' suggests, collective memory is constantly 'in the works' and, like a swimmer, has to keep moving even just to

stay afloat. To bring remembrance to a conclusion is de facto already to forget. (Rigney 2008a, 346)

Understanding the *lieu de mémoire* not as a stable entity but as fundamentally a mnemonic *process*, Rigney (2005, 18) emphasizes that 'sites of memory are constantly being reinvested with new meaning' and that they thus 'become a self-perpetuating vortex of symbolic investment'. She advocates the study of *lieux de mémoire* in the wake of what she terms a 'shift from "sites" to "dynamics" within memory studies [which] runs parallel to a larger shift of attention within cultural studies from products to processes, from a focus on cultural artifacts to an interest in the way those artifacts circulate and influence their environment' (Rigney 2008a, 346; see also 2008b).

All in all, it can be said that while Nora's *lieu de mémoire* is certainly the most prominent and internationally most frequently practised approach to cultural remembrance, it also constitutes one of the most sorely undertheorized concepts of memory studies. On top of this, it carries with it some old-fashioned and ideologically charged assumptions about the nature of memory, history and the nation, which memory studies had better shed if it wants to capitalize on the great inspirational value of the idea of the *lieu de mémoire* in order to study the increasingly globalizing processes and constellations of cultural memory (see chapter III.1.6).

II.4   Aleida and Jan Assmann: The Cultural Memory

The theory of 'Cultural Memory' (*das kulturelle Gedächtnis*), which was introduced by Aleida and Jan Assmann at the end of the 1980s, has proved to be the most influential approach of memory studies in the German-speaking world. (To distinguish it from a more generic use of the term 'cultural memory', this text capitalizes 'Cultural Memory' when referring specifically to the Assmanns' concept.) One of its central achievements is to describe the connection between culture and memory in a systematic, conceptually nuanced and theoretically sound manner. In particular through its accent on the interdependences among cultural memory, collective identity, and political legitimation, the Assmanns' theory makes it possible to deal with a range of phenomena which have been of increasing interest in the humanities and the social sciences since the 1980s. The theory of Cultural Memory has generated a shared field of research and brought together under one roof such disparate academic fields as history, anthropology, archaeology, religious studies, media theory, literary studies and sociology.

II.4.1   Communicative Memory and Cultural Memory

The starting point of the theory of Cultural Memory is the distinction between two registers of Halbwachs's collective memory. Jan and Aleida Assmann's concept, which is in many aspects indebted to Halbwachs's findings, is grounded in the insight that there is a qualitative difference between a collective memory that is based on forms of everyday interaction and communication and a collective memory that is more institutionalized and rests on rituals and media. In response, they differentiate between two 'memory frameworks' – communicative memory on the one hand and the Cultural Memory on the other.

Jan Assmann (1992, 56) pointedly contrasts characteristics of communicative memory and Cultural Memory, in order to show that the contents, forms, media, temporal structure and carriers of these two memory frameworks are fundamentally different from one another (see also Table II.2):

- *Communicative memory* comes into being through everyday interaction; its contents consist of the historical experiences of contemporaries and it thus always refers only to a limited, shifting temporal horizon of about eighty to one hundred years. The contents of communicative memory are changeable and not ascribed a determined meaning. Within this framework, everyone is considered equally competent in remembering and interpreting the common past. Communicative memory, according to Jan Assmann, belongs to the field of oral history. The Assmanns use communicative memory as a contrasting term to better demarcate the field of Cultural Memory, which represents the actual focus of their research.
- *Cultural Memory* is a memory which is tied to material objectivations. It is purposefully established and ceremonialized. Remembering within the framework of the Cultural Memory takes place in what Jan Assmann calls the 'temporal dimension of the festival' (while communicative memory is tied to the 'temporal dimension of everyday life'. Cultural Memory transports a fixed set of contents and meanings, which are maintained and interpreted by trained specialists (for example, priests, shamans, or archivists). At its core are mythical events of a distant past which are interpreted as foundational to the community (for example, the exodus from Egypt or the Trojan War). Between the time remembered in the framework of the communicative memory and that remembered in the Cultural Memory, thus, there is a gaping hole, or – using the term coined by the anthropologist Jan Vansina – a shifting 'floating gap' that moves along with the passage of time.

Table II.2 Comparison of communicative memory and Cultural Memory
(J. Assmann 1992, 56)

	Communicative memory	Cultural Memory
Content	historical experiences within the framework of individual biographies	mythical past/ancient history, events from an absolute past
Forms	informal, loosely shaped, natural, created through interaction and everyday experience	consciously established, highly formalized, ceremonial communication, festival
Media	living memory in individual minds, experience, hearsay	established objectivations, traditional symbolic encoding/ staging in word, image, dance, etc.
Temporal structure	80–100 years, a temporal horizon of three or four generations that shifts with the passage of time	absolute past of a mythical ancient time
Carriers	non-specific, eyewitnesses within a memory community	specialized carriers of tradition

In an essay entitled 'Collective Memory and Cultural Identity' (published in German in 1988 and in English in 1995), Jan Assmann coined the term 'Cultural Memory' and offered the following definition:

> The concept of cultural memory comprises that body of reusable texts, images, and rituals specific to each society in each epoch, whose 'cultivation' serves to stabilize and convey that society's self-image. Upon such collective knowledge, for the most part (but not exclusively) of the past, each group bases its awareness of unity and particularity. (1995, 132)

A cluster of central characteristics establishes the meaning of the term 'Cultural Memory' (J. Assmann 1995, 130–2):

- *Concretion of identity* means that social groups constitute a Cultural Memory, from which they derive their collective identity.
- Cultural Memory's *capacity to reconstruct* takes into account the insight that every memory is related to the present situation: Cultural Memory is a retrospective construction.
- *Formation* is the first distinctive characteristic that distinguishes between the frameworks of communicative and Cultural Memory. Cultural Memory requires the continuation of meaning through

established, stable forms of expression; communicative memory is more flexible. One of Cultural Memory's methods of stabilization is the creation of 'memory figures' (*Erinnerungsfiguren*), the amalgamation of an image and a term or a narrative (as, for example, in the memory figure of 'Exodus'; see J. Assmann 1992, 37).

• *Organization* refers to the institutionalization of Cultural Memory and the specialization of its carriers. These gatekeepers of memory are usually elites, such as shamans, priests, or professors of history.

• The *obligation* of Cultural Memory 'engenders a clear system of values and differentiations in importance' (J. Assmann 1995, 131) for the group.

• The characteristic of *reflexivity*, lastly, points to the fact that Cultural Memory reflects the group's lifeworld and its self-image, and is moreover self-reflexive.

Such a bisection of Halbwachs's collective memory has proven to be highly suggestive for numerous authors and it turns up again and again, in one form or another, as *milieux de mémoire* and *lieux de mémoire* (Pierre Nora), as 'vernacular' and 'official' memory (John Bodnar), and as 'lived' and 'distant' memory (William Hirst and David Manier). This tendency to further subdivide cultural remembrance into two modes likely results from the need to differentiate between the reference to events of one's own epoch and the reference to more distant epochs; between unofficial and official forms of commemoration; between modifiable, negotiable everyday memory and meaning-laden traditions; between oral forms of remembrance and a memory which relies on other, more elaborate media technologies; and thus also, as Aleida Assmann puts it, between the relative fluidity and fixity, the more liquid and the more stable forms of cultural memory (see A. Assmann 1991).

However, at first glance, the Assmanns' use of the terms 'cultural' and 'communicative' may seem confusing. The adjective 'cultural' in the context of their theory does not denote a broad understanding of culture, that is, the totality of human self-interpretations in a given context, but rather the area which Aleida Assmann (1991) calls 'culture as monument' (as opposed to 'culture as lifeworld', the staged, stylized, observer-oriented areas of (high) culture). This use of the term 'culture' is not fully compatible with the current anthropological understanding, which also encompasses practices of everyday life and popular culture. 'Cultural Memory' does therefore *not* describe all manifestations of 'memory in culture'; rather it represents a subset of this: the societal construction of normative and formative versions of the past.

In fact, the attribute 'cultural' in the broad anthropological sense can be applied to both the communicative as well as the Cultural Memory, as both are certainly phenomena of culture. The opposite also holds true: Both Cultural and also communicative memory are 'communicative' as it is only through media communication that memory can be conveyed intersubjectively.

And, of course, Jan Assmann's distinguishing criteria – contents, media, forms, time structure, carriers – cannot really be unambiguously assigned to one or the other framework of memory. Life experience, for example, is nowadays by no means transmitted solely through oral everyday speech, but also through a host of mass media and the so-called new media (for example, in blogs and on Facebook). And equally, in the age of the Internet and formats such as Wikipedia there is an increased blurring of the distinction between specialists and laymen of the Cultural Memory.

Relativizing his polarizing contrast of Cultural and communicative memory, Jan Assmann (1992, 51) explains: 'At stake here are two modes of remembering, two functions of memory and the past – "uses of the past" – which one must first carefully distinguish, even if they permeate one another in manifold ways in the reality of a historical culture.' Working from this insight, Cultural Memory and communicative memory should be conceived of as two *modi memorandi*, modes of memory, possible horizons of reference to the past. Their distinction depends upon the (conscious or unconscious) decision as to which mode will be applied for the remembering – the mode of the 'foundational' or the 'biographical memory' (ibid.). This means that in a given historical context, the same event can become simultaneously an object of the Cultural Memory *and* of the communicative memory. Such a scenario is not an exceptional borderline case, but is rather a recurrent characteristic of modern memory culture. In societies which have experienced massive changes in recent times, it is in fact the rule. For example, the French Revolution around 1800 and the First World War in the 1920s were objects of both the Cultural and also the communicative memory. The Second World War and the Holocaust still are today. In this sort of historical constellations we are dealing with a 'simultaneity of the non-simultaneous' (Wilhelm Pinder) evoked through concurrent yet divergent modes of imagining the past.

As part of life experience, of a 'lived' or 'experienced history' (Halbwachs's *histoire vécue*), such historic events are the content of communicative generational memories. They are understood as a component of temporally limited, group-specific worlds of experience, as events which had an effect on individuals' lives. Memories in accordance with communicative memory belong, in Aleida Assmann's (1991, 12) words, to the everyday 'near horizon' of a time perceived as the 'present'. The rememberers connect the memories with their lifeworld: 'The lifeworld context is a near horizon, which tightly and flexibly encloses the present.' As objects of 'foundational remembering', the same events have very different implications. They are part of a cultural 'distant horizon'. Remembering in accordance with the Cultural Memory means the 'transformation of the past into foundational history, that is, into myth' (J. Assmann 1992, 77).

The 'distant horizon' of Cultural Memory, however, can, in terms of historical-chronological time, be extremely near. Not only has foundational history, at least since the beginning of modernity and the associated experience of an 'acceleration of time' (Koselleck) in the eighteenth century, as well as the founding of nation-states in the nineteenth century, slipped largely into the area of historical time, but its most significant elements even arise from a very close historical past. The French Revolution took on the character of a foundational event almost immediately. The same holds true for the founding of the German Reich in 1871, for the world wars in the twentieth century, and last but not least for '9/11'. Such ad hoc transformations of events barely past into foundational history share basic characteristics with the memory of 'distant', 'mythical' times and fulfil the same functions. The mode of Cultural Memory generates meaning which, first, is to a greater extent binding and obligatory than is the case for the mode of communicative memory, and which, second, claims to be valid for very large mnemonic communities (religious groups, societies, and so on). Connected with Cultural remembering are usually political or ideological functionalizations of the past. Cultural Memory therefore has to be legitimized (which is not necessarily the case with communicative memory). To this end, foundational events are tied to events of a distant past and/or visions of a distant future.

The central criterion to differentiate the 'Cultural' from the 'communicative' mode of remembering is therefore, it seems, not the measurable time (the chronological distance of the remembered events from the present in which the act of remembering takes place). It is rather the way of remembering chosen by a community, the collective *idea* of the meaning of past events and of their embeddedness within temporal processes, which makes a memory 'Cultural' or 'communicative'. Thus the distinction between the two modes rests not primarily on the *structure* of time (a universal, measurable category), but rather on the *consciousness* of time (a culturally and historically variable phenomenon of the mental dimension of culture). The criterion 'consciousness of time' also overrules the strict differentiation between the media associated with each of the two frameworks of memory. Neither is the production of communicative memory limited to orality, nor do all texts and images automatically belong to Cultural Memory. The deciding factor is rather the media *usage*.

II.4.2   Cultural memory, writing, and political identity

In Germany, the most influential book in the area of cultural memory studies is arguably still Jan Assmann's *Das kulturelle Gedächtnis* ('The Cultural Memory,' 1992), in which he addresses the connections between memory, the formation of collective identity, and the exercise of political power, and also the differences and similarities between oral and written cultures. 'Societies imagine their self-images and maintain an identity over the course of generations by developing a culture of memory, and they do this in *entirely different ways*', Jan Assmann emphasizes (ibid., 18). His goal is to illustrate these differences in the 'connective structure' of societies (that is, a structure that brings together different times – past and present – as well as different groups of a society through acts of remembering; see ibid., 16), by creating a typology of cultures. The Egyptologist Assmann uses as examples the early eastern and western civilizations – Egypt, Israel, the Hittites, and Greece.

The two central media of Cultural Memory, orality and literacy, can fulfil fundamentally the same functions, as far as the creation of cultural coherence is concerned: They are *functionally* equivalent. However, the introduction of writing does influence the *forms* through which the past is envisioned in a culture. Assmann speaks of the ritual coherence of oral cultures and of the textual coherence of literate cultures. Oral cultures depend on the relatively exact repetition of their myths, since the Cultural Memory is stored in the organic memories of the singers or shamans and any variation could endanger the tradition. Textual coherence, on the other hand, relies on the outsourcing of cultural meaning into the medium of writing. By means of such medial externalization, it becomes possible to transmit more than that which the individual is able to keep in his or her memory. However, the obligatory, canonical texts of Cultural Memory must be re-appropriated by later generations. Their meaning has to be laid out, interpreted: Textual coherence thus goes hand-in-hand with the cultural techniques of commentary, imitation or critique.

Drawing on a distinction made by Claude Lévi-Strauss, Jan Assmann names two possible strategies of memory policy: the 'hot' and the 'cold' options. Hot cultures, such as ancient Israel, are dynamic societies which make memory the engine of their development. Alternatively, societies can 'freeze' historical change through remembering an eternally unchanged past. Examples of such cold cultures are ancient Egypt or medieval Judaism.

The Cultural Memory is founded on 'myths', stories about a common past, which offer orientation in the present and hope for the future. These stories can (as in the case of ancient Egyptian culture) feature elements of an absolute past, of mythical time; but they can also (as in the case of ancient Israel) deal with a relative past, with history. No matter whether they rest on facts or fiction, either way, the myths of the Cultural Memory fulfil a specific function: 'Myth is a story one tells oneself in order to orient oneself in the world; [it is] a truth of a higher order, which is not simply true but in addition makes normative claims and possesses a formative power' (ibid., 76).

Myths tend to exhibit both a foundational as well as a contra-present dynamic. The myth provides the fundament for and legitimizes existing systems when it is perceived by society as an expression of a common history, from which present circumstances derive. In contrast, the myth can also take on a contra-present and potentially delegitimizing meaning if it serves to contrast a 'deficient present' with the memory of a past, better era.

The case studies in the second part of *Das kulturelle Gedächtnis* show that writing, cultural memory, and political identity are quite closely entwined. Shared, identity-forming cultural meaning is established and maintained in literate cultures through normative and formative texts. '*Normative* texts codify the norms of social behaviour. *Formative* texts formulate the self-image of the group and the knowledge that secures their identity' (J. Assmann 2006, 104). The former answer the question of 'what should we do?'; the latter that of 'who are we?' Such texts constitute the monumental discourse of Egypt, are the prerequisite for religious memory as resistance in Israel, and cultivate the ethnogenesis, the birth of a culture, in Greece.

II.4.3   Memory as *ars* und *vis*, functional memory and stored memory

Aleida Assmann prefaces her book *Erinnerungsräume* (1999, 'Memory Spaces'), which further develops the theory of Cultural Memory, with a fundamental distinction: memory as *ars* vs memory as *vis*. The concept of memory as *ars*, as art or technology, goes back to the topological model of ancient mnemonics (see chapter III.2.1). Memory as *ars* appears as a storehouse of knowledge, in which information can be deposited and later recalled in the same form. The concept of memory as *vis*, an anthropological 'force', in contrast, accentuates the temporal dimension and time's transformative effect on the contents of memory, thus highlighting memory's processual nature and its reconstructive activity. Memory as *vis* always also implies forgetting, since from the plethora of things that could be remembered only a few elements can be chosen which speak to the present situation.

Assmann uses these two traditional conceptions of memory as a basis for a typology of cultures: It is the period 'around 1800' – when the ancient mnemotechnics became less prestigious, Locke had developed his philosophy of identity, the bourgeois subject had come into being, and finally the 'romantic concept of identity-through-memory' was arising – which she identifies as the turning point: The previously dominant concept of memory as *ars* is now replaced by an understanding of memory as *vis* (ibid., 89–113). During the nineteenth century, then, the philosopher and cultural critic Friedrich Nietzsche became the 'patron of the paradigm of identity-creating memory' (ibid., 29).

To describe how the contents of the Cultural Memory are activated and deactivated, Assmann makes one further distinction, that between functional and stored memory (or: working and archival memory). Functional memory is the 'inhabited memory'. It consists of 'meaningful elements' which can be configured to form a coherent story. Functional memory is characterized by its 'relevance to a group, selectivity, its relation to shared values and an orientation towards the future'. The stored memory, on the other hand, is the 'uninhabited memory', 'an amorphous mass' of unconnected, 'neutral elements', which do not exhibit any 'vital connection' to the present (ibid., 134f.).

> On a collective level, the stored memory contains that which has become unusable, obsolete, or foreign; the neutral, identity-abstract factual knowledge; but also the repertoire of missed opportunities, alternative options, and unused chances. The functional memory, in contrast, is an acquired memory, which emerges from a process of choosing, connecting, and constituting meaning. Unstructured, disconnected elements enter the functional memory composed, constructed, and connected. Meaning emerges from this constructive act, a quality which the stored memory fundamentally lacks. (ibid., 137)

Aleida Assmann describes the relationship between these two areas of the Cultural Memory as 'perspectival'. The functional memory should be seen as existing in the foreground, silhouetted against the background of the stored memory (see also A. Assmann 1996b).

While the functional memory fulfils such important tasks as identity construction or the legitimization of an existing societal form, the stored memory is no less important. It serves as a 'reservoir for future functional memories', as a 'resource for the renewal of cultural knowledge' and thus as a 'condition for the possibility of cultural change' (ibid., 140). The elements of the stored memory can – should they acquire an additional dimension of meaning for society – cross over into the functional memory. The decisive aspect is thus not only the contents of the two areas of Cultural Memory, but also the degree of permeability between them, as this determines the possibilities for change and renewal (see Table II.3).

The distinction between a stored and a functional memory allows an explanation of processes of change within the Cultural Memory. In *Erinnerungsräume*, Assmann recounts the history of such changes from ancient to postmodern times.

Aleida Assmann's concept of Cultural Memory as the totality of stored *and* functional memory entails an enormous expansion of the phenomena that can be studied from a memory studies perspective. All objectivations which a given culture preserves now come into sight: not only the central 'reusable' texts, images and rituals, but also documents stored in archives, long-forgotten works of art, scarcely heeded

Table II.3   Differences between stored and functional memory (Assmann and Assmann 1994, 123)

	Stored memory	Functional memory
Content	'the Other', transcending of the present	'the Self', the present rests on the fundament of a specific past
Temporal structure	anachronous: dual temporal horizon, the past exists alongside the present; contra present dynamics	diachronic: continuity between past and present
Forms	inviolability of texts; documents have autonomous status	selective = strategic, perspectival use of memories
Media and Institutions	literature, art, museums, science	festivals, public rituals of collective commemoration
Carriers	individuals within a cultural group	collectivized subjects

buildings, and so on. The bundle of characteristics suggested by Jan Assmann in his 1988 essay clearly applies only to the core area of functional memory – to the Cultural Memory in the narrow sense – which has merely one characteristic in common with Cultural Memory in the broader sense, namely that of 'formation'. The distinction between functional and stored memory further clarifies why the Assmanns' concept is not merely a 'reissue' of the study of tradition. Cultural Memory, in contrast to tradition, exists not only 'in the modus of actuality', but also in the 'modus of potentiality as an archive, as a "total horizon"' (J. Assmann 1988, 13). The concept of tradition brings only the actuality of memory culture into focus. The Assmanns' concept not only describes a larger field than could be grasped with research on tradition or on *lieux de mémoire*; it also allows for a description of the reservoirs, origins, dynamics, and changes of cultural recall.

III
The Disciplines of Memory Studies

Since the 1980s, with the emergence of the 'new' cultural memory studies, 'memory' has widely been understood as a genuinely transdisciplinary phenomenon whose functioning cannot really be understood through examination from one single perspective. Cultural memory studies is therefore not merely a multidisciplinary field, but fundamentally an interdisciplinary project. Nonetheless, many concepts of memory have evolved over the past two or three decades which are specific to individual disciplines. In fact, within historical studies or the social sciences, literary studies or psychology, 'memory' is nowadays constituted in such widely varying manners that it seems that we are dealing with a different object on each occasion – with 'memories', as a matter of fact. Nevertheless, the disciplines of memory studies are steadily moving towards one another, and scholars are increasingly interested in the possibilities offered by interdisciplinary exchange. Successful cross-fertilization, however, presupposes a knowledge of discipline-specific concepts, methodologies and background assumptions. The focus of this chapter is therefore on both the approaches to memory taken within specific disciplines and also the possibilities of designing interdisciplinary and integrative models of memory in culture.

III.1 Historical and social memory

Historical studies and the social sciences not only laid the foundations for interdisciplinary memory studies; today they are still the most active in memory research. (For an overview of historical memory studies, see also Cubitt 2007; on social memory studies Misztal 2003.) Of course, this is not too surprising, as historical consciousness and remembering in a social context are two of the central components of cultural memory. Maurice Halbwachs's *mémoire collective* and Pierre Nora's *lieux de mémoire*, the two most important concepts of social and historical memory research, have already been introduced in chapter II. This chapter looks more closely at the discipline-specific concerns and debates about memory that are carried out in historical studies and the social sciences. The chapter closes with what can be identified as a new field of convergence in memory studies: research on transcultural and globalizing memory.

III.1.1 History and/or/as memory

A question which to a certain extent stands at the beginning of recent historical memory research is that of 'history and/or/as memory'. Since the beginning of the 1970s historians have been increasingly interested in the relation of history and memory. The debate centres around the question of whether historiography itself is not a form of cultural memory. After all, even historical sources are cultural artefacts which do not reflect a past reality, but rather re-construct it. In addition, the activity of historians by no means lives up to the naïve ideal of objectivity which Halbwachs still posited as the basis of his polemical contrast between uninvolved history and evaluative memory. Historians are bound to their historical position and their personal perspective. They select certain historical events and exclude others; they transform the chronicle of events into a meaningful story by means of narrative structuring and rhetorical devices; and in doing so inevitably interpret it (see White 1973). In short, just like remembering, all history writing is a constructive, narrative process, deeply imbued with – often unacknowledged – patterns of culture and ideology.

Then there is the question of which social functions should be assumed by historiography: Should it attempt a fairly objective and uninvolved reconstruction of the past, or should it undertake a debate with history which takes sides, bears witness, and 'has an agenda' in the present? In other words, does historiography have a dominant scholarly function or a dominant memorial function? (Habermas 1988) In the German 'historians' dispute' (*Historikerstreit*, 1986–87), and perhaps even more so in the framework of the 'historicization debate' (*Historisierungsdebatte*, 1985–88), exemplified by the correspondence between Martin Broszat and Saul Friedländer (1990), the main issue was this tension between 'objective-scholarly' and 'subjective-memorial' forms of approaching the Holocaust.

In France, questions of memory versus history are tied up with heated public debates and with veritable wars fought over the past – the so-called *guerres de mémoires*. Pascal Blanchard and Isabelle Veyrat-Masson (2008, 17), editors of a volume of the same title, assert that 'the opposition between history and memory has become one of the major paradigms of current intellectual debates'. However, it is not only in France, but virtually all across the globe, that 'memory wars' are taking place and politically highly charged notions of 'memory' (connoting 'counter-memory', 'memory from below', 'the victims' memories' are used in the public arena by various identity groups) and pitted against 'history' (implying official versions of the past and historiographies written from western, white, male, middle-class perspectives), in order to follow specific aims in the present, such as the recognition of colonial injustice, the inclusion of women's writings into the literary canon, or the restitution of victims of war and genocide. Addressing this issue, Pierre Nora (2006, 9) speaks of the 'tyrannie de la mémoire', even of memory's 'terrorisme', and feels that French society is menaced by the rewriting of history from the point of view of different identity groups, such as 'les ouvriers, les juifs, les femmes, les Corses, les Noirs etc.'. How can memory researchers deal with such inordinate rhetoric? The highly charged opposition of 'history versus memory' can only be critically assessed by, first of all, taking a very close look at what exactly is meant by the two terms, history and memory.

Arguably, to no other field is the connection between culture and memory as central as it is to historical studies; and it is at the same time nowhere as hotly debated (see also the discussions in the journals *History and Memory* and *History & Theory*). The memory discourse is particularly loaded in historical studies, because with it the very self-understanding of the field would seem to be at stake. As Marcus Sandl (2005, 95f.) has pointed out, the 'concept of memory seemed to many historians to be the Trojan horse of the postmodern criticism of historical grand narratives, or at least to be the attempt to popularize the historical'. From a more optimistic perspective, memory research could be seen as making possible for historians both a study of the past and at the same time an acknowledgement of the insights of poststructuralism. Consequently, memory is seen by some historians as a new key concept within a theoretically reflected New Cultural History (see the seminal essays by Confino 1997; Megill 1998; Kansteiner 2002), which proceeds from the insight that, as stated by Raphael Samuel stated *Theatres of Memory* (1994, 25), we live 'in an expanding historical culture, in which the work of inquiry and retrieval is being progressively extended into all kinds of spheres that would have been thought unworthy of notice in the past'. Jan Assmann (1997, 9) has introduced the term 'mnemohistory' and emphasized that this kind of research 'is not the opposite of history, but rather is one of its branches or subdisciplines, such as intellectual history, social history, the history of mentalities, or the history of ideas'.

Some of the most significant positions in the discussion of 'history and/or/as memory' will be briefly considered on the following pages. The spectrum extends from attempts to demonstrate the similarities, or indeed identity, between history and memory – *History as an Art of Memory*, to use the term coined by Patrick Hutton (1993) – all the way to the emotionally charged insistence that they are in fact incompatible (here Halbwachs's and Nora's contributions are constitutive; see chapter II).

In *History and Memory* (1992; orig.: *Storia e memoria*, 1977ff.) Jacques Le Goff provides one of the most pertinent histories of memory from the ancient world to the present (on his history of media, see also chapter V.2). In the preface, Le Goff offres a brief sketch of his understanding of the relationship between the two forms of reference to the past. Here, it becomes clear that they are for him two distinct, albeit mutually influential, processes to organize knowledge. For Le Goff, the discipline of history must

> seek to be objective and ... remain based on the belief in the historical 'truth.' Memory is the raw material of history. Whether mental, oral, or written, it is the living source from which historians draw. ... Moreover, the discipline of history nourishes memory in turn, and enters into the great dialectical process of memory and forgetting experienced by individuals and societies. The historian must be there to render an account of these memories and of what is forgotten, to transform them into something that can be conceived, to make them knowable. (xi–xii)

Similarly, David Lowenthal, in his fundamental work *The Past is a Foreign Country* (1985), draws a clear distinction between memory and history. In a famous phrasing, he emphasizes that 'the past is a foreign country whose features are shaped by today's predilections, its strangeness domesticated by our own preservation of its vestiges' (ibid., xvii). 'Memory and history are processes of insight; each involves components of the other, and their boundaries are shadowy. Yet memory and history are normally and justifiably distinguished: memory is inescapable and prima-facie indubitable; history is contingent and empirically testable' (ibid., 187). This is the received historian's notion about memory as 'the Other' of history, which has, however, been much complicated in memory studies since.

'History *or* memory' is an alternative which, according to Yosef Hayim Yerushalmi, the Jewish people were faced with in the course of their millennia of history. His classic book, *Zakhor: Jewish History and Jewish Memory* (1982), centres on a mnemonic community in which the injunction to remember (*zakhor!*) plays a prominent role. In four lectures, Yerushalmi shows that the written fixation of current events as provided by historiography and memory as lived tradition are, in the case of Jewish mnemohistory, mutually exclusive. The Biblical texts, Yerushalmi argues, still exhibit a certain sense of historical time and historical change. But after the Biblical canon is completed, the Jews practice virtually no historiography any longer. Jewish memory, in the centuries after the destruction of the second temple, is represented in the ahistorically structured rabbinical writings: The events recounted in the Bible become archetypes for every later historical event. As a result, Jews in the Middle Ages abstain completely from recording current events. It is not until the nineteenth century that scholarly research into Jewish history is first undertaken. Yet, as a result of secularization, the rise of modern Jewish historiography is accompanied by the decline of Jewish memory, which was a living tradition, yet lacking what would today be called 'historical consciousness'. However, modern historiography cannot constitute a memory that provides orientation, because 'those who are alienated from the past cannot be drawn to it by explanation alone; they require evocation as well' (Yerushalmi 1982, 100).

The origins of the opposition 'history *versus* memory' so prevalent in current public debates can be traced back to the debates elicited by revisionist work of social historians in the 1960s who, in writing 'history from below' (Thompson 1963), usually in a Marxist or Gramscian tradition, pitted 'people's memory' (local versions of the past, often of 'subalterns', that is, people outside the hegemonic power structure and without agency) against the official records of the past. Postcolonial historiography, notably the Subaltern Studies Group, rewrote colonial history from the perspectives of colonized peasants or 'doubly marginalized' women. Combining approaches from anthropology and history, using written and oral evidence, they tried to read colonial records 'against the grain' (in Walter Benjamin's sense), focusing on silences and omissions (Guha 1983; Amin 1995). 'Memory' in this tradition of historiographical work designates 'counter-memory' (on the delegitimation of the hegemonic memory through *contre-mémoire*, see Foucault 1977). Working with 'memory' in this tradition means the recovery of past experience that was forgotten or repressed by official historiography.

A different approach to the problem of history and memory was taken by Bernard Lewis who pointed out as early as 1975 that there are functions of 'historiography *as* memory'. He distinguishes between: (1) remembered history, that is, collective memory as defined by Halbwachs; (2) recovered history, the historiographical reconstruction of elements of the past suppressed by the collective memory (which Lewis sees as a modern and European phenomenon); and (3) invented history, the version of history which pursues a (novel) ideological aim.

One of the most thought-provoking considerations of the relation of history and memory is Peter Burke's seminal article 'History as Social Memory' (1989), which anticipated many later developments of cultural memory studies. Burke clearly opposes the 'traditional account of the relation between memory and written history, in which memory reflects what actually happened and history reflects memory' (ibid., 97). On the contrary, 'current studies of the history of historical writing treat it much as Halbwachs treated memory, as the product of social groups such as Roman senators, Chinese mandarins, Benedictine monks, university professors and so on' (ibid. 98). Both the selection and the interpretation of historical events in historiography are socially and culturally determined. Burke thus professes to a 'historical relativism' (ibid., 99), yet without renouncing a claim to the specific possibilities that the discipline of history has at its disposal to create methodologically sound – 'reliable, plausible, perceptive' (ibid.) – accounts of the past. Burke calls for a 'social history of remembering' guided by the questions 'who wants whom to remember what, and why? Whose version of the past is recorded and preserved?' (ibid., 107).

According to Jörn Rüsen, 'historical memory' is an integral part of 'historical culture', which in turn can be defined as 'the very field of human life where history is a part of social reality' (2005, 4). History is a 'meaningful nexus between past, present and future' (25). Historical consciousness – which is always formed by narrative and 'based on the agency of memory' – 'deals with the past qua experience; it reveals to us the web of temporal change within which our lives are caught up, and (at least indirectly) the future perspectives toward which that change is flowing' (ibid.). Thus, one central function of historical consciousness consists in 'temporal orientation' (ibid.). (For more on 'historical consciousness' as a link between history and collective memory, see Funkenstein 1989.) Rüsen distinguishes between an aesthetic, a political, and a cognitive dimension of dealing with the past (5). It is only the last of these that he assigns to the field of historical studies, which is distinguished from all other forms of conscious memory work in that it specifically claims to be scientific: 'Truth claims and rationality constitute historical studies as an academic discipline or as a 'science' in a broader sense' (ibid., 2).

In the ongoing memory debates among historians, increasing importance is placed on the way that historical memory is represented in individual minds. History culture and historical consciousness necessarily have to be actualized in organic memories in order to have any effect (see Crane 1997). And in turn, it is individual minds which produce – by means of the medial externalization of organic memories – what is later used as historical sources (letters, archival documents, and so on). How such processes of internalization and externalization in the production of history can be described is a question which can only be answered through collaborative research carried out by historians, psychologists, and neuroscientists (for some interdisciplinary models of cultural memory, see chapter III.3.3).

To sum up, many problems have arisen in the discussions surrounding 'history and/or/as memory' because the two terms tend to be treated in parallel, in order to then postulate their difference or identity. Yet this approach, inherited from Halbwachs, popularized by Nora, and continued in many current publications, leads from the very first step to a precarious situation, as it forms an unfruitful – and indeed misleading – opposition. In his critical survey of the recent appearance of the concept of 'memory' in historical discourse, Kerwin Lee Klein (2000, 128f.) summarizes the situation: 'Where history is concerned, memory increasingly functions as antonym rather than synonym; contrary rather than complement and replacement rather than supplement.'

And where the concept of cultural memory is already notoriously multifarious, in discussions among historians it is moreover very often not clear which aspects of 'history as a collective singular' (Koselleck 2004, 195) are actually contrasted with it:

- selective and appropriated memory vs the totality of 'raw' *historical events*?
- 'authentic', immediate memory vs mediated, ideologically fraught models, images or *narratives of history*?
- methodologically unregulated, identity-related, subjective and unreliable memory vs scholarly, ostensibly neutral, and objective *historiography*?
- memory as the layman's pastime vs history as an *academic subject*?

- memory and its broad and heterogeneous group of carriers vs the institutionalized guild of *historians*?
- memory as a private undertaking vs history as *the official version of the past*?
- memory as counter-memory and the victims' version of the past vs the 'grand narratives' and the *'history of the victors'*.

The list of fallacious oppositions could go on. This book abandons the antagonism of 'history versus memory'. Instead, it uses 'cultural memory' as a broad cover term and understands historical reference to the past as *one* mode of cultural remembering (which only emerged around 1800 and is thus specific to the modern era). Historical memory takes place within comprehensive memory cultures, which usually also feature many other ways of remembering. 'History' is thus *one* symbolic form of reference to the past. In addition to history, other symbolic forms, such as religion, myth, and literature, contribute to the production of cultural memory. Likewise, historiography is *one* medium of cultural memory alongside other media, such as novels, architecture or rituals.

III.1.2   The 'Shoah' as test case and other topics of mnemohistorical research

Mnemohistorical research has been flourishing since the 1980s. Today, it is generally accepted that there are no transhistorically valid answers to the question of how groups and societies refer to the past. As a result, historical studies focus on specific constellations of collective remembering and ask how these change over time. They also address the historical variability of the very concepts of 'history' and 'memory'. Mnemohistory is thus interested in the cultural practices of memory as well as in memory cultures' self-reflexivity. Moreover, it also applies the insights of memory studies to the discipline of history itself: Not only the objects of study (for example, Jews in the Middle Ages, the French Third Republic, Vietnam War veterans), but also the contexts within which the research takes place are understood as specific, historically situated memory cultures, which have a significant influence on the selection and interpretation of past events.

A topic which has been the focus of especially intensive mnemohistorical research is the Shoah and its consequences for the formation of cultural memory. Here in particular the limits of a purely scholarly-historiographic approach to the past come to light. The Shoah has proved a test case for historical memory. In his preface to the edited volume *Probing the Limits of Representation* (1992, 2f.), now a classic of Holocaust studies, Saul Friedländer points out that in the extermination of the Jews 'we are dealing with an event which tests our traditional conceptual and representational categories, an "event at the limits"'. He emphasizes also that 'there are limits to representation *which should not be but can easily be transgressed.*' The contributors to his collection of essays – Hayden White, Amos Funkenstein, Carlo Ginzburg, Dominick LaCapra, Dan Diner, Geoffrey H. Hartman and others – all address the dilemma of 'a need for "truth"' on the one hand, and 'the opaqueness of the events and the opaqueness of language' on the other (ibid., 4). In *Memory, History and the Extermination of the Jews of Europe* (1993, x), Friedländer further examines the difficult relationship between public memory and historiography of the Shoah and points out that 'we are confronted with an insoluble choice between the *inadequacy* of traditional historical representation and the need to establish as reliable a narration as possible. At the same time we must comply with the most rigorous requirements of scholarship in order to keep records of events which are constantly challenged by a negationist trend' (1993, x; for similar concerns, see also Hartman 1994).

In discussions about the Holocaust and (the limits of) historical representation, the issue of trauma has become a central paradigm. In *Holocaust Testimonies* (1991), the psychoanalyst Lawrence Langer focuses on oral testimonies of Holocaust survivors, and further develops Charlotte Delbo's concept of a traumatic 'deep memory' which is distinct from the survivors' more detached 'common memory'. Dori Laub and Shoshana Felman (1992) explore the nexus between witnessing, testimony, and the transgenerational transmission of traumata, using an interdisciplinary methodology which brings together psychoanalysis and literary and historical studies.

Psychoanalytical approaches to historiography and historical consciousness have in particular been developed within the field of Holocaust studies. The combination of psychoanalysis and mnemo-history has engendered a set of new questions about the Shoah – for example, in relation to the latent motivations of historical actors (suppression, projection, or sublimation). Dan Diner (1986) detects 'screen memories' of the Holocaust – that is, the substitution and concealment of problematic experiences with the memory of unimportant events – on both the German and the Jewish sides. Henry Rousso (1991) identifies a 'Vichy syndrome' in French society, as a result of the trauma of the Second World War, occupation, and of the deep rift in society between collaborators and *Résistance*. In *Representing the Holocaust: History, Theory,*

Trauma (1996, xif.), Dominick LaCapra asks whether psychoanalysis 'should itself be understood not primarily as a psychology of the individual ... but as an inherently historicized mode of thought intimately bound up with social, political and ethical concerns'. He investigates the 'transferential relation between the historian or theorist and the object of analysis'. Although proponents of psychoanalytical memory studies like LaCapra emphasize the aim 'to articulate the relationship between history and psychoanalysis in a manner that does not eventuate in a dubious pathologization of historical processes or personalities but instead links historical inquiry to explicit ethical and ethicopolitical concerns bearing on the present and future' (LaCapra 1998, 180), the approach is not unproblematic (see chapter IV.1).

Part of psychoanalytically inspired historical studies is also the work on the memory of perpetrators. This, however, proves to be quite problematic as soon as it goes beyond a determination of a possible traumatization of the perpetrators (and their children) and also suggests the comparability of the experiences of perpetrators and victims. (For new perspectives on 'perpetrator memory' and 'memory about perpetrators', see *Memory Studies* 3.2 (2010).)

Further prominent topics in mnemohistory include – to offer just a small selection from a field so broad it is hard to get a clear overview – the memory of the world wars and other major upheavals since the early twentieth century, such as revolutions, decolonization, mass migration, and terror. From an early stage studies of the First World War have been connected to questions of memory (Fussell 1975; Mosse 1990; Winter 1995; Winter and Sivan 1999). Further challenging work has been done on the memory of Stalin (Roth 1995); on commemorative practices in the United States (Kammen 1991; Bodnar 1992); on Germany as a 'culture of remembrance' (Confino 2006; Kansteiner 2006); on South Africa's memory cultures before and after apartheid (Coombes 2003; Witz 2003); on memories in late socialist Vietnam (Tai 2001b); and on the genealogy and characteristics of what is understood as a specifically 'modern memory' (Matsuda 1996; Fritzsche 2004).

Such a list of the topics of historical memory research could be continued indefinitely. Mnemohistory has so heavily proliferated, also internationally, that it can no longer be meaningfully organized by its objects of attention. And besides this pragmatic reason there are also theoretical considerations against such an organization of the field. Alon Confino has taken a decided stance against a 'topical definition' of cultural memory, and drawn attention to the problem that thematically defined memory studies would quickly become a mere aggregation of research about various epochs, media, and events, 'a field with neither a center nor connections among topics' (Confino 1997, 1387). Instead of *topics*, thus, the following discussion foregrounds the field's specific analytical perspective and attempts to chart the *concepts* of memory studies. The focus is on approaches which have been developed for the study of mnemohistory on 'both sides of the floating gap', approaches, that is, which – to use the terminology of Aleida and Jan Assmann – help us to understand forms of remembering within the broad temporal horizon of the Cultural Memory ('*memoria*', 'memory cultures', 'invented traditions', the 'archive' and 'heritage'), as well as within the more narrow horizons of communicative memory (contemporary history, oral history, and generational memory).

III.1.3 Concepts: *Memoria*, memory cultures, invented traditions, archive and heritage

'*Memoria*', 'memory cultures', 'the invention of traditions', the 'archive' and 'heritage' are – in addition to the previously mentioned *lieux de mémoire* – four of the central, albeit extremely varied, concepts of memory research to have emerged internationally from the field of historical studies. All four concepts were developed for the analysis of long-term cultural memory – that is, for periods that go beyond the limits of generational memory. Research connected with these concepts is thus more strongly oriented towards more distant historical epochs (such as antiquity, the Middle Ages or the era of nation-states) than towards contemporary history.

Medievalist *memoria* research interprets medieval commemoration of the dead in rites and liturgy as a social act which constitutes a community of the living with the saints and the dead, or, as is formulated by Gerhard Oexle, which evokes the 'presence of the dead'. This branch of research looking at medieval memory goes back to the 1950s and the group of scholars associated with the medievalist Gerd Tellenbach in Freiburg, Germany. (For the history of memoria research, see Borgolte 2002.) Its focus were the *Libri Memoriales*, memorial books, of which Oexle (1994, 308) writes: 'These were always records of names, as it is the act of naming names, the recitation of names, that constitutes *memoria*.' While the medieval historians first addressed such obvious text types as memorial books, necrologies, and annals of the dead, it soon became clear, as their work on medieval memory became more interdisciplinary, that *memoria* in fact permeated medieval culture as a whole (see also Althoff, Fried and Geary 2002; Geary 1994).

With his concept of 'memoria as culture' Oexle (1995) firmly locates this research, once limited to the Middle Ages and the discipline of history, in a much broader transdisciplinary context. He understands 'memoria as a 'total' social phenomenon (Marcel Mauss) which encompasses all dimensions of life and has an impact on every area of life – not only religion, but also the economy, everyday life, philosophy, art, historiography, human relationships, social behaviour, and action as a whole' (Oexle 1994, 301). Oexle (ibid., 299) distinguishes this type of scholarly work on the social dimension of medieval *memoria* from studies on *ars memorativa*, on the rhetorical, literary, and artistic manifestations of the ancient art of memory in the Middle Ages, which will be presented in the following chapter (III.2.1) as key to art historical and literary memory studies. New approaches to medieval *memoria* focus further on the concept of 'ritual' (see van Bueren and van Leerdam 2005; Rose 2009) or study the preservation of medieval knowledge and the passing on of stories from one generation to the next (Houts 2001). Late medieval and early modern *memoria* is investigated by Gordon and Marshall (2000), and insights into the effects of the plague epidemic on Renaissance *memoria* practices are provided by Cohn (1992).

The concept of 'memory cultures', developed in Germany in the late 1990s, aimed to enable historical memory research across a wide spectrum of periods and cultural contexts. 'Memory Cultures' (*Erinnerungskulturen*) was the title of an interdisciplinary research centre established at the Justus Liebig University Giessen (Germany) in 1997. Its goal, as expressed in its first application for funding from 1996, was 'a thorough historicization of the category of memory' (*Erstantrag*, 11). The Giessen approach emphasizes the dynamic, creative, and processual nature, and, above all, the plurality of cultural memory. The use of the plural – memory cultures – is a token of the variety and historical as well as cultural variability of the many practices and concepts of memory. Thus, 'speaking of memory cultures in the plural does not just signify an accumulation, but rather is applied in a theoretically reflected manner' (ibid., 16). A model to study different memory cultures (from antiquity to the postmodern age) from an historical viewpoint was devised, the goal of which was 'not a synthesis or unity of the object ..., but rather the search for operative factors and transversal lines which open up various possibilities for the thematic, methodical, and theoretical preparation of the topic' (Sandl 2005, 108). In this vein, Giessen scholars focused, for example, on the 'challenges' faced by a memory culture, on questions of 'memory sovereignty' in a society (ranging all the way from 'hegemonic' to 'competing'), on the 'memory interests' of various social groups (which can compete, but also exist alongside each other, overlap or permeate one another), on 'technologies of memory,' (namely a society's mnemonic strategies, ways of communicating, and media) and, finally, on different 'types of memory work' (from 'scholarly-discursive' to 'imaginative-fictive' strategies).

A much more specific concept is that of 'the invention of tradition', a perspective developed by British Marxist historians interested in the emergence of nationalism. In their anthology *The Invention of Tradition* (1983), Eric Hobsbawm and Terence Ranger showed that the national memories of the late nineteenth century were social constructions, based on traditions invented by elites. They distinguish between changeable 'customs' on the one hand and generally invented, yet always static 'traditions' on the other. Scotland, Wales, the British monarchy, Victorian India and colonial Africa all have their specific invented traditions. The era of the nation-states in Europe between 1870 and 1914 is the zenith of this practice. Hobsbawm lists three types – or three functions – of invented traditions since the Industrial Revolution (ibid., 9): (1) 'establishing or symbolizing social cohesion'; (2) 'establishing or legitimizing institutions, status or relations of authority'; and (3) 'the inculcation of beliefs, value systems and conventions of behavior'.

According to Hobsbawm, invented traditions are 'responses to novel situations' (ibid., 2). They might refer to past events, people, or institutions formerly not granted much importance, or they might actually construct new pasts. In either case, it is a matter of 'the use of ancient materials to construct invented traditions of a novel type for quite novel purposes' (ibid., 6). Hobsbawm and Ranger's model of the emergence of national memory is closely correlated with that of Benedict Anderson's (1983) idea of nations as imagined communities. Both concepts are located within the context of Anglo-American historical studies and both take Marxist approaches to the study of nationalism (for new perspectives on the 'memory-nation connections', see Olick 2003).

Concepts of the archive as the 'memory of dominance and power' come predominantly from the historical and philosophical currents of French poststructuralism and are connected with the theories of Michel Foucault, Jacques Derrida and Giorgio Agamben. These are critical currents which challenge the idea of neutral data and the objectivity of their institutionalized collection and storage – that is, the archive. This line of attack appears first in Michel Foucault's *The Archaeology of Knowledge* (1972; orig.: *L'archéologie du savoir*, 1969), a type of alternative historiography of the field of history. In place of the guiding concepts dominant in the classic hermeneutic approach, all of which imply ideas of continuity – such as tradition, influence, development, evolution, mentality and spirit of the age – Foucault introduces to historical analysis terms such as break, discontinuity, and limit. He understands 'the archive' metaphorically, that is, *not* in its material and institutional dimension, but rather as the general system of the formation and trans-formation of discourses, as the 'law of what can be said, the system that governs the appearance of statements as unique events' (ibid., 145).

In 'Archive Fever: A Freudian Impression' (1995, 11) the philosopher Jacques Derrida confirms the link between the archive and power: 'There is no political power without control of the archive, if not of memory. Effective democratization can always be measured by this essential criterion: the participation in and the access to the archive, its constitu-tion, and its interpretation.' But he also understands the archive as a psychological drive, similar to Freud's death drive. Derrida thus identi-fies 'archival fever' as a contradictory drive, or desire, to collect and remember and at the same time to repress, destroy, and forget. Against the backdrop of transition and reconciliation in South Africa and the realization that also 'the country's archives require transformation, or refiguring', Hamilton et al. (2002, 7) bring together key texts and dis-cussions about the archive. (For a new approach on the Dutch colonial archive, see Stoler 2008.)

Within memory studies, the archive as a storage mechanism is often contrasted with acts of remembrance. In this way, Aleida Assmann refers to 'the actively circulated memory that keeps the past present as the *canon* and the passively stored memory that preserves the past past as the *archive*' (2008, 98). Jan Assmann's (2002, 246) further distinction between archive and crypt is intended to accommodate the forms of the cultural unconscious. The crypt houses 'the apocryphal, excluded, and forbidden'. With a nod to Sigmund Freud's psychoanalysis, he speaks of the 'cultural creation of crypts' when areas of cultural tradition are 'suppressed, marginalized, shunted to sub-cultural folklore, or down-right criminalized'. While the Assmanns' distinction is based on the *uses* of mnemonic material, Diana Taylor, in *The Archive and the Repertoire* (2003, 19f.), focuses on its specific *mediality* and distinguishes between two types: '"Archival" memory exists as documents, maps, literary texts, letters, archeological remains, bones, videos, CDs, all those items supposedly resistant to change,' while the repertoire 'enacts embodied memory: performances, gestures, orality, movement, dance, singing – in short, all those acts usually thought of as ephemeral, nonreproducible knowledge.' With the digital revolution, fundamentally new forms of the archive have emerged (see Ernst 2004, 2007), which challenge the assumptions made by Foucault and others about the hierarchical and exclusionary nature of the archive. It seems that, on the contrary, digital archives, such as YouTube and Google Books, and social networks, such as Facebook, are participatory, communicative and inclusive. But they also raise new questions about accessibility, authenticity, power and legality (see Jimerson 2009; see also chapter V.5).

The interest in 'heritage' finally, brings historians together with colleagues from art and architectural history, anthropology, archaeology and sociology in the interdisciplinary convergence field of 'heritage studies' (Sørensen and Carman 2009). This field is characterized by its concern not only with the scholarly investigation of heritage, but also with its creation, curating and marketing. In the late 1980s 'heritage' was identified by historians as a new obsession with the past (Lowenthal 1996), directed equally towards serious and banal sites of memory, 'from Euro-Disney to the Holocaust Museum, from Balkan enmities to the Northern Irish troubles, from Elvis memorabilia to the Elgin marbles' (ibid.). British historians' approaches to heritage (Wright 2009 [1985]) addressed the national, even imperial, nostalgia of the 1980s, the Thatcher era, and uttered a harsh critique of the emergence of a veritable 'heritage industry' (Hewison 1987), which capitalizes on such forms of nostalgia (see also Shaw and Chase 1989). Gilroy (2004) widened the perspective on problems of 'postcolonial melancholia' to critically discuss the state of multicultural Britain. But there is also a critical potential to nostalgia, namely the way in which is keeps constructions of a 'past future' alive and measures them against the present. In this sense, Lowenthal (1985, 9) has argued that what actually 'pleases the nostalgist is ... not so much the past itself as its supposed aspirations, less the memory of what actually was than of what was once thought possible.'

Heritage sites are both a result and a trigger of nostalgia. In the framework of memory studies, Boym (2001, xv) has defined nostalgia as 'a yearning for a different time' and as 'the ache of temporal distance and displacement'. She distinguishes between two types of nostalgia: The first is the 'restorative' type, which is directed backwards, towards origins, truth, and a lost 'home' (*nostos*) – thus nourishing national heritage, the emergence of which Boym traces back to the nineteenth century and its institutionalization of nostalgia in museums and memorials (see ibid., 15). The second type is 'reflective nostalgia,' which accepts the ambivalences of modernity, displays irony, and potentially unfolds a utopian dimension (ibid., 41–56; see also Wilson 2005).

In today's practice of cultural memory, heritage and (restorative) nostalgia tend to be performed through tourism. Sturken (2007) has shown how in American memory-tourism to sites of terrorism mourning and remembering are bound up with consumerism. Research in 'dissonant heritage' (Tunbridge and Ashworth 1996) and 'difficult heritage' (Macdonald 2009) addresses the ethics and pragmatics of presenting sites of atrocities, disease, and death to observers. And studies in 'dark tourism' (Lennon and Foley 2000) show how prisons, concentration camps, and places of genocide, terror, and injustice are marketed as 'heritage sites' and attract worldwide consumers.

The UNESCO World Heritage Convention (1972) defined 'monuments', 'groups of buildings' and 'sites' as components of 'cultural heritage'. Its aim is 'to encourage the identification, protection and preservation of cultural and natural heritage around the world considered to be of outstanding value to humanity' (http://whc.unesco.org/). With its focus on 'shared heritage' and 'universal value,' the UNESCO led the way early on to perceiving of cultural memory through a global lens (see also chapter III.1.6). However, the UNESCO's projects find themselves increasingly faced by the questions of ethics and (dark) tourism raised above. One example are the world heritage sites in West Africa which are connected with the memory of slavery. Slave castles on the Ghanaian and Senegalese coasts are now the destination of slave-route tourism and 'pilgrimages' by members of the African diaspora. However, such sites appear to be geared to ideas of heritage prevalent in western audiences and to say little to the African residents in Ghana and Senegal (see Holsey 2008). The UNESCO Convention on the Safeguarding of the Intangible Cultural Heritage (2003) was a measure to acknowledge non-western manifestations of heritage, for example, indigenous practices of memory in Africa or South America (see Smith and Akagawa 2009). But the concept has sparked controversial discussions, as it may be reinforcing the very binary logic (between 'western and Indigenous,' tangible and intangible) that it seeks to counteract.

III.1.4   This side of the 'floating gap': Contemporary history, oral history and generational memory

The concepts discussed above can be applied in analyses of those institutionally safeguarded and transmitted national, religious, political and ethnic memories which may reach back hundreds and even thousands of years. Contemporary history, generational history, and oral history, on the other hand, address the communities of memory on 'this side of the floating gap' (Niethammer 1995). That is, they look at the construction and interpretation of more recent events, spanning the time from the immediate present to about 80 to 100 years in the past. Here the focus is on history as life experience, on the transmission of versions of the past through everyday communication and interaction, in short: on the 'communicative memory'.

The manifold mutual permeations of history and memory become particularly evident in the area of contemporary history (see Laqueur 2004). There is a saying that the witness is the 'natural enemy of the contemporary historian' – a reference to the competition between 'living memory' and scholarly historiography as two forms of reference to the past. Living memory enjoys a productive use as an historical source, however, within oral history (see Perks and Thomson 1998; Ritchie 2010). The goal of this approach is to add a different type of source material to historiography, which usually resorts to written documents only: oral speech. Oral historians thus deal with organic memory; they study knowledge about the past which is anchored in individual minds and orally circulated in small communities such as families, veterans, or colleagues.

The methodology of oral history consists in conducting life-history interviews and analysing how historical events are perceived by witnesses. Oral history began to be established in the USA as early as the 1950s, and slightly later in Great Britain, with the History Workshop founded in 1966 and designed to reconstruct the history of the working classes, thus adding a new methodology to the project of writing peoples' history 'from below' (see Thompson's *The Voice of the Past*, 1978, and the *History Workshop Journal*, launched in 1976). In Germany and Italy, the study in working-class memories was often combined with an interest in the ways that fascism and national socialism were remembered (Passerini 1987; Niethammer 1995). Oral history as a methodology to approach contemporary history has spread virtually worldwide, and much fascinating work is done in countries in transition, e.g. in South Africa (Field, Meyer and Swanson 2007) or in Eastern Europe (Mihkelev and Kalnačs 2007).

At the beginning it was problematic that oral historians simply collected these testimonies, without 'having at their command any feasible theory of memory', and that they often – to quote Ruth Klüger – reduced contemporary witnesses to 'raw material' (Wischermann 1996, 78). A critical reflection of the practice of oral history started in the late 1980s. *The Myths we Live By* (Samuel and Thompson 1990) brings together different strands of oral history and emphasizes the importance of shared 'myths' in the construction of histories (see also Portelli 1990; Frisch 1990). Sean Field summarizes the epistemological challenges of oral history thus:

> If you are only seeking verifiable factual evidence, then memories presented through oral histories will sometimes give you facts and

at other times they will not. But if you are trying to understand how and why people believe what they believe, think what they think, and – most crucially – why people act in the ways that they do, then memories and oral narratives or texts are of vital research significance. (Field, Meyer and Swanson 2007, 9)

Recent studies in oral history which are informed by theories of cultural memory and place more reliance on biography research emphasize that memories, and especially the autobiographical memories which we shape into our life histories, are retrospective constructions. They often have much less to do with the past reality than with the here and now of the interview situation. Oral history thus is always recording not just contemporary history but also current ways of remembering, that is, memory culture (see Green 2004; Hamilton and Shopes 2008). In this vein, scholars have addressed the significance of narrative in oral histories (Chamberlain and Thompson 1998) and the performative aspects of oral history (Pollock 2005). Increasingly, oral historians also acknowledge the extent to which literary templates shape personal memories and oral life stories. For his book on private memories of the Stalin era, *The Whisperers* (2007), Orlando Figes conducted thousands of interviews with survivors and perpetrators of the Stalinist repressions and realized that

> In the 1970s and 1980s, when books like *The Gulag Archipelago* circulated in samizdat, many victims of Stalinist repression identified so strongly with their ideological position ... that they suspended their own independent memories and allowed these books to speak for them. ... The published Gulag memoirs influenced not only the recollection of scenes and people, but the very understanding of the experience. (Figes 2007, 634–6)

Much fundamental research on 'gendered memories' has been conducted within the framework of oral history. At the forefront of the study of women's memories were oral historians focussing on women's recollections of war, totalitarianism, countries in transition, migration, and transnational identities in the twentieth century (see Leydesdorff, Passerini and Thompson 1996; see esp. the new introduction 'Gender and Memory. Ten Years On,' 2005). In recent work, new combinations of theories and concepts are being formed to study the relation of gender and memory (Neubauer and Geyer-Ryan 2000; Hirsch and Smith 2002). There are family studies, auto/biography studies as well as broader media-cultural approaches to gendered memories (for example, on the 'social inheritance of the Holocaust', see Reading 2002).

Located between oral history, social science, and social psychology we find research on intergenerational family memory. Angela Keppler (1994), for example, has shown through conversational analysis that the unity of family memory rests not so much on the consistency of the oral stories that are being told, but instead in the continuity of the opportunities for and acts of shared remembering. Harald Welzer, Sabine Moller, and Karoline Tschuggnall, in their book *'Opa war kein Nazi'* (2002; 'Grandpa was not a Nazi', present the results of a multi-generational study on the transmission of historical consciousness. Family memory as arguably the most important site of communica-tive memory is a significant framework for an understanding of 'how learned historical knowledge is interpreted and applied' (ibid., 13). In intergenerational communication, memories of the past are gener-ated according to the storyteller's current needs to create meaning – as shown in interviews in which grandparents, parents, and grandchildren were supposed to tell the same story (along the lines of the 'telephone game'). Welzer and his research group observed a 'cumulative heroiza-tion' in the rendering of the grandparents' experiences in the 'Third Reich.' 'The tendency to heroize the grandparents' generation makes manifest the effect, not to be underestimated, that loyalty to loved ones has on historical consciousness and on the respective constructions of the past' (ibid., 64).

Remembering on 'this side of the floating gap' is performed in both explicit and implicit ways. There are intentional, conscious, even reflected, articulations of the past within the framework of communica-tive memory. But there are also unintentional, not conscious, and unre-flected, constructions of the past – phenomena which Harald Welzer (2001, 12) has called the 'social memory,' the 'universe of remembering *en passant'* (see also Welzer 2010). Arguably, implicit communicative memories (for example, the passing-on of narrative patterns between generations) may be just as powerful as explicit memories – and even more so, because they operate in unacknowledged ways.

In contrast to approaches to *inter*generational memory, which focus on the formation of memory between the generations, studies of *intra*generational memory see age groups as communities of memory. Common labels such as 'baby boomers', the '68ers', the 'Generation X', or the 'Generation @' show that historical research is thus dealing with a currently very popular terrain. Research on generationality, the memory-based self-images of generations, often refers to the work of

Wilhelm Dilthey and Karl Mannheim. In his essay 'The Problem of Generations' (1928/29), the sociologist Mannheim made statements about generational identity and generation-specific memory which are held valid still today. For example, it is generally assumed that the formative period in a person's life falls approximately between the ages of 17 and 25 – a time in which political views typical for a generation are developed (see, for example, Schuman and Scott 1989). Historians have looked particularly at the connection between the experience of war and the formation of generation-specific memory cultures (Wohl 1979; Reulecke 2008). Generational memories are moreover closely connected to social and cultural factors, such as gender, class, and ethnicity (Edmunds and Turner 2002; Sollors 1988). Sigrid Weigel, finally, has studied 'generation' as a central 'symbolic form' of culture (2002).

The study of communicative memory to date has been the domain of contemporary history. But it is certainly not limited to this field, as there are not only contemporary, but also historical communicative memories – say, the generational memory of the Romantic poets, or family memories in the Middle Ages. Because the methodology of the oral history-interview cannot be applied to study such constellations (they are no longer 'living memory'), historians have started developing new methodologies. To investigate communicative memories of Dutch people in the seventeenth century, for example, early modern historian Judith Pollmann examines a wide range of media and memory practices. 'This side' and 'that side' of the floating gap are therefore merely constructs of memory studies which have emerged from the practice of historical research so far. But just as in the way that we can study communicative memories of the early modern period, it is also possible to use the concepts developed for *longue durée*-memory processes (the cultural canon, national archives, or invented traditions) to further an understanding of today's practices of everyday remembering. It is towards such intersections and overlappings between different mnemonic registers and scholary methodologies that memory studies as a convergence field is steadily moving.

III.1.5 Social memory studies

Not only historical studies, but also the social sciences have seen a significant increase in memory research since the 1980s. What can be subsumed under the term social memory studies – to use the wording of American sociologists Jeffrey K. Olick and Joyce Robbins (1998) – has branched out in many directions internationally. Memory research undertaken within such disciplines as sociology, anthropology, political science, and political philosophy is characterized by the unanimous recourse to Maurice Halbwachs. Another fundament of social memory studies lies in the sociological and philosophical thought of the Frankfurt School, especially in the writings of Hannah Arendt and Theodor W. Adorno (see Arendt 1951; Adorno 2010).

The key question of social memory studies is – as formulated in the title of Paul Connerton's study (1989) – 'how societies remember.' In their eponymous co-authored book Fentress and Wickham (1992) define social memory as 'an expression of collective experience; social memory identifies a group, giving it a sense of its past and defining its aspirations for the future'. Bruce Smith, in his *Politics and Remembrance* (1985, 7), argues that, historically, republics were understood as mnemonic structures, based on the 'injunction to remember'. Predominantly, the social sciences focus on the role of 'public memories' (Phillips 2004) and on connections between memory and the creation of collective identities (see Gillis 1994; Ben-Amos and Weissberg 1999). Case studies of social memory research include, for example, work about Watergate and Abraham Lincoln in American memory (Schudson 1992; Schwartz 2008), the USA's politics of apology to Oneida Indians and Japanese Americans (Weiner 2005), about the memory of slavery and the formation of African-American identity (Eyerman 2001), and German memories of guilt and defeat (Olick 2005). Cultural sociology addresses questions of 'cultural trauma' (Alexander et al. 2004); the sociology of religion studies 'religion as a chain of memory' (Hervieu-Léger 2000).

If Halbwachs bequeathed social memory studies the concept of collective memory, then Peter L. Berger and Thomas Luckmann's legacy to the field is the theoretical framework of social constructionism. Addressing questions of the sociology of knowledge, Berger and Luckmann's seminal study, *The Social Construction of Reality* (1966), is both a foundation and fund for all disciplines involved in memory studies. Societies, as the authors show, construct for themselves a reality which soon appears to be the only given reality; this, in turn, reinforces the constructors' perception of it. Three stages within this process are of significance: first, externalization ('externalization of subjective meanings', ibid., 48); second, objectivation ('the process by which the externalized products of human activity attain the character of objectivity'; ibid., 57); and, third, internalization ('by which the objectivated social world is retrojected into consciousness in the course of socialization'; ibid.). Sedimentation and tradition are two aspects of the process of the institutionalization of social knowledge about reality. In order to pass knowledge on from one generation to the next – and it is only through this transition from individual memory to tradition that societal reality is created (ibid., 66) – semiotic operations and media are necessary: 'Intersubjective sedimentation can be called truly social only when it has been objectivated in a sign system of one kind or another, that is, when the possibility of reiterated objectification of the shared experiences arises' (ibid., 63).

Anthropology's contributions to memory studies are manifold. From research on orality and literacy and their impact on memory emerged J.A. Barnes's (1990 [1947]) concept of a structural amnesia: In non-literate cultures, only the socially relevant aspects of the tribal history are passed on. There is no room for anything else in the collective memory, as there is no possibility to store anything on external media (for a critique, see Goody 2000). This concept as well as Jan Vansina's work on *Oral Tradition* (1965) laid the groundwork for the Assmanns' distinction between Cultural and communicative memory (see chapter II.4.2). A similar differentiation is made in Michael Herzfeld's (1991) seminal study on 'social' and 'monumental time':

> Between social and monumental time lies a discursive chasm, separating popular from official understandings of history. Social time is the grist of everyday experience. ... Monumental time, by contrast, is reductive and generic. It encounters events as realizations of supreme destiny, and it reduces social experience to collective predictability. (Herzfeld 1991, 10)

In the ethnography of memory in non-western societies, the method of oral history is put to use and combined in challenging ways with research on other mnemonic media and practices. Examples include studies on memory in South Africa (Bozzoli and Nkotsoe 1991; Hofmeyr 1994), China (Jing 1996), and Japan (Yoneyama 1999). Anthropology moreover teases out the intersections between memory studies and postcolonial studies (Werbner 1998), studies the intergenerational transmission of violence (Argenti and Schramm 2010), or dedicates itself to the connections between bodily experiences and cultural remembering, as, for example, in Sutton's (2001) anthropology of food and memory. (For an overview of anthropology's concern with cultural memory, see Berliner 2005.)

The ethical implications of remembering and forgetting are considered in research located at the border between the social sciences and political philosophy, such as Paul Ricoeur's *Memory, History, Forgetting* (2004) and Jeffrey Blustein's *The Moral Demands of Memory* (2008). In *The Ethics of Memory* (2002, 51f.), Avishai Margalit distinguishes between common and shared memory, the latter implying a certain convergence of view-points: A common memory 'is an aggregate notion. It aggregates the memories of all those people who remember a certain episode which each of them experienced individually.' 'A *shared* memory, on the other hand, is not a simple aggregate of individual memories. It requires communication. A shared memory integrates and calibrates the different perspectives of those who remember the episode ... into one version.'

Past crimes and injustices, memory and moral responsibility are at the heart of social memory studies today. Zygmunt Bauman (1989) considers the possibilities of a sociology after Auschwitz and arrives at a sociological theory of moral responsibility. Of particular importance has been the topic of 'coming to terms with the past' (*Vergangenheitsbe-wältigung*), the problems of remembering collective crimes and atrocities (Cohen 2000), and of ensuing public acts of 'apology' (Tavuchis 1991), 'restitution' (Diner and Wunberg 2007), and 'forgiveness' (Shriver 1995). Jeffrey Olick introduced the concept of a 'politics of regret' (2007, 14), with which he describes 'the rise of ... a new framework for confronting past misdeeds,' regret nowadays being characterized by its 'ubiquity and elevation to a general principle' (see also Tavuchis 1991). An emerging field connected with these questions is genocide studies, which is increasingly comparative in nature and sensitive to issues of cultural memory (Bloxham and Moses 2010).

At the end of the twentieth century, the issue of transitional justice and the work of truth and reconciliation commissions have become matters of particular interest to scholars of sociology and political science (for a comparative overview Kritz 1995; for a historical perspective Elster 2004). Truth and reconciliation commissions are at work in countries with as diverse histories as Argentina, Canada, Ghana, Rwanda, Morocco, and East Timor. While the South African Truth and Reconciliation Commission, established by Nelson Mandela after the apartheid era, has gained great prominence as a model institution (Bell and Ntsebeza 2001), today there are very different modes of addressing past crimes, entailing, for example, pursuing criminal prosecution or dispensing with it, working at national or local levels, and using different media and methods.

A systems-theory perspective on cultural memory has been introduced by Elena Esposito (2002, 2008). 'Memory' can be understood from a systems-theory standpoint, following Niklas Luhmann (1997, 585), as an abbreviated expression for the recursivity of communicative operations. The main function of memory is forgetting, that is, 'preventing the system from blocking itself with the concretion of the results of earlier observations' (ibid., 579). Remembering is thus an exception rather than the rule. Systems-theory approaches therefore focus on what Esposito calls 'social forgetting.' Systems theory, in addition, calls for a strict separation between social and cognitive systems. Thus, the term used is *'social* memory,' without taking into account social memory's representations in individual memories. Society consists of communications. The memory of society emerges from communications referring to communications. The result are 'semantics,' that is, 'topics which can be the subject of communication and the terms one can use in the expectation that one will be understood' (Esposito 2002, 21). In this view, the memory of society depends on the available communication technologies. Esposito emphasizes that 'there exists a circular connection of mutual influence between memory and the media of communication.' (2002, 10; see also chapter V.2).

To sum up, social sciences today assume a 'mnemonic socialization' in 'mnemonic communities' through the way in which a 'sociobiographical memory' is passed on and appropriated, a process which always operates in narrative form (Zerubavel 1996, 2003). Further areas of research of social memory studies, according to Olick and Robbins (1998), include contested memories and the negotiation of memory conflicts (Zemon Davis and Starn 1989; Nuttall and Coetzee 1998; Radstone and Hodgkin 2003), the 'malleability' and 'persistence' of memory cultures, as well as practices of memory in the sciences themselves (Bowker 2005). Olick and Robbins particularly emphasize processual and narrative approaches to the study of cultural memory. In fact, it is especially the field of narrative theory (as will be seen later, in chapter III.3.3) offers important points of contact between memory research in the social sciences, in psychology, and the humanities.

III.1.6   Global memory studies

It is roughly since the turn of the millennium that 'global memory studies' has become a burgeoning new convergence field in memory studies. Three in many ways connected strands of this research area can be distinguished: (1) 'Global memory studies' is a shorthand formula for what should more precisely be called 'the study of memory in the global age'. This concerns approaches which are interested in present-day forms of remembering and ask what happens to memory when it is confronted with the effects of contemporary economic and cultural globalization. (2) A slightly different direction is taken in research on 'transcultural memory', that is, the translocal, transnational, and global circulation of mnemonic contents, media, and practices. This kind of research directs its attention away from static 'sites' and towards the dynamic 'movement' of memory across time and space. It understands the circulation of memory not as a specifics of the present age but takes a decidedly historical perspective on the matter. (3) Thirdly, the formula of 'global memory studies' also hints at the increasing scope of the research field itself, i.e. the manifold collaborations and exchanges of concepts across the borders of national academias. This is turning 'memory studies' into a truly international research field – a project which is admittedly only in its infancy, the attempt to bring together various western perspectives alone being a great challenge. All three strands have in common that they work against the 'methodological nationalism' prevalent in memory studies so far (which is perhaps best exemplified by Pierre Nora's *lieux de mémoire*); and they do so in the conception of their research objects as well as in their research practice.

The defining work of 'global memory studies' has emerged from sociology, namely Daniel Levy and Natan Sznaider's *The Holocaust and Memory in the Global Age* (2006 [2001]; for new approaches see Assmann and Conrad 2010). It is perhaps no wonder that this book is on the subject of Holocaust memory, which is, in fact, the very paradigm of a global object of remembrance. As an historical event, the Holocaust affected many different nations and ethnicities, and today it is commemorated in many places around the world. The Holocaust has become a global site of memory, an example of, as Levy and Sznaider emphasize, a 'de-territorialized, transnational, and globalizing memory'. As the founding myth of global justice, the Holocaust has effected the emergence of 'cosmopolitan memory cultures' (ibid., 2). It is the worldwide remembrance of the extermination of the Jews which led to the transnational establishment, legitimation and adherence to a set of normative rules concerning democracy, tolerance and humanism, most notably in the form of the Universal Declaration of Human Rights in 1948.

According to Levy and Sznaider, the cosmopolitan memory of the Holocaust was created by a 'dual process of particularization and universalization' (ibid., 13), by an interaction between local relevance and global reference. The Holocaust functions as a 'transnational symbol' for the violation of human rights. Therefore, in the fight for recognition, victim groups often present their experience in analogy to the Holocaust and draw parallels between the perpetrators and the Nazis. In this way, terms like 'Kosovoaust,' 'Indian Holocausts', 'African Holocausts' and the 'Red Holocaust' (referring to Stalin) have been coined. And even the Palestinian 'Nakbah' ('catastrophe')-remembrance imitates some of the rituals associated with Jewish Holocaust remembrance, such as the two-minute sounding of sirens (ibid., 200). In this process, the Holocaust has become a global narrative template. Levy and Sznaider argue that 'paradoxically, it is precisely the Holocaust's limits of representation that have contributed to its decontextualization, enabling it to function as a model for "good and evil" or "guilt and innocence" in general. In this sense, the Holocaust provides a global point of reference for memory' (ibid., 132).

The fact that the globalization of Holocaust memory inevitably seems to imply its decontextualization and relativization can be viewed as problematic: The slots of a global memory schema – 'perpetrator' and 'victim' in the case of Holocaust-memory – can also be filled in a perverted manner (for example, when groups of perpetrators fashion themselves as victims); or the schema can simply circulate in its most rudimentary form, emptied of meaning, as a form of banal memory. In his *Urban Palimpsests* (2003, 99), Andreas Huyssen comes to a similar conclusion when he writes that the Holocaust 'attaches itself like a floating signifier to historically very different situations.' However, Huyssen also emphasizes the productivity of such a dynamics, when he argues that 'Holocaust commemoration ... has functioned like a motor energizing the discourses of memory elsewhere' (ibid.).

A similar road into understanding the significance of Holocaust memory in the globalizing age is taken in Michael Rothberg's *Multidirectional Memory* (2009). The concept is directed against Eurocentrist notions of cosmopolitan memory as well as against the idea that memory operates according to the 'scarcity principle' (ibid., 3), for example, that recalling one victim group necessarily seems to reduce the possibility of remembering another victim group. Rothberg proposes an alternative way of thinking about memory and focusses on how one discourse of memory can *enable* other discourses of memory (ibid., 6). Rather than understanding memory as competitive, therefore, he conceives of it as 'multidirectional, as subject to ongoing negotiation, cross-referencing, and borrowing' (ibid., 15). His specific concern is the way in which 'Holocaust memory emerged in dialogue with the ... struggles that define the era of decolonization' and thus an 'unacknowledged history of cross-referencing' (ibid., 7). Multidirectional memory, in Rothberg's view, 'has the potential to create new forms of solidarity and new visions of justice' (ibid. 5). (For a similar concept, see also Nancy Wood's 'vectors of memory'; Wood 1999)

One perspective on global memory which emerges from political science and is tied up with the discourses of witnessing and testimony initiated by Laub and Felman (see chapter III.1.2) was put forward by

Fuyuki Kurasawa (2009, 95) who suggests conceiving of bearing witness 'as a globalizing mode of ethico-political labour'. He identifies a

> web of transnational testimonial practices structured around five dialectically related tasks and perils: giving voice to mass suffering against silence (what if the message is never sent or does not reach land?); interpretation against incomprehension (what if it is written in a language that is undecipherable?); the cultivation of empathy against indifference (what if, after being read, it is discarded?); remembrance against forgetting (what if it is distorted or erased over time?); and prevention against repetition (what if it does not help to avert other forms of suffering?).

Another strand of global memory studies is concerned with expanding and complicating Pierre Nora's notion of *lieux de mémoire*. Andreas Huyssen has criticized the nation-centredness of Nora's sites of memory and argued that 'the *lieux de mémoire* today function not just in an expanded field but in a field altered by globalization' (2003, 97; see also Legg and chapter II.3). There are now new ways of conceiving of transnational *lieux de mémoire*. The articles in Hebel (2009), for example, show the fundamental transnational nature of American memories; and Indra Sengupta-Frey (2009) deals with the logic of memory sites in colonial and postcolonial contexts. Much work is currently being done on the case of Europe, with the aim of conceiving – and indeed actively constructing – European memories and identities beyond the nation-state (see Eder and Spohn 2005; Assmann 2007; Passerini 2009). The sociologist Harald Welzer (2007) and his group have conducted interviews in different European states and shown through their comparative research how Holocaust memory is refracted according to different nations and generations.

As postcolonial studies have always been dealing with shared, entangled and contested pasts as well as with equally complex, often hybrid, practices of remembrance in (post)colonial and multicultural societies – in what one could call 'mnemonic contact zones' –, many of their contributions to memory studies have fallen under the 'global memory' paradigm all along. In *Forgetting Aborigines* (2008), Chris Healy considers 'the intercultural space of Aboriginality as constituted by strange and transient patterns of remembering and forgetting' (ibid., 5). He starts from the paradox that in Australia 'Aborigines are remembered as absent in the face of a continuing and actual indigenous presence' (ibid., 12) and assumes that 'the performance and organisation of social memory provides one way of thinking about why Aborigines keep on disappearing' (ibid., 10).

Migrant memories and diasporic memory (Mageo 2001; Baronian et al. 2007) constitute another burgeoning field of global memory studies; and much of what is written about current forms of nostalgia (Boym 2001), memory tourism, and the construction and marketing of heritage in the age of globalization is perceived through the transnational lens (on 'recombinant history' in Vietnam see Schwenkel 2006; on India see Hancock 2008).

In dealing with frameworks such as these, researchers working from anthropological, historical, literary and cultural studies perspectives increasingly favour the term 'transcultural memory' (see Crownshaw 2010). As I have suggested elsewhere (Erll 2010, 2011), this term allows us to move away from the methodological nationalism, and especially the 'nation–culture bind', that has characterized much of memory studies to date, and instead to focus on those aspects of remembering and forgetting which are located between, across, and beyond what we construct as 'cultures'. What we can see with the 'transcultural lens' is, firstly, the many fuzzy edges of national cultures of remembrance, the many shared sites of memory that have emerged through travel, trade, colonialism and other forms of cultural exchange; secondly, the great internal heterogeneity of national culture, its different classes, generations, ethnicities, religious communities, and subcultures, which will all generate different, but in many ways interacting frameworks of memory; and, thirdly, the relevance that formations beyond national culture have for memory, such as the worldwide Umma, Catholicism, or the European Left, but also football, music culture, and consumer culture.

What the discourses of globalization and 'global memory' sometimes tend to overlook – and what a decidedly historical perspective on memory will quickly bring to light – is that transcultural remembering has a long genealogy. It is actually since ancient times that contents, forms and technologies of memory have crossed the boundaries of time, space, and social groups, and been filled in different local contexts with new life and new meaning. (A practice that was arguably screened in the era of the nation-states – the effects of which still shape our thinking about memory today.) The 'transcultural' is therefore not only a category for studying memory in our current globalizing age, but also a perspective on memory that can in principle be chosen with respect to all historical periods.

To describe processes of transcultural memory, I draw on James Clifford's (1992) metaphor of 'travelling culture' and speak in terms of 'travelling memory'. Adapting the anthropologist's famous dictum, it can indeed be said that 'memories don't hold still for their portraits'. On the contrary, memory seems to be constituted in the first place through the movement of people, objects and media. What we are dealing with is not so much (and perhaps not even metaphorically; see IV.1) 'sites' of memory (*lieux de mémoire*), but rather with the 'travels' of memory (*voyages* or *mouvements de mémoire*). The ubiquitous contexts of such movement range from everyday interaction among different social groups to transnational media reception and from trade and travel to migration and diaspora, to war and colonialism. With Paul Gilroy one could argue that cultural memory can be studied through the reconstruction of its mnemonic 'routes' the paths which has been taken by certain stories, rituals and images – and not so much by echoing what social groups may claim as their 'roots', the alleged origins of a seemingly stable cultural memory. In fact, the very fundaments of what we assume to be the Western Cultural Memory are usually products of transcultural movements. There is the Persian influence on the Old Testament; Egyptian fairy tales in Homer's *Odyssey*; Islam's substantial contribution to the European Renaissance; or the French origins of the Grimm brothers' German fairy tales. Even the 'first memories' of a cultural formation are often likely the effect of transcultural travel. (On travelling memory, especially by means of premediation and remediation, see Erll 2009b; and chapter V.5.3.)

Transcultural memory in the sense delineated here is therefore *not* simply a special case of cultural memory. It is a certain research perspective, a specific curiosity or focus of attention, which is directed towards mnemonic processes unfolding across time and space, between and beyond cultural formations. Transcultural memory means transcending the borders of traditional cultural memory studies by looking beyond our established research objects and methodologies. It is based on the insight that memory – individual as well as social – is fundamentally a transcultural phenomenon.

III.2 Material memory: Art and literature

Not only academic discourses, but also art and literature, are involved in the current 'memory boom'. Painting, sculpture, architecture, Internet art, movies and novels all address themes such as the fragility of memory and the ideological implications of public commemoration. It would seem that we are witnesses to one of those epochs in which science, art and societal discourse offer mutual stimulation and enrichment to one another, and the exchange of memory concepts is by no means a one-way street. This is evident in the prominent position that scholarly texts on cultural memory (for example, A. Assmann 1999) and the psychology of individual memory (for example, Schacter 1996) award to literary texts, from Marcel Proust to Julian Barnes, and to recent memory art, for example to works by Anselm Kiefer, Mildred Howard, Sigrid Sigurdsson, and Anne and Patrick Poirier.

Not just literature and art but also literary studies and – to a lesser degree – art history have provided a variety of contributions to issues of cultural memory. While *Memory and Oblivion* (Reinik and Stumpel 1999) provides an insight into the entire spectrum of possible relations between art and memory, the focus of art historical research has so far been on contemporary memory art (*Kunstforum International* 1994; Wettengl 2000; Saltzman 2006; Gibbons 2007), on art as 'technology' and 'performance' of memory (Smith 2006; Plate and Smelik 2009) and on the museum (Crane 2000) and architecture (Boyer 1994) as media of cultural memory. A first overview of the intersections between literature and cultural memory was offered by the volumes published in the series *Literature as Cultural Memory* (2000). They show address literary memories of colonialism (D'haen and Krüs 2000) and of traumatic experiences (Ibsch 2000); they study translation as a form of cultural remembrance (D'Hulst and Milton 2000), genres as 'repositories' of cultural memory (van Gorp and Musarra-Schroeder 2000), the mnemonic dimension of travel literature (Seixo 2000); and, finally, they look at the possible methods literary studies can employ to analyse memory (Vervliet and Estor 2000).

Today, we are faced with an abundance of individual contributions to the relation of literature and memory. With their varying theoretical and methodological approaches, they constitute a highly heterogeneous field that may loosely be called 'literary memory studies'. Nevertheless, from a survey of existing research, diverse concepts of memory in literary studies can be derived (Erll and Nünning 2005a,b; Erll and Rigney 2006). Such concepts span the spectrum from more narrowly philological analyses to approaches that are strongly influenced by cultural studies and interdisciplinary work. Five directions in the study of the connection of literature and memory will be distinguished here (which can largely be applied to the relation of art and memory, too): First, 'literature as *ars memoriae*' captures research on memory which explores literature's role in cultural mnemonics. The focus of interest has been on the art of memory of the Middle Ages and early modern period. Second, a 'memory *of* literature' is highlighted in studies that look at the return of elements from earlier works of art. This return is often conceived of in terms of intertextuality and intermediality. An important forerunner of this research direction is the art historian Aby Warburg. Third, 'memory *of* literature' can also denote processes of canon formation and literary historiography. Fourth, the concept of 'memory *in* literature' captures work done on the forms of the aesthetic representation, or: staging, of memory. Fifth, 'literature as a medium of cultural memory' is used here to designate a direction of research which is interested in literature as an active force in memory culture. Chapter VI will be dedicated to this question.

III.2.1   Foundation: Art of memory – *ars memoriae*

Unlike historical studies and the social sciences, where research on memory focuses on the constructive and identity-creating appropriation of the past in social contexts, memory research in art history and literary studies has long been dedicated to the significance of ancient mnemonics (*ars memoriae*) for art and culture. Memory in art and literature, thus – to use Aleida Assmann's words (see chapter II.4.3) – is primarily studied as *ars* (artificial, spatially oriented memory), while history and social memory are conceived of as *vis* (natural, temporally oriented memory).

Particularly suggestive for art history and literary studies is the close connection between space and image that underlies *ars memoriae*. The founding myth of mnemonics was recorded by Cicero in *De Oratore*. It is the story of the Greek poet Simonides of Ceos (ca. 557–467 BCE), who was able to identify the guests at a banquet who had died in a catastrophe, because he remembered who had been sitting where. The realization that spatially ordered images retained in the mind can serve as an aid to memory is supposed to have inspired the poet to invent the art of memory (see Yates 1966).

Ancient mnemonics functions according to the principle of *loci et imagines*: To a series of real or imagined places (*loci*) in one's imagination, one adds images, ideally very vivid pictures (*imagines agentes*), which refer to the things to be remembered. One can later traverse this path in one's mind, and 'collect' the images and thereby that which one wanted to recall. In other words, this technique is a sort of 'mental writing', which in ancient times was primarily used to memorize speeches. As a result, the ancient art of memory has come down to us solely in writings on rhetoric: from Cicero, Quintilian, and in the anonymous *Rhetorica ad Herennium*. It is one of the five elements of the speech: *inventio* (invention), *dipositio* (arrangement), *elocutio* (style), *memoria* (memorization), *actio* (delivery).

It was the literary historian Frances Yates who established *ars memo-riae* as an object of research within modern cultural studies. Her work, *The Art of Memory* (1966), is a history of mnemotechnics from ancient times to the early modern period. Yates recalls the largely forgotten *ars memoriae*, and argues that art, the organization of knowledge, and systems of thought in the Middle Ages and the Renaissance draw materially on the classical, ancient art of memory, but at the same time reshape it dramatically: The medievals took recourse to Roman sources and connected them to Platonic writings as well as to the body of Christian thought. Artificial memory thus takes on an entirely new dimension, a moral function: Scholastics such as Albertus Magnus or Thomas Aquinas grasp *memoria* as an aspect of *prudentia*, one of the four cardinal virtues. According to Yates, the most impressive imagery in Dante's *Divine Comedy* (around 1310), Gothic architecture, or paintings by Giotto or Titian can be better understood when they are taken to be an expression of a medieval art of memory. They represent a Christian form of platonic recollection (*anamnesis*) – of paradise and hell, vices and virtues – and accomplish this through the aid of the mnemonic system, recorded in the ancient sources, of connecting places with *imagines agentes*. Yates's account of the history of the art of memory from the mnemonics of the ancient world to the imagery of the Middle Ages all the way to the magical-hermetic memory systems of Giulio Camillo, Giordano Bruno or Robert Fludd in the Renaissance and early modern period make clear that the art of memory was a living and remark-ably versatile tradition which served not only rhetorical goals but also Christian remembrance, the cultural organization of knowledge, and as a possibility for artistic expression. (For an anthology of material, see Carruthers and Ziolkowski 2002.)

Mary Carruthers shows in *The Book of Memory* (1990), qualifying Yates's theses, that in the Middle Ages the printed page itself becomes a mnemonic memory space. This marks the beginning of the transition from a spatially oriented memory moulded by images in the ancient and medieval world to a memory moulded by writing in the early modern period, and thereby also from rhetoric and memorization to hermeneutics. Although *ars memoriae* disappears from cultural prac-tice around 1800, it nonetheless continues to have an effect, and has ensured itself a lasting presence, especially in art and literature. This is shown by studies such as that by Stefan Rieger (1997), who argues that mnemonics as a deep structure can still be perceived in modern systems of organizing knowledge; or in that by Patrick Hutton (1987), who holds the view that mnemonics as a way to interpret reality even influenced Freud's psychoanalysis; and in that by Anselm Haverkamp and Renate Lachmann (1991), who interpret the connection of images and places as a fundamental literary method.

An alternative model to ancient mnemonics with its teaching of *loci et imagines* is represented by the art of meditation in the medieval and early modern periods (Butzer 2000). The monastic tradition of the early medieval period linked *memoria* and meditation for the purpose of studying the Holy Scripture: 'The practice of meditation is imagined as an act of mental and bodily appropriation of the text and connected with the image of a ruminating animal' (ibid., 1018). Augustine understands writing as the stomach of memory, reading and hearing as eating, and reflecting as ruminating. Meditation as a method of introspection, finally, plays a significant role for the development of individuality in the early modern period. Literary studies with a focus on *meditatio* as a literary genre (which develops in the eleventh century) have contributed to medievalists' interdisciplinary research on *memoria* (see chapter III.1.3).

III.2.2   Memory *of* literature I: Topoi and intertextuality

Talking about a 'memory *of* literature' means using a strongly metaphorical expression, and this term has therefore been criticized time and time again: Literature, of course, cannot 'remember' in the sense that individuals recall the past (for more on metaphors in memory research, see chapter IV.1). Concepts of the 'memory of literature' are instead based on the assumption that literature can only be grasped adequately when seen in its diachronic dynamics. Two aspects of the expression 'memory of literature' can be distinguished: The use of the term as (a) a *genitivus subjectivus* (through intertextuality literature 'remembers itself'); and as (b) a *genitivus objectivus* (in a socially institutionalized manner, literature is remembered, for example through canon formation and the writing of literary histories). In the first case, literature is seen as a symbol system, in the second as a social system (for more on this distinction, see Schmidt 2000).

When used as *genitivus subjectivus*, the concept of the 'memory of literature' points to the idea of an inner-literary memory, a memory of literature as a symbol system, which is manifested in individual texts. In a work of literature, earlier texts are 'remembered' through intertextual references. Literary studies approaches which consider intertextuality as a literary 'practice of memory' have tended to use the *ars memoriae* as an inspiration, interpreting it broadly and connecting it with various other concepts to form novel theories. The goal is to describe the return of aesthetic forms.

Studies which look at the continuities and changes in art and literature and describe these as an effect of 'memory' stand in the tradition of Aby Warburg's Mnemosyne project and his concept of a 'social memory' (see chapter II.2). Warburg's work is still relevant today, particularly to semiotic approaches which grasp literature and culture as a continual process of 'de- and resemiotization' (Lachmann 1993, xviii). The 'memory of literature' is based on a resemiotization of signs, on a 're-charging' of elements from old works with new meaning. The phenomenon which Warburg observed and called 'social memory' is discussed in literary studies as 'intertextuality' in the broadest sense – as a recourse to existent topoi, as references to individual texts or to genres.

The historical topic of Ernst Robert Curtius, which the scholar of Romance languages and literatures developed in his monograph *European Literature and the Latin Middle Ages* (1953), is arguably also founded on the concept of a 'memory of literature'. Curtius dedicated his book to, among others, Aby Warburg, whom he had met in 1928 in Rome, when Warburg was hoping to find people with whom he could discuss his Mnemosyne project. The theory and method of the historical topic must be located within the early phase of cultural memory research that took place during the period between the two world wars. Curtius (1953, 12) sees Europe as an historical and intellectual (*geistesgeschichtliche*) unity: European literature 'embraces a period of some twenty-six centuries (reckoning from Homer to Goethe)'. Limiting studies of literature to certain epochs and nations, Curtius argues, thus means ignoring important traditions and connections. To uncover continuities and changes in literary forms, he focuses his attention on topoi, that is, on the commonplaces or set schemata of thought and expression which were part of the *inventio* of ancient rhetoric. Curtius includes in this category rhetorical topics such as the topos of affected modesty or the inexpressibility topos, and concepts such as that of the *mundus inversus* (the world upside-down), but in a broader understanding also metaphors such as 'life as a voyage' or 'the world as a theater'. Curtius pursues two goals with his historical topic: First, he is interested in a history of genres and forms, the 'knowledge of the genetics of the formal elements of literature' (ibid., 82). Second, he is led by his interest in the history of intellectual ideas, since he argues that a study of the return of literary forms of expression contributes to an 'understanding of the psychological history of the West' (ibid.) – a focus which, in the wake of current global memory studies, would certainly have to be widened to include wider transcultural perspectives (see chapter III.1.6).

Curtius's historical topic provides a fundamental insight into the processes of a 'memory of literature'. It shows that all artistic activity is an act of memory, as it necessarily falls back on elements of cultural tradition. Literary *inventio* is based on *memoria*. Curtius's topos research also makes clear that literature has a diachronic and transcultural dimension. Just as pathos formulas store the energy of the cultural memory of images, the literary memory finds its expression in topoi. Curtius's somewhat vague and conservative concept of the topos has been the subject of sharp criticism from other literary scholars. Peter Jehn (1972, x), for example, remarks: 'Curtius's topos ... is a protean concept, whose identity is not truth, but rather the false result of an ahistorical equation of different terms of rhetoric.' Yet at the same time, Curtius's concept has had a significant impact and has enjoyed a renaissance especially in the context of recent cultural memory research (see Berndt 2005).

The origins of poststructural concepts of memory-as-intertextuality, as advanced by Harold Bloom and Renate Lachmann, can also be traced back to the 1920s – to Mikhail Bakhtin's concept of 'the dialogic imagination' (1981). Julia Kristeva, building on Bakhtin's theory of the novel, coined the term 'intertextuality' (Kristeva 1969; Allen 2000). The 'memory of literature', from the perspective of poststructural theory, appears as a reference to cultural pretexts manifested on a text-internal level, and as the actualization and transformation of those texts.

Harold Bloom, in *The Anxiety of Influence* (1973, 5), addresses 'intrapoetic relationships'. Using the poetry of English Romanticism as an example, he shows that the anxiety of influence (Bloom thinks in Freudian terms and describes with the 'anxiety of influence' the fear that a young poet – *ephebe* – displays in the face of a seemingly overpowering 'father poet') is what makes literary production possible in the first place: 'Poetry is the anxiety of influence' (ibid., 95). This anxiety leads to literary defence mechanisms, above all to 'misreading' (Bloom 1975). Bloom affirms: 'Every poem is a misinterpretation of a parent poem' (1973, 94). He distinguishes among various 'revisionary ratios' (ibid., 14) – forms of intertextual actualization and variation of elements of the literary tradition which are recognizable in the text as rhetorical strategies.

As early as 1919, in his essay 'Tradition and the Individual Talent', T.S. Eliot (1975) had drawn attention to this competitive dimension of the 'memory of literature'. Eliot argued that a literary text can only be truly new and original if it acknowledges and engages with tradition.

Conversely every new, 'great' literary work has an effect on the existing order of classical or canonical texts:

> The existing monuments form an ideal order among themselves, which is modified by the introduction of the new (the really new) work of art among them. The existing order is complete before the new work arrives; for order to persist after the supervention of novelty, the *whole* existing order must be, if ever so slightly, altered; and so the relations, proportions, values of each work of art toward the whole are readjusted; and this is conformity between the old and the new. (Eliot 1975 [1919], 38; see also Smith 1996)

While the abovementioned approaches dealt with but never explicitly mentioned 'cultural memory', Renate Lachmann deliberately introduced the notion of memory into her poststructuralist theory of intertextuality. Her monograph *Memory and Literature* (1997) has proved to be a fundamental contribution to literary memory studies. Key to Lachmann's approach is her equation of memory with the category of intertextuality: 'The memory of a text is its intertextuality' (ibid., 15). On the relationship of *ars memoriae* and literature, Lachmann notes: 'For literary criticism, the crucial problem here is to define the way in which mnemic *imaginatio* and poetic imagination interact' (ibid., 14). Literary texts 'construct an architecture of memory into which they deposit mnemonic images based on the procedures of *ars memoriae*' (ibid., 15). Literature is thus in many ways related to cultural memory: It is a 'mnemonic art par excellence. Literature supplies the memory for a culture and records such a memory. It is itself an act of memory. Literature inscribes itself in a memory space made up of texts, and it sketches out a memory space into which earlier texts are gradually absorbed and transformed' (ibid.).

The approaches presented so far show some important commonalities in the way they address the 'memory *of* literature'. Literary studies has frequently made use of terms and ideas which have their origins in the art of rhetoric. This recourse is, moreover, usually tied to a productive appropriation and (often far-reaching) changes of the ancient tradition. Literary memory research has undertaken two important modifications of *ars memoriae*. First, the process of combining *loci* and *imagines*, originally abstract and oriented towards the individual memory, gains – in a literary studies perspective – a collective, medial, and diachronic dimension: Literary traditions and their changes are described by means of mnemonic concepts. Second, literary studies conceives of the five steps of ancient rhetoric as a circle; in this understanding, *memoria* does not mean the mere memorization of something which already exists, but instead provides the basis for the creation of new literature. *Inventio, dispositio, elocutio* are all based on *memoria*. Every new literary text refers to existent texts, to culturally available genre patterns, to literary forms and tropes. In addition, the studies by Warburg, Curtius, Bloom and Lachmann show that the interest within art and literary studies in memory is itself strongly oriented towards the then-dominant theories of memory and discourses of the past: While Warburg explained his observations using the engram theory of the psychologist Richard Semon and the contemporary notion of *mémoire involuntaire*, Curtius, in the era of the world wars, conjures up a conservative image of European continuity and unity. Bloom's and Lachmann's theories of intertextuality, finally, are based on elements of both poststructuralist and also psychoanalytic theory. And, last but not least, concepts of individual and collective remembering, biological and medial processes, are often intertwined in the approaches to cultural memory taken by art and literary studies.

Moreover, memory studies has, for the last few years, placed increasing emphasis on 'memory genres' and 'genre memories' (Olick 1999b). These are phenomena closely connected with the 'memory *of* literature', because intertextuality means reference not only to individual texts, but also to genres. The very existence of literary genres is an effect of intertextual processes, of 'literature's memory'. 'Genre' and 'memory' are linked on several levels: First, the historical novel, different forms of 'life writing' (Saunders 2008), and testimony (A. Assmann 2006a), but also more traditional and less openly memory-related genres, such as comedy, pastoral poetry and the romance, can be understood as generators, media and products of cultural memory. A second aspect of the relationship between genre and memory is that the realization of a genre requires a 'readers' memory'. Only when authors and recipients of a mnemonic community share the knowledge of genre conventions (and suspect, for example, that at the end of a detective novel the murder case will be solved) can one speak of the existence of a genre. Third, certain genres, such as biography, comedy or tragedy, are the source of conventionalized, generic schemata for the coding of versions of the past. We draw on such patterns when we tell the stories of our lives as well as in the writing of historiography (see Eakin 1999). Genre schemata are, however, not neutral containers to be filled with specific memories. Instead, they are charged with ideological meaning. Genres such as epic poetry, tragedy and romance carry values, norms and worldviews. (For more, see chapter VI.1.1.)

III.2.3 Memory *of* literature II: The canon and literary history

While theories of intertextuality view literature as a *symbol* system, research into the canon allows for insights into literature as a *social* system: Canon formation and the writing of literary history are central mechanisms on the basis of which the 'memory of literature' is upheld in societies. Institutions are necessary in order to select a corpus of texts to be remembered from the breadth of available literary works, and to organize these texts and ensure their being handed down.

The canon is not only of interest to literary studies. In fact, it is primarily scholars of religious studies, archaeology, and history who have occupied themselves with canon formation as a central process in the creation and maintenance of a cultural memory (see J. Assmann 2006). The canon – a term originally applied to the corpus of recognized holy texts – has a significant societal and cultural relevance. Among the functions that canon formation can fulfil are, as is shown by Jan and Aleida Assmann, the creation of collective identities, the legitimization of political power, and the upholding or undermining of value systems. With their corpus of 'reusable texts' (Jan Assmann), communities describe themselves, and as the concepts of identity and the value structures of a community are transformed over time, so also will its canon change.

The beginning of the 1970s saw growing criticism of the old-fashioned ways of canon formation in the field of literary studies. In the wake of the critique of ideology and feminist research (Ezell 1993), the criteria underlying the western canon were challenged. A revision of the literary canon was called for, one that would open up the dominantly white, male and bourgeois elite canon and that would also take into account previously marginalized authors. Following the paradigm of poststructuralism, a complete renunciation of any sort of canon formation was even called for. These debates, which made waves in the press under the names 'The Great Canon Controversy' (Casement 1996) or 'Culture Wars' (Jay 1997), had an enormous resonance, in the United States in particular.

Although the canon debate is inherently concerned with processes of remembering – what should be selected and thus remembered, what should be forgotten? – there is nonetheless seldom explicit mention of memory in this context. One interesting and rather controversial example of a memory-sensitive perspective on canon formation is, however, Harold Bloom's 1994 monograph *The Western Canon*, a reaction to the heated debate in the United States about canon revision. Bloom not only discusses in a highly selective manner the works of 26 authors (including Shakespeare, Goethe, Tolstoy, and Proust), but also responds to the canon-critical 'School of Resentment' with a reading list which is included in his book. Bloom makes conscious recourse to concepts of ancient mnemonics to explain and support the correctness and importance of canon formation and thus a 'memory of literature'. Yet while in the abovementioned approaches the importance of the canon for cultural memory (religious, ethnic or national) is stressed, Bloom, interestingly, elucidates the canon's important role on the level of individual memory of both author and reader: 'The Canon, once we view it as the relationship of an individual reader and writer to what has been preserved out of what has been written, and forget the canon as a list of books for required study, will be seen as identical with the literary Art of Memory, not with the religious sense of canon' (Bloom 1994, 17). This take on the canon's function sees 'the Canon as a memory system' (ibid., 37). Just as in the classical *ars memoriae*, in the canon-supported memory of the individual reader, *loci* and *imagines* enter into an alliance:

> [W]hat I believe to be the principal pragmatic function of the Canon: the remembering and ordering of a lifetime's reading. The greatest authors take over the role of 'places' in the Canon's theater of memory, and their masterworks occupy the position filled by 'images' in the art of memory. Shakespeare and *Hamlet*, central author and central drama, compel us to remember not only what happens in *Hamlet*, but more crucially what happens in literature that makes it memorable and thus prolongs the life of the author. (ibid.)

A final research framework to be mentioned here is that of literary historiography. Against the backdrop of the 'linguistic turn' and the discussion about the possibilities and limits of representing history, literary studies started to scrutinize its own practice of history writing and pointed to the processes which underlie the creation of literary historiography – processes of retrospective insight, representation and interpretation. Starting from an understanding of the constructed nature of every literary history, there was an examination of selection criteria and construction mechanisms. The theory of literary history converges with cultural memory studies in more recent research on national specificities and mnemonic functions of literary historiography (Grabes 2001).

As is evident from the debates about canon revision and the constructed nature of literary history, literary studies create and maintain cultural memory. Because canon formation and literary historiography have always belonged to the central tasks of the discipline, the institutionalized 'memory *of* literature' is a phenomenon which has – implicitly, but with a lasting impact – always shaped and still continues to shape the practice of literary studies. In this sense, literary studies is, at its very heart, memory studies. In recent decades the mechanisms and the varied social functions of the field's reference to the past have come to the forefront of disciplinary self-reflection. As a result, literary studies today is increasingly interested not only in the making of canons and literary histories, but also in the critical reflection of such construction processes. The field thus observes its own activity – the bringing forth and passing on of cultural memory – from the perspective of memory studies.

III.2.4   Memory *in* literature: The staging of memory

Research on intertextuality and the canon deals largely with the diachronic dimension of memory and literature. The study of the literary representation of memory, on the other hand, foregrounds the synchronic, dialogical relation between literature and extra-literary memory discourses. It starts from the premise that literary works refer to cultural memory, 're-present' (or 'stage', or 'perform') cultural remembrance, and thus make it observable in the medium of fiction.

It is at least since Marcel Proust's *A la recherche du temps perdu* (1913–27) that the relationship of literature to the discourse of memory has been a central area of interest in literary studies (see Terdiman 1993). In Proust's famous 'memory novel', ideas about 'involuntary memory' which had been circulating at the beginning of the twentieth century (such as in Sigmund Freud's concept of 'the unconscious' and Henri Bergson's *mémoire involontaire*) are staged with specifically literary forms, in particular through first-person narration, with a dominant narrating (or rather: remembering) 'I'. A number of studies in recent years have been dedicated to the analysis of how memory is represented in fiction. Using examples from various periods and national literatures, genres and authors, it has been shown that memory plays an important role in literature, both structurally and thematically (Wägenbaur 1998; Middleton and Woods 2000; Nalbantian 2003; Ender 2005; Nünning, Gymnich and Sommer 2006; Favorini 2008).

Much of poetry, certain forms of drama, and a significant amount of fiction can actually be described as the literary representations of individual memory. It is narrative texts in particular which exhibit forms that show a special affinity to memory. Therefore, it is unsurprising that, for example, the narratological distinction between an 'experiencing I' and a 'narrating I' already rests on a (largely implicit) concept of memory, namely on the idea that there is a difference between pre-narrative experience on the one hand, and, on the other, narrative memory which creates meaning retrospectively (see Erll 2009a). The occupation with first-person narrators is thus always an occupation with the literary representation of individual remembering. Adopting concepts from cognitive psychology, the 'narrating I' and 'experiencing I' can moreover be understood as forms of representing 'observer memories' and 'field memories' (on these two terms, see chapter III.3.1). The representation of consciousness is a further example of literature's ability to stage memory: Psycho-narration, free indirect discourse, and interior monologue bring conscious and unconscious processes of individual remembering to light. Such forms of staging internal memory processes belong to literature's 'fictional privileges' (Ansgar Nünning). Monika Fludernik (1996, 27) maintains: 'As Käte Hamburger first suggested, narrative is the one and only form of discourse that can portray consciousness, particularly *another's* consciousness, from the inside, and it is this capacity ... that provides narrative with a niche in the field of competing discourses.' Referring to these and other literary forms, Martin Löschnigg (1999) subsumes under the term 'rhetoric of memory' those narrative means with which the illusion of an authentic memory is created, for example in Charles Dickens' famous memory novel, *David Copperfield* (1850). (For narratological approaches to the literary representation of cultural memory, see Birke 2008, Neumann 2008, and chapter VI.2.4.)

Aleida Assmann, in *Erinnerungsräume* (1999), grapples with forms of the literary representation of the Cultural Memory, considering, for example, Shakespeare's historical dramas and how they represent memory and identity, history and nation: The 'actual actors in these dramas [are] memories' (ibid., 64; see also A. Assmann 2006b). With the Romantic period, a literary concept of memory emerges which is no longer primarily dedicated to the storing of knowledge (*ars memoriae*), but instead accentuates forgetting and the construction of individual identity through the selective and constructive reference to the past. Assmann shows how the competition among different ideas of memory around 1800 can be illustrated with a poem by William Wordsworth which is aptly called 'Memory'. Lastly, Assmann also considers how concepts of memory were represented in literature around 1900, using as an example a short story by E.M. Forster ('Ansell'). Here, the burden of historicism is represented by an extremely heavy box of books which in the end falls into a gorge. The story thus illustrates 'the burden of knowledge and the blessings of forgetting' (ibid., 128). Assmann's interpretations show that art can take on a critical and reflexive function in memory culture. 'Artistic creation plays an important part in the renewal of memory, in that it challenges the firmly drawn border between what is remembered and what forgotten, continually shifting it by means of surprising compositions' (Assmann 2000, 27).

Metaphors of memory, a fundamental literary form, have always been and still are a preferred way of illustrating processes of remembering and forgetting. In attempts to approach the unobservable organic memory, linguistic images were always in play: memory as a wax tablet (Plato), as a seal (Aristotle) or as a 'magic tablet' (Freud's *Wunderblock*), for example. Douwe Draaisma (2000), scholar of the history of psychology, has shown impressively that since antiquity, the media technology dominant at any given time was pressed into service to form that era's metaphors of memory (from writing to phonographs and photography all the way to computers). Literary studies has also contributed to the systematization of the metaphors of memory (see Weinrich 1964; on metaphors of forgetting see Weinrich 2004). Aleida Assmann (1999) distinguishes between metaphors of writing and spatial and temporal metaphors. In a somewhat different direction of enquiry, literary studies is also interested in how metaphors *for* memory, as powerful linguistic images, shape our ideas about history and thus contribute to the formation of cultural memory. ('The British empire as a family' is one of these memory-making metaphors; see Nünning 2002.)

The approaches presented so far suggest that literary representations of memory are characterized by their complex interrelations with memory discourses of other symbol systems, such as psychology, religion, history, and sociology. Literary works can vividly portray individual and collective memory – its contents, its workings, its fragility and its distortions – by coding it into aesthetic forms, such as narrative structures, symbols, and metaphors. Literary representations of memory not only exist in a dynamic relationship to cultural concepts of memory; they also change along with them. (More on the literary representation of memory can be found in chapter VI.2.)

The possibilities and limits of literary representation are gauged when it comes to the memories of violent history, such as war, terror, and genocide. Recent studies, often comparative in their approach, have looked at the literary memory of the world wars, of colonial experiences, dictatorship, and of global terror (for example, Avelar 1999; Peitsch, Burdett and Gorrara 1999; Cohen-Pfister and Wienröder-Skinner 2006; Suleiman 2006).

The study of Holocaust literature has emerged as the most prominent field of literary memory studies, and the extensive body of critical writing is hard to assess (for an overview, see the handbook by Friedman 1993). Recent contributions include Bigsby (2006) who identifies a 'chain of memory' going from writers such as W.G. Sebald and Peter Weiss to Anne Frank and Elie Wiesel; and Banner (2000), who differentiates between survivors' testimonies (for example, Primo Levi) and writers of the second generation (for example, Art Spiegelman), and examines how the memories of the former group were transmitted to the latter. Indispensable for a critical understanding of artistic representations of the Holocaust – literature being one among them – is James E. Young's work on Holocaust writing (1988) and on the art history of Holocaust monuments and memorials (1993). Young shows that Holocaust representations (literary, artistic, and architectural) manifest themselves differently across the world and take on locally different shapes.

It is especially within American discussions that the notion of trauma as a 'crisis of representation' has gained great prominence. This idea was introduced to literary studies in the framework of poststructuralist thinking, notably by Cathy Caruth's *Unclaimed Experience* (1996) (for notions of trauma in historical and psychological memory research, see ch III.1.2 and chapter III.3.1). In her clear-sighted, critical survey of the field, Ruth Leys (2000, 267f.) identifies at the heart of literary trauma studies the concern with the 'constitutive failure of linguistic representation in the post-Holocaust, post-Hiroshima, post-Vietnam era'. In poststructuralist trauma discourse, 'the Holocaust is held to have precipitated, perhaps caused, an epistemological-ontological crisis of witnessing, a crisis manifested at the level of language itself'. In a deconstructivist mode of arguing, scholars like Caruth link trauma with the general limits of signification. Ruth Leys explains that, in trauma studies, the 'gap or aporia in consciousness and representation that is held to characterize the individual traumatic experience comes to stand for the materiality of the signifier', very much in the sense of Paul de Man 'who theorized a "moment" of materiality that on the one hand belongs to language but on the other is aporetically severed from the (speech) act of signification or meaning' (Leys 2000, 266). Questions of the transmissibility of trauma were raised by Felman (1995, 14) who asks, with a view to the teaching of literature: 'How is the act of *writing* tied up with the act of bearing witness – and with the experience of the trial? Is the act of *reading* literary texts itself inherently related to the act of *facing horror*? If literature is the *alignment between witnesses*, what would this alignment mean? And by virtue of what sort of agency is one *appointed* to bear witness?'

A critique of poststructuralist trauma concepts was articulated by Kansteiner and Weilnböck (2008, 237). The authors emphasize that great theoretical and epistemological difficulties arise from the fact that, in current discourse, 'cultural trauma' constitutes a 'vague, metaphorical concept ... which equates the concrete suffering of victims of violence with ontological questions concerning the fundamental ambivalence of human existence and communication'. And indeed, what we are facing today is a veritable trauma industry, proliferating in public discussions, literature, film, and academia. The ethical consequences of literary trauma studies' tendency to personify texts, to conflate literary works with real people, have been considered by Hungerford (2003; for further discussion see also Crownshaw 2010).

Although postcolonial studies' work on the persistence, or 'working-through', of the colonial past in literature as well as some of its key concepts, such as 'writing back', the Middle Passage as 'traumatic event', or 'colonial nostalgia', clearly display a cultural memory-dimension, the connections between these two relatively young research fields have seldom been reflected explicitly. However, a complex of themes that memory studies increasingly focuses on is the literary representation of inter- and transcultural memory. Literary works play an important role in the depiction and construction of ethnic identities, in American ethnic literature (Singh, Skerrett and Hogan 1996) as well as in Black British literature (Rupp 2010). With a view to South African fiction, Sarah Nuttall has developed valuable concepts, such as 'negotiation' and 'entanglement', which help address literary responses to the divergent and contested memories arising from different racialized identity groups (Nuttall and Coetzee 1998; Nuttall 2009). Literary works also play a crucial role in the articulation of postcolonial, migrant and diasporic memories, and in the emergence of 'multidirectional memory' (Rothberg 2009). With this kind of research, literary memory studies also contributes to current discussions about 'world literature' (Damrosch 2003) and global memory (see chapter III.1.6).

More and more, finally, the connections between literature, mediality and memory are coming to the fore in memory studies. Of particular interest have been the interplay and the transitions between orality and literacy, text and image (the latter especially with a view to W.G. Sebald, see Horstkotte 2009). Scholars have also started to look at the 'memory work' done by literary-aesthetic media in the broadest sense – from Hollywood movies to graphic novels to Internet narratives (see Morris-Suzuki 2005).

Today, there is a lively exchange among literary and media studies in the common goal to understand 'mediated memory'. In this context, intermediality and remediation are understood as effective techniques of cultural remembering in literature and other media (see chapter V.5).

The effective presence of literature in memory culture – what I call literature as a medium of cultural memory –, finally, is a phenomenon which is crucial to current discussions about the impact of media on memory, yet remains sorely underexamined. However, it is precisely insights into the power of art and literature as media which *actively shape* cultural remembrance on which the opportunity for literary and art history to engage in the ongoing interdisciplinary dialogue of memory studies depends. It is in this area that a productive exchange with history, sociology, and psychology is most likely to be engendered. (For this reason, chapter VI.3 is dedicated to this question.)

III.3   Mind and memory: Psychological approaches

It was not until the end of the nineteenth century that psychology became established as a science. Until that point, theories of individual memory were primarily the realm of philosophical and proto-psychological thinkers. Around 1900 the ways of thinking about memory ranged from philosophy and psychoanalysis to literature all the way to empirical research. Sigmund Freud's psychoanalytical concepts (such as transference; the importance of the unconscious mind; the mechanisms of denial and repression, condensation and displacement; secondary revision; and screen memory) have become central tropes in certain parts of current cultural memory studies (see III.1.2). Today, psychological approaches to memory are highly diversified, ranging from social and cognitive psychology all the way to the neurosciences. It is increasingly psychologists who suggest interdisciplinary approaches to the study of 'memory in culture', thus enabling collaborative research with colleagues from the humanities and the social sciences.

III.3.1   Memory in cognitive psychology, social psychology, and the neurosciences: History and key concepts

The beginnings of experimental psychology of memory date back to Hermann Ebbinghaus (1964 [1885]) and his attempts to observe the process of memory in its 'pure form' by memorizing nonsense syllables and measuring his ability to retain them in his memory. The British psychologist Sir Frederic C. Bartlett carried out studies diametrically opposed to those designed by Ebbinghaus; these focused on the productive rather than the reproductive aspects of memory. In *Remembering* (1932), his classic study which combined elements of experimental and social psychology, Bartlett showed that all cognitive processes must be understood as an 'effort after meaning' (ibid., 44). Using an experiment in which participants were supposed to remember an unfamiliar story, he proved that memory is shaped by distortions—leveling, accentuation, assimilation. Bartlett agreed with Halbwachs insofar as he argued that constructive processes play a role in memory: 'Remembering ... is an imaginative reconstruction, or construction' (ibid., 213). That said, however, he also pointed out that the concept of *mémoire collective* needed to distinguish between 'memory *in* the group' and 'memory *of* the group' (ibid., 296). The latter he held to be an interesting, but in the end unprovable speculation. The first point, however—that sociocultural contexts have a constitutive meaning for individual memory—appeared to him to be quite evident.

Arguably, Bartlett's most important contribution to cultural memory studies is his popularization of the notion of 'schemata'. Schemata are patterns and structures of knowledge on the basis of which presuppositions regarding specific objects, people, and situations as well as regarding the nature of their relationship can be made. They reduce complexity and guide perception and remembering. Schemata are acquired through socialization. They are thus not universal, but culture-specific (this is what Bartlett's experiment with the unfamiliar story showed: the participants recalled the story according to their culturally shaped ideas about what 'good' stories should be like). Contemporary psychology assumes that

> [schemata consist] of slots and conditions governing what can occupy these slots (and thus, what can, according to the schema, be comprehended, perceived, remembered, or anticipated). Schemata thereby have an economical function for memory, as now not all the details have to be remembered; instead just the particular slots of the particular schema currently activated have to be concretely filled. ... [In this way] schemata make it possible for various pieces of information to be *meaningfully* related to one another and organized. (Pethes and Ruchatz 2001, 520)

Bartlett's studies did not attract much attention among his contemporaries. The behaviourist approach dominant in psychology until the 1960s, which focused solely on measurable, external behaviour, found more to work with in Ebbinghaus's memory research. Today, however,

Bartlett is seen as an important trailblazer for later approaches within psychology which explore the sociocultural dimension of memory.

Not until behaviourism made way for other approaches, in the course of the 'cognitive turn' in psychology, were internal processes of perception and cognition of interest again. Humans were now understood as information-processing creatures, and the main metaphor of memory became the computer. 'Memory' was treated as a three-step process of encoding, storing and retrieving information. In this context, the reconstructivity of memory so strongly emphasized by both Halbwachs and Bartlett came more to the fore: Ulric Neisser, one of the founders of cognitive psychology, compared the process of remembering with the attempt by a paleontologist to recreate the form of a dinosaur using fossil remains: 'The model of the paleontologist ... applies ... to memory: out of a few stored bone chips, we remember a dinosaur' (Neisser 1967, 285).

Since the 1970s, the ground-breaking research done by Endel Tulving (whose main work is *Elements of Episodic Memory*, 1983) has advanced cognitive psychology's understanding of various systems of memory. Psychologists distinguish among ultra-short-term memory, short-term (or working) memory, and long-term memory. Long-term memory is in turn also subdivided into different systems, according to the criterion of their dissociability: In specific experiments or through the observation of memory disorders, it becomes clear that the systems operate independently of each other. 'Two systems of memory are dissociable, when constraints can be specified which benefit or inhibit one of the two memory systems, while having no effect on the other' (Erdfelder 2002, 199). The following systems of long-term memory are currently distinguished in the psychology of memory (Schacter, Wagner and Buckner 2000; Schacter 1996):

Explicit (or declarative) memory systems

(a) Semantic memory. 'Semantic memory' contains conceptual and factual knowledge. In this memory system, we remember learned, symbolically represented knowledge (for example that 'the earth is round'). Semantic knowledge is not tied to a specific time or context. It consists to a significant extent of schemata. This memory system is, in addition, identified with 'noetic' (knowing) consciousness. In retrieving information from the semantic memory, we have the subjective feeling of *knowing that.*

(b) Episodic memory. 'Episodic memory' is tied to a specific time and context. It encompasses memories of life experience (for example,

'the first day of school'). In calling up episodic memory, we have the subjective feeling of *remembering*. Tulving (1983, 124), on whose work the distinction between semantic and episodic memory is based, describes memory in the framework of the latter as 'mental time travel': 'Remembering, for the rememberer, is mental time travel, a sort of reliving of something that happened in the past.' Identified with this system is an 'autonoetic' (self-perceiving) consciousness (see Wheeler 2000). Episodic memory has a unique subjective coloring, and is additionally – in contrast to semantic memory – strongly affective.

Episodic memories are further subdivided into 'field memories' and 'observer memories': Daniel Schacter (1996, 21) asks – 'Do you see yourself in the scene?' This is the question to identify an observer memory. 'Or do you see the scene through your eyes, as if you were there and looking outward, so that you yourself are not an object in the scene?' This would indicate that an episodic memory is represented as a field memory. Field memories are connected with a particularly emotional intensity, and observer memories with a certain distance to the past events.

Recent memory research works from the assumption that episodic memory is above semantic memory in the hierarchy. Even episodic, self-referencing information must first pass through the semantic memory system in the course of its serial encoding: 'Without the possibility of embedding self-referential experiences in a socially shared system of rules and frameworks, the event would not take on any form in a person's consciousness and would not become an experience to be remembered' (Welzer 2002, 104; see also Tulving and Markowitsch 1998).

'Autobiographical memory' is based on processes of the narrativization of episodic memories to form life stories (see Rubin 1996; Fivush 2008). Its function had been described by the English philosopher John Locke in *An Essay Concerning Human Understanding* (1690): For Locke, memory is the condition for individual identity and responsibility. It is through remembering that individuals experience the continuity of their selves and are able to orient themselves on the basis of previous experience in the world. Today a distinction is made among various levels of autobiographical knowledge:

- 'Lifetime periods': 'lengthy segments of life that are measured in years or decades, say, going to college, living in Arizona, or working at a particular place' (Schacter 1996, 89)
- 'General events': 'extended, composite episodes that are measured in days, weeks, or months, such as going to football games during freshman year [or] vacationing at the Grand Canyon' (ibid.)

- 'Event-specific knowledge': 'individual episodes that are measured in seconds, minutes, or hours, such as ... the moment you first laid eyes on the Grand Canyon' (ibid., 90)

On the first two of these levels, the autobiographical memory also exhibits semantic aspects. Schacter (1996, 151) therefore assumes: 'Perhaps lifetime periods and general events are part of semantic memory, while event-specific knowledge is part of episodic memory and preserves the details of individual experiences.' This illustrates how closely the systems of memory cooperate with one another.

Implicit (or non-declarative) systems of memory

Semantic and autobiographical memories are consciously brought about and are thus part of the 'explicit memory'. Yet at the same time, we find ourselves continually influenced by past experience, without our being aware of it. This is an effect of 'implicit memory' (Schacter 1996, 161–91). There are two central forms of implicit memory:

(a) Procedural memory.   As early as 1896, Henri Bergson (1988) called attention to the 'procedural memory', with his concept of *mémoire habitude* (as opposed to the explicit *mémoire souvenir*). This system of memory allows automatic actions that occur without any conscious reflection. Motor skills and habits such as riding a bicycle or playing the piano are examples of procedural memory. In contrast to the 'knowing that' of the semantic memory, here we have the feeling of *knowing how*.

(b) Various forms of priming (perceptual and conceptual).   The term 'priming' refers to the higher likelihood that we will recognize a stimulus which we have already unconsciously perceived at some earlier point. Advertising uses perceptual priming when it repeats images; unconscious stereotypes or unintended plagiarism can be a result of semantic-conceptual priming.

Cognitive psychology certainly does not understand memory according to a simple 'storage and retrieval' model; on the other hand, memory is also not seen through the lens of radical constructivism as purely a product of the present without any reference to past events. It instead takes the middle road, represented by the concept of 'ecphory' (Tulving 1983): The psychology of memory posits the existence of 'engrams', or memory traces, a term which was introduced, along with 'ecphory', by Richard Semon (1921) in 1904 (for a philosophical history of the term see Sutton 1998). At least as important for remembering, however, are retrieval cues. These can be external stimuli, but also internal cues – emotional, cognitive, or motivational, for example. Ecphory means that each memory is the result of a synthesis of engram and cue, of stored information regarding past experience and the conditions at the time of recall: 'The cue combines with the engram to yield a new, emergent entity – the recollective experience of the remember – that differs from either of its constituents' (Schacter 1996, 70).

The fact that differing versions of the past can be modelled on the basis of one and the same engram raises the question of the 'veridicality' of memory, of its 'truth'. This question is nowhere more pressing than in the context of the false memory debate, which was sparked at the beginning of the 1990s in the USA as a result of spectacular court cases in which witnesses testified to the best of their knowledge, in good conscience, and yet nonetheless reported false memories. The possibility of memories being false has been debated particularly in connection with the memory of traumatic experiences, such as sexual abuse (see Schacter 1995).

The term 'trauma' is used to refer to experiences which, as a result of their extreme emotional intensity, cannot be worked through sufficiently, meaning they cannot be narrativized. Mechanisms of traumatic memory include suppression, dissociation from the experience already during its encoding, as well as the involuntary and compulsive reproduction of fragments of memory (see Williams and Banyard 1999; Schooler and Eich 2000). However, inaccurate memories of traumatic experiences can evidently also be induced, for example through suggestive questioning and false information (Loftus and Ketcham 1994).

Cognitive science, a relatively new field that emerged in the mid-1970s, accommodates the insight that the study of memory requires interdisciplinary research which overcomes the polarity of the natural sciences and the humanities (see Maturana and Varela 1992). Psychologists, computer scientists, linguists, social scientists, philosophers and neurologists cooperate in the attempt to understand cognitive processes and structures of knowledge in humans and to put this to productive use in the development of artificial systems of intelligence.

In the USA the 1990s was dubbed the 'decade of the brain'. Neuroscientific memory research has shown through the measurement of neuronal activity that memory has no fixed location in the brain (see Markowitsch and Nilsson 1999). Every region of the brain appears to be involved in processes of remembering, a fact which speaks for the theories of connectionism or for certain forms of the neuronal-network model, which posit that memory is not a storehouse, but rather consists of enduring cognitive structures constructed in the nervous system (see McClelland 2000). Remembering thus proves to be the activation of neuronal patterns. It is continually created anew within an autopoietic system. The neuroscientists Gerald M. Edelman and Giulio Tononi thus emphasize that 'a memory is not a representation; it is a reflection of how the brain has changed its dynamics in a way that allows the repetition of a performance' (Edelman and Tononi 2000, 95). A comprehensive neurobiological definition of memory still valid today is that of Rainer Sinz:

> Memory is the learning-dependent storage of ontogenetically acquired information. This information is integrated selectively and in a species-specific manner into the phylogenetic neuronal structures and can be retrieved at any given time, meaning that it can be made available for situation-appropriate behavior. Generally formulated, memory is based on conditioned changes of the transfer properties in the neuronal 'network' whereby under specific circumstances the neuromotoric signals and behavior patterns corresponding to the system modifications (engrams) can completely or partially be reproduced. (Sinz 1979, 19; quoted in Markowitsch 2008, 275–6)

What is the contribution of brain research to interdisciplinary memory studies? Through various neuroimaging techniques, memory systems can now be studied from the perspective of cognitive psychology *and* the neurosciences (see Schacter, Wagner and Buckner 2000; Roesler et al. 2009). With an eye towards autobiographical memory, functional imaging has shown that different regions of the brain are activated during the recall of positive vs negative experiences, from the more recent vs more distant past, or of imagined vs actually experienced events – in other words, that our brain differentiates in reference to affect, time, and facticity of what is being remembered (see Markowitsch 2002, 132–3). Many brain researchers also emphasize that we have long fallen for *Descartes' Error* (Damasio 1994), namely the assumption that reason and emotion are mutually exclusive. On the contrary, emotions – themselves obviously socially and culturally formed – appear to shape to an extraordinary degree our consciousness, our memory, and our actions. The autobiographical memory in particular is unthinkable without emotions (see also LeDoux 1996).

The psychology of memory has expanded today into a number of subdisciplines; *The Oxford Handbook of Memory* (Tulving and Craik 2000) and *The Science of Memory: Concepts* (Roediger, Dudai and Fitzpatrick 2007) offer useful overviews. The subdisciplines of a broadly defined psychological memory studies – from cognitive psychology to social and developmental psychology all the way to neurobiology and cognitive neuroscience – for a long time proceeded in parallel, but are now increasingly coming together in an interdisciplinary dialogue.

III.3.2 Remembering in a sociocultural context: Ecology, communicativity and narrativity of memory

Memory as a social and cultural phenomenon has attracted increasing attention since the mid-1980s, a time when pure cognitivism was under attack and there were calls for an expanded view that also took into account contextual factors. Neisser (1982, 4) offered the provocative summary: 'If X is an interesting or socially significant aspect of memory, then psychologists have hardly ever studied X.' So-called ecological approaches turn away from traditional experimental research in the laboratory, and look at the interactions between the individual and the sociocultural environment: other people, things, places, media such as text and image – all of which can act as triggers for remembering (see Bruce 1985; Neisser and Winograd 1989; Graumann 1997). The 'extended mind' model assumes that there are not only 'engrams', which represent experiences on the neuronal level, but also, with a term coined by Merlin Donald (1991, 308–33), 'exograms', that is, external memory representations, from body decorations to hieroglyphics, books and movies. Connected notions are that of embodied or distributed cognition, developed in cognitive science and philosophy (Lakoff and Johnson 1999; see Sutton 2006).

Social-psychological and discourse-oriented approaches pursue questions of interpersonal memory activity. They look at the interdependence of individual and group in the collective construction of memories within a framework of conversational or group remembering – for example, when family members look at old photos: 'The point is to create a socially shared and validated *version* of the past out of previously individual experiences' (Bangerter 2002, 191; see also Clark and Stephenson 1995). In studies of conversational remembering it has been shown that through memory talk and the cross-cuing that emerges as a result it is not so much that *more* is remembered, but first and foremost that the participants remember *differently*: Episodic memories are adjusted according to criteria of relevance specific to the group. 'Audience tuning' determines the selection of and perspective on what is remembered. The shared elaboration can have such an influence that a source amnesia makes second-hand experiences become part of a person's own life history, indistinguishable from first-hand memories (see Echterhoff, Higgins and Groll 2005). In the collective discursive negotiation of memory, thus, not only mnemic factors play a role, but also social, linguistic, rhetorical, and, last but not least, aesthetic-narrative factors.

Narrative psychology recognizes the prominent role narrative structures play in remembering (Bruner 1991). In a productive application of Bartlett's studies, David E. Rumelhart reintroduced the notion of 'story schemata' in 1975. Today, narration is conceived of as a ubiquitous format for the creation of meaning (Schank and Abelson 1995). Gerald Echterhoff and Jürgen Straub (2003–04) list the diverse functions of narrative for the human mind: the constitution of human time, the creation of meaning and handling of contingency, basic mental abilities (perception and reception, thought and judgement, memory and remembering, motivation and personal goals, emotion and affect), the creation and representation of identity, and communicative and social-interactive functions.

Life experience, in particular, is given meaning first through narrative emplotment. In this context, Donald E. Polkinghorne (2005, 8) speaks of processes of 'symbolic transformation' and explains: 'Narrative knowing … is a reflective explication of the pre-narrative quality of unreflective experience.' It is

> not a simple recall of the past. Narrative comprehension is a retrospective, interpretive composition that displays past events in the light of current understanding and evaluation of their significance. While referring to the original past life events, narrative transforms them by ordering them into a coherent part-whole plot structure. (ibid., 10)

The fact that life stories are always reconstructed in retrospect, from a provisional end point, inspired in Jens Brockmeier the concept of a 'retrospective teleology' (Brockmeier and Carbaugh 2001, 247–80). In the subsequent moulding of pre-narrative experience, various forms of 'narrative smoothing' can be observed, which Polkinghorne (2005, 9) summarizes as follows: 'In configuring a story of a life episode, narratives often omit details and condense parts ("flattening"), elaborate and exaggerate other parts ("sharpening"), and make parts more compact and consistent ("rationalization") to produce a coherent and understandable explanation.'

The sociocultural dimension of narrative remembering can be considered under many different aspects: Patterns of narration are, first, following Bartlett, to be understood as culture-specific schemata, which already pre-form every single experience we have. The cultural context thus influences *what* can be narrated and remembered and *how* this can be done. From the perspective of discourse-oriented psychology, narration appears, second, as a fundamental practice of the shared creation of memory within the framework of conversational remembering. The autobiographic remembering self, as 'totalitarian ego' (Greenwald 1980) changes, third, its life story according to current sociocultural contexts and the demands for meaning that result from the experience of the present.

III.3.3 Psychology and cultural memory studies: Integrative models

Genuinely transdisciplinary memory research, which combines approaches from cultural history, social sciences, literary and media studies with research in psychology, psychoanalysis and neurosciences, has gradually taken root since the beginning of the 1990s (see, for example, Middleton and Edwards 1990; Antze and Lambek 1996; Pennebaker, Páez and Rimé 1997; Straub 2005; Tomasello 1999; Echterhoff and Saar 2002; Boyer and Wertsch 2009). The theoretical and methodological possibilities and limitations of such combinations have since been a frequent topic of debate. The spectrum of psychological contributions to this discussion spans all the way from a critical distancing from the concept of 'collective memory' to a presentation of various integrative models which demonstrate the interfaces of historical, social, literary, and psychological memory research.

In an article called 'Searching for Cultural Memory,' Jens Brockmeier (2002) suggests 'hybrid perspectives that aim to overcome categories and research agendas set up by what Latour called the "work of purification"' (ibid. 12). One of the 'underlying assumptions' of such hybrid memory studies is the conviction that

> there is no principal separation of what traditionally is viewed as individual or personal memory from what traditionally is viewed as social, collective or historical memory. ... As a consequence, the investigative focus shifts to the forms of interaction and co-construction, interplay and mutual dependence, fusion and unity between the previously separated spheres of the individual and the collective, the private and the public, the timeless and the historical. (ibid., 9)

One of the most comprehensive examples thus far for such a synthesis has been put forth by James Wertsch who, in his *Voices of Collective Remembering* (2002), draws on psychology, history, literary theory, semiotics, sociology and political science to provide a sophisticated theoretical model of collective memory as multivoiced and distributed 'mediated action' (ibid., p. 6). Another example for truly integrative work on memory is the research conducted by the social psychologist Harald Welzer. In his book *Das kommunikative Gedächtnis* (2002, 'The Communicative Memory'), Welzer combines insights of neuroscientific research, developmental psychology and social psychology with the results he gained in oral history interviews in order to highlight and theorize the social and communicative aspects of individual memory (for a concise summary of his work, see Welzer 2008).

In designing models for research that integrate psychology and cultural studies, many psychologists start with the distinctions among various systems of memory. Harald Welzer and the neuroscientist Hans J. Markowitsch, for example, foreground the autobiographical memory. They outline a 'bio-psycho-social developmental model of the autobiographical memory' which is based on the discovery of the 'plasticity of the brain', that is, the fact that environmental influences exert an enormous influence on the brain's form and functioning:

> The finding that a significant part of the development of the neuronal network patterns and decisive phases of the organic development of the brain take place after birth, that is, under social and cultural influences, marks from our point of view a central interface between research done on memory and remembering in the social sciences and that in the natural sciences. (Welzer and Markowitsch 2001, 206)

In contrast, Edgar Erdfelder (2002), a representative of experimental memory psychology, makes an argument for conceiving of the semantic memory as a junction between the individual and the collective memory, that is, as 'the part of the individual memory in which collective and cultural memory are mirrored, partly incompletely and partly also idiosyncratically warped' (ibid., 199). Integrative models of psychological memory research, thus, look at the sociocultural and communicative creation of episodic-autobiographical memory as well as the representation of history and cultural knowledge in the semantic memory of the individual.

Combining both perspectives, the social psychologists David Manier and William Hirst have proposed a 'cognitive taxonomy of collective memories' (2008). They proceed from cognitive psychology's differentiation of various systems of memory (see chapter III.3.1) and distinguish between three forms of the representation of collective memory in individual minds:

1. Collective-episodic memory: This includes memories that members of a social group unanimously hold of their shared experiences (say, a picnic); everyone remembers the specific context, time, and place of the event. Such memories can even become a collective-autobiographical memory if everyone in equal measure locates the shared experience within the framework of a specific narrative which helps establish a collective identity. Determining the rules which govern the creation of collective-episodic memory is the object of studies on conversational remembering (see chapter III.3.2).

2. Collective-semantic memory: This is the memory of historical events not personally experienced. Manier and Hirst distinguish between 'lived semantic memory' and 'distant semantic memory'. An example of the former would be memories many Americans over age fifty have of the Vietnam War. Even those who did not actively participate in the fighting followed the events in the press and discussed them with their friends. The deciding factor for lived semantic memory is precisely its 'lived quality' (ibid., 258). As an example of distant semantic memory, Manier and Hirst cite the memory of Washington's crossing of the Delaware; this is also indirect knowledge, but in this case, the feeling of vitality and immediacy which characterize lived semantic memories are lacking during the recall of this more distant event. Lived semantic memory is a typical object of the memory that is formed between generations, while distant semantic memory is communicated by means of institutions. The transitions between the two forms of memory are, however, never truly distinct.

Clearly, these terms introduce yet again a distinction that would be marked in the Assmanns' terminology as 'communicative vs Cultural Memory'. The contrast is memory of recent events on the one hand and history, myth, and tradition on the other – a difference which, in one form and under one label or another, is a common thread in many studies of collective memory (see chapter II.4.1).

With both forms of collective-semantic memory, as Gerald Echterhoff (2004, 79f.) points out, the importance is 'on the one hand the explicit reference to past (historical) events, and on the other hand the "valence" or relevance of these contents in light of current actions'. 'The retrieved and invoked events from the past are anything but neutral historical data; they are used for orientation in the current context, useful, and thus also valuable' (ibid.). In addition, Echterhoff calls attention to the central intersection between memory research in social psychology and cultural studies' interest in media and institutions of remembering: Collective-semantic bodies of knowledge become such only 'as the result of a series of social processes of construction and validation' (ibid., 78). Thus 'the collectivization of what are at first simply contents of the semantic memory are presumably tied to a number of cognitive, technical, social, and societal conditions' (ibid., 82).

3. Collective-procedural memory: In this last category, Manier and Hirst subsume traditions and rituals, which the individual often carries out and passes on without being aware of it. 'Rituals and traditions, or more generally, procedural memories, can serve as mnemonic tools that shape the collective identity of their practitioners, collectively reminding them of declarative memories' (Manier and Hirst 2008, 259).

To sum up, in recent decades almost no other topic has inspired such a stimulating and productive interdisciplinary dialogue, one which also blurs the boundaries between the humanities and the natural sciences. Of course, the fact that 'memory' figures as a shared object of study for disciplines with significantly different basic assumptions, research interests, and methods can have explosive results. And, of course, it is also true that researchers are far from establishing a 'super theory' of memory which would perfectly interweave the 'two cultures'. However, many scholars and scientists have at least cast off some of their reservations and shown themselves to be open to 'memory as a convergent field' (Welzer 2008, 295) and the interdisciplinary exchange that goes along with it, so that we can look forward to interesting new developments.

IV
Memory and Culture: A Semiotic Model

In light of the broad multidisciplinarity of memory studies and the great variety of concepts of memory it has yielded, should one even attempt a definition of 'cultural memory'? Nicholas Pethes and Jens Ruchatz find this goal neither realistic nor desirable. Thus, they did not even include entries for 'memory' or 'remembering' in their interdisciplinary encyclopedia (2001) of the same name. They certainly have a point. The 'supertheory' of memory that integrates all the existing approaches has yet to be conceived (on some far-reaching attempts, though, see chapter III.3.3). The goal of this chapter is to outline an heuristic model of cultural memory. This model is rooted in anthropological and semiotic approaches to culture, but at the same time it should leave room for as many points of contact with other approaches as possible.

We cannot conceive of memory without using metaphors; in fact, throughout history, the phenomenon of 'memory' has itself generated a great many metaphors. In a first step, therefore, the possibilities, limits, and dangers of the metaphorical reference to cultural memory will be carefully examined and two fundamentally different uses of Halbwachs's term 'collective memory' – *collective* and *collected* – will be explained. A second step then introduces categories of cultural semiotics and distinguishes among three dimensions of memory culture (material, social, and mental). Third, concepts of cognitive psychology are transferred to the level of culture, in order to locate acts of remembering within a framework of various systems of cultural memory. And fourth, the relationship of memory to the neighboring terms 'identity' and 'experience' is considered.

IV.1   Metaphors – productive, misleading and superfluous, or: How to conceive of memory on a collective level

One of the established criticisms levelled against theories of cultural memory contends that they are based on an improper transference of concepts of individual psychology to the collective level. Marc Bloch (1925), in his response to Halbwachs's theses, was the first to point out the problems that arise when terms such as 'memory', 'remembering' and 'forgetting' are simply furnished with the adjective 'collective' in order to transfer to sociocultural phenomena the insights gathered in studying individuals. It is certainly true that there exists no form of collective consciousness (outside of individual minds) to which one could ascribe acts of remembering and forgetting, an unconscious, or the suppression of memory.

Cultural memory, *collective* remembering, or *social* forgetting are *metaphors* – as has been emphasized repeatedly (be it as a reproach or as a justification for cultural studies' approaches to memory). They are linguistic cognitive models with heuristic value, as Harald Weinrich pointed out as early as 1976: 'We cannot conceive of an object such as memory without metaphors. Metaphors, particularly when they occur in the consistency of semantic fields, are valuable as (hypothetical) cognitive models' (294) (see also Lakoff and Johnson 1980). Memory, remembering and forgetting have been paraphrased with metaphors since Plato and Aristotle – from wax tablet, seal, and aviary to storehouse and theatre all the way to photography and the computer. Thus, as Douwe Draaisma (2000, 3) points out, 'ever-changing images are projected onto our theories of memory, a succession of metaphors and metamorphoses, a true *omnia in omnibus*'. The classical metaphors of memory have always referred to the individual level. This means that when we draw on the concept of memory, we are using a term which is already associated with a range of metaphors. Metaphorizing this term even further – that is, taking the previous tenor (or: target domain) 'individual memory' and making it a vehicle (or: source domain) for an understanding of social phenomena such as processes of canonization or public commemorations – can be very suggestive, but also harbors the danger of producing endlessly meandering catachreses, chains of mixed metaphors.

To be exact, in speaking of 'cultural memory' we are only sometimes dealing with metaphors proper, but always with tropes, that is, with expressions that have a figurative meaning. Yet not every concept of cultural memory exhibits the same degree of tropology. Basically, there are two different uses of tropes in cultural memory studies which should be distinguished: 'cultural memory' as metaphor and as metonymy.

- Metonymy: When 'cultural remembering' is conceived of as an individual act, when the focus is on the shaping force that sociocultural surroundings exert on organic memory – that is, when we speak of 'memory as a phenomenon of culture' (see J. Assmann 2006, 170) –, then we are dealing with a literal use of the term 'memory' and with a metonymic use of the attribute 'cultural' (which stands for sociocultural contexts and their influence on individual memory).
- Metaphor: In contrast, it is a metaphorization of the term 'memory' when we speak of the 'memory of culture', 'a society remembering' or the 'memory of literature'. These are linguistic images for the organized archiving of documents, for the establishment of official commemoration days, or for the artistic process of intertextuality – in short for 'culture as a phenomenon of memory' (ibid.). The term 'memory' itself becomes a metaphor.

Thus there are two fundamentally different ways of conceiving of the relationship between culture and memory, both of which can be found already in Halbwachs's work on *mémoire collective*. However, there they are not discussed separately nor clearly distinguished from each other. It is the American sociologist Jeffrey Olick (1999a) who has pointed with the necessary clarity to the difference between what he calls a 'collected' and a 'collective' memory. He speaks of the 'two cultures' of memory research: 'two radically different concepts of culture are involved here, one that sees culture as a subjective category of meanings contained in people's minds versus one that sees culture as patterns of publicly available symbols objectified in society' (ibid., 336). Drawing on Olick, we can therefore distinguish between

- '*collected* memory' as the socially and culturally formed individual memory. We remember with the aid of culturally specific schemata; we act according to collectively shared values and norms; we assimilate second-hand experiences into our personal wealth of experience. Halbwachs would call these instances *cadres sociaux de la mémoire*. Olick uses the metaphor of 'collecting': The individual mind appropriates various elements of the sociocultural environment. Cultural studies research on *collected* memory is often engaged in a dialogue with social psychology and can even profit from the insights of the neurosciences; and

- *'collective* memory' (in the narrower sense), which refers to the symbols, media, social institutions, and practices which are used to construct, maintain, and represent versions of a shared past. History, sociology, literary and media studies (including the influential approaches by Nora and the Assmanns) have traditionally addressed this second level of *mémoire collective.*

The two forms of collective memory can thus be separated analytically; however, they exert their influence only through their continual interaction, through the interplay of the individual and collective levels. There is no pre-cultural individual memory. But neither is there a 'Collective Memory' that is totally detached from individuals and embodied solely in media and institutions. Just as the social environment and cultural schemata shape the individual memory, the 'memory' of a sociocultural formation must be actualized and realized in, or appropriated through, organic minds. Otherwise commemorative rituals, archival material, and media representing the past will be useless and ineffective – dead material, failing to have any impact in memory culture.

Olick's distinction between *collected* and *collective* memory corresponds to Elena Esposito's (2002, 17) systems-theory approach and her differentiation between memory on the cognitive level and memory on the social level: 'Only by maintaining the differentiation between the two forms of memory can one focus an analysis on their mutual influence.' It is only through the interaction of cognitive and social memory that memory culture emerges.

Throughout this book I will call the two aspects of cultural memory that should be analytically distinguished 'cultural memory on the individual level' on the one hand and 'cultural memory on the collective level' on the other. Figure IV.1 sums up the key characteristics of and differences between those two levels.

Another frequent objection to the concept of cultural memory has been that it is a superfluous trope. These critics argue, first, that individual memory is still individual memory, even when its cultural aspects are emphasized, and, second, that cultural memory on the level of the collective is a bad metaphor, because it lumps together heterogeneous phenomena which could just as easily be replaced by the familiar terms 'tradition', 'myth' or 'historical consciousness'. In this vein, Noa Gedi and Yigal Elam (1996, 47) have asked 'Collective Memory – What Is It?' and arrived at the answer that '"collective memory" is but a misleading name for the old familiar "myth" … Indeed, collective memory is but a myth'.

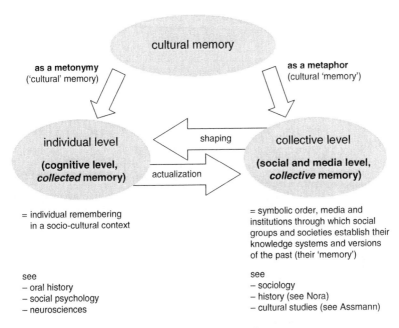

Figure IV.1   Two uses of the term 'cultural memory'

Indeed, it is the case that 'cultural memory' is a broad umbrella term, under which a number of cultural, social, cognitive and biological phenomena can be subsumed: tradition, archive, canon, monuments, commemorative rituals, communication within the family circle, life experience and neuronal networks. Critics point out that concepts of collective or cultural memory thus blur the fine gradations between all these phenomena (see ibid., 30). What these criticisms overlook, however, is their integrative power. It is exactly the umbrella quality of the term 'cultural memory' which helps us see the (sometimes functional, sometimes analogical, sometimes metaphorical) relationships between phenomena which were formerly conceived of as distinct, and thus draw connections between tradition and canon, monuments and historical consciousness, family communication and neuronal circuits. Therefore, the concept of cultural memory opens up a space for interdisciplinary perspectives in a way none of these other (albeit more specific) concepts can.

Nonetheless, the criticism does make clear that cultural memory studies must draw an important distinction, namely that between productive and misleading metaphors. As a productive metaphor, 'cultural memory' is a sensitizing concept (Olick 1999a), a concept which draws our attention to previously unrecognized structural similarities and functional relations. On the other hand, the term 'memory' should at least be put in quotation marks when it serves as a metaphorical expression for the role of media and institutions in the collective construction of the past. Otherwise, we would indeed seem to 'enter a new age in which archives remember and statues forget', as the historian Kerwin Lee Klein complains (2000, 136). He is seconded by the psychologist Wolfgang Schönpflug (2002, 224), who emphasizes: 'External relics and systems have no memory and are not memory', And also Wulf Kansteiner (2002, 189) finds such statements 'at best metaphorical and at worst misleading'. In the cases mentioned by Klein, the term 'memory' is used not only as a metaphor, but also as an abbreviation. Applying it in this manner means skipping over several stages of complex cultural processes. Statues and literature are not 'memory', but rather *media* of cultural memory, which encode information and can prompt remembering or forgetting (see chapter V); archives and universities are likewise not themselves memory, but rather can serve as *institutions* of cultural memory, which gather, preserve, administer, and impart culturally relevant information about the past.

The memory metaphor becomes completely misleading, however, when it is used to apply the entire conceptual logic of individual psychology to culture. Although certain characteristics of individual memory (such as the nexus between memory, narration, and identity) seem to function analogously on the level of culture, it must be stated very clearly that in principle, 'from the functioning of the brain and consciousness *nothing* can be deduced regarding the functioning of society' (Esposito 2002, 18; my emphasis). In this regard psychoanalytical concepts in particular are as suggestive as they are potentially misleading. One can, it is true, observe processes on the level of society which correspond to individual repression, displacement, or screen memories: for example, censorship, selective and biased historiography, or the creation of fictive myths. But when it comes to the effects of such processes (as postulated by Freud and other psychoanalysts) the matter looks altogether different: Denial and repression might well make an individual organism sick, but not necessarily a society. 'Nations *can* repress with psychological impunity: their collective memories can be changed without a "return of the repressed"' (Kansteiner 2002, 186). Even Dominick LaCapra (1998, 23), one of the pre-eminent figures of psychoanalytically inspired cultural memory studies, is concerned that 'there is a great temptation to trope away from specificity'. In particular, the poststructuralist-psychoanalytical metaphor of cultural trauma has more often elicited misunderstandings in the field than yielded insights into processes of cultural memory. The notion of cultural trauma is, as Wulf Kansteiner (2004) sums up in his critical survey of trauma research in philosophy, psychology and cultural studies, a 'category mistake', derived from a misleading metaphorization of concepts which describe mechanisms of individual memory.

To sum up, the 'cultural' memory of the individual and the cultural 'memory' of social groups and societies are two possible ways to describe (and study) 'memory in culture'. Neither of the areas thus constituted can be viewed exclusively, since *collected* and *collective* memory, the cognitive and the social (and media) level, can only be understood through their interaction with each other. In both cases, the term 'memory' has a tropological dimension, and both are legitimate. However, when employing metaphors and metonymies it is important to be aware of the direction and degree of the transfer of meaning, the productivity of the trope for the specific research question, and also the chance that the logic of the figurative term could lead us astray.

IV.2   Material, social and mental dimensions of memory culture

As announced in the introduction, this book is based on a broad understanding of cultural memory. This means that unlike in Halbwachs's or Nora's work, 'memory' is not narrowly defined as group memory or national memory and contrasted to history. Nor does the term carry any specific positive or negative connotations (neither as the refuge of an 'original' version of the past nor as its biased distortion). The umbrella term 'cultural memory' unites all possible expressions of the relationship of culture and memory – from *ars memoriae* to digital archives, from neuronal networks to intertextuality, from family talk to the public unveiling of a monument. Cultural memory can thus broadly be defined as the sum total of all the processes (biological, medial, social) which are involved in the interplay of past and present within sociocultural contexts. It finds its specific manifestation in memory culture.

Because of the significance of cultural sign systems in all forms of remembering, the model developed here draws on research done in the field of cultural semiotics. In a similar vein, James Wertsch (2002, 26) has proposed placing 'semiotics front and centre' in theories of collective remembering and focusing on memory's 'semiotic mediation' (ibid., 52). From a semiotic viewpoint, culture is the result of the diachronic dimension of semioses (that is, of sign processes). The condition for the development and viability of culture in this understanding is the lasting effect of codes and of 'texts' (that is, cultural artefacts). To conceive of this fundamentally temporal aspect of culture, semioticians like Jurij Lotman and Boris Uspenskyij integrated the idea of memory into their theory early on: 'We understand culture as the *nonhereditary memory of the community*' (1978, 213; emphasis in the original; see also Lotman 1990 on the relation between 'cultural memory, history, and semiotics').

A theory of culture which integrates anthropological and semiotic perspectives has been developed by Roland Posner. He conceives of culture as a system of signs which has three dimensions:

> Anthropology distinguishes between social, material, and mental culture, and semiotics systematically connects these three areas in the way it defines a social culture as a structured set of users of signs (individuals, institutions, society); the material culture as a set of texts (civilization); and mental culture as a set of codes. (Posner and Schmauks 2004, 364; see also Posner 2004)

The three dimensions of culture postulated by cultural semiotics are dynamically interrelated, since users of 'signs' (social dimension) are dependent on 'codes' (mental dimension) if they want to understand 'texts' (material dimension). In a specific cultural formation, codes manifest themselves in social interaction as well as in media and other artefacts; and at the same time, it is here that culture is continually created anew.

As in the case of culture at large, it is useful to distinguish among different dimensions (material, mental and social) when considering memory culture. Positing such a three-dimensionality of memory culture is especially helpful in light of the disparity of the field of memory studies, where representatives of individual disciplines tend to focus on one of these three dimensions and render it in terms of absolutes. Thus it is no surprise that social scientists – ever since Maurice Halbwachs – have developed concepts which foreground the social dimension of memory culture (Olick 2008). Scholars in the fields of art and literature, from Aby Warburg to Mieke Bal et al. (1999) and Renate Lachmann (1997), on the other hand, point to the importance of the material dimension (paintings, literary texts) for acts of cultural recall. The mental dimension of memory culture, lastly, is underscored by scholars interested in the history of mentality (see Confino 2008) as well as – albeit not in a semiotic but in a biological understanding – by psychologists and neuroscientists. All of these branches have provided important impulses for cultural memory studies. Nonetheless, a one-sided focus on a 'social memory', a 'material memory' or a 'mental memory' threatens to hide from view the complexity of cultural processes. It is only through the constant, processual, and dynamic interaction of all three dimensions that cultural memory is produced (see Figure IV.2):

- The material dimension of memory culture is constituted by mnemonic artefacts, media, and technologies of memory, ranging from symbols and landscapes to architecture and books to film and photography.
- To the social dimension of memory culture belong mnemonic practices and the carriers of memory: commemorative rituals; forms of production, storage, and recall of cultural knowledge; and the persons and social institutions involved in these processes.
- The mental dimension of memory culture, finally, includes all the shared schemata, concepts, and codes which enable and shape collective remembering through symbolic mediation, as well as all the

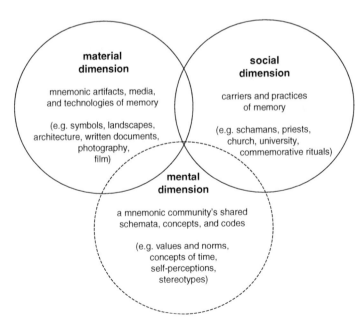

Figure IV.2   Three dimensions of memory culture

effects that the activity of remembering has on the mental disposi-
tions predominant in a community – such as ideas about time and
history, values and norms, self-perceptions and the perception of
others.

As a (however imagined) 'whole' cultural memory is elusive. Researchers
can only study discrete acts, or performances, of memory. These may
derive from either the material or the social dimension of memory
culture (say, in the shape of a religious tract or a burial ceremony);
and they may give rise to hypotheses about its (unobservable) mental
dimension.

All acts of cultural remembering (commemorative 'minutes of
silence', conversations with family members about a recent vacation,
the production and circulation of a historical study of the Middle Ages)
show a specific mediality. It is only through media in the broadest sense
that contents of cultural memory become accessible for the members of
a mnemonic community. Media not only connect the three dimensions
of memory culture; they are also the interface between the *collected* and
collective, the cognitive and the social/media level of memory (see also
chapter V.1).

The coding of knowledge about the past occurs not only with the
help of specific media, but also always within the framework of a
symbolic form, or a symbol system. According to the cultural philosopher Ernst Cassirer (1944), symbolic forms are independent forms of
understanding the world. Religion, history, the natural sciences, law,
and art are some of the symbolic forms available to memory culture.
Whether a piece of information to be remembered is encoded in the
symbolic forms of academic history or Christian religion, of Islamic law
or western literature is a crucial question, since the choice of symbol
system also changes the quality of that which is remembered.

Media and symbol systems are two of the coordinates which play a
significant role in determining in which 'mnemonic mode' the past is
being remembered (see II.4.1). Our memories (individual and collective) of past events can vary to a considerable extent. This holds true
not only for *what* is remembered (facts, data), but also for *how* it is
remembered – that is, for the quality and meaning the past assumes. As
a result, there are different modes of remembering identical past events.
A war, for example, can be remembered as a mythic event ('the war as
apocalypse'), as part of political history (the First World War as 'the great
seminal catastrophe of the twentieth century'), as an ethically charged
traumatic experience or event ('the horror of the trenches', 'the lost

generation'), as a part of family history ('the war my great-uncle served in'), as a focus of bitter contestation ('the war which was waged by the old generation, by the fascists, by men'), or as a piece of good entertainment ('the war I saw at the movies'). Mythical, politicized, traumatic, familial, generational, genealogical, contested, aestheticizing, and entertaining memory are all different modes of referring to the past.

In the following chapters, particular attention will be paid to these coordinates of cultural memory – media, symbolic forms, and modes. Chapter V deals with the relationship of media and memory. Chapter VI is dedicated to an analysis of literature as a symbolic form of cultural memory, and Chapter VI.2.4 addresses the modes of literary memory from a narratological point of view. But first, some of the major systems of cultural memory will be explained.

IV.3   Autobiographical, semantic and procedural systems of cultural memory

Psychologists differentiate among several memory systems: Explicit systems (semantic, episodic, and autobiographical memory) are distinguished from implicit systems (procedural memory and priming). Social psychologists have productively adapted this classification to explain '*collected* memory' (see chapter III.3). Drawing on the work by Hirst and Manier (and slightly changing their terminology to fit the distinction between *collected* and *collective* memory), I use the terms 'collected-episodic', 'collected-semantic' and 'collected-procedural' memory to describe the sociocultural aspects of individual remembering. To these psychological categories for describing *collected* memory this book adds an (admittedly metaphorical) cultural-studies systematization of *collective* memory. Various procedures by which groups and societies refer to temporal processes are understood here as an expression of different collective systems of memory. Such a metaphorical transfer of memory systems distinguished with a view to individual remembering to the level of the social and medial cannot be rendered in absolute terms and must be taken with a grain of salt; but it may nonetheless prove useful, as this allows for the multitude of heterogeneous acts of collective remembering to be more clearly differentiated.

I use the term 'collective-autobiographical memory' to refer to the collective remembering of a shared past. Psychological studies of the individual autobiographical memory emphasize its dynamic, creative and narrative nature, as well as its identity-creating functions. On the social and media level, too, 'autobiographical' versions of the past are highly constructive and fulfil the function of self-description ('our past, our identity'). Through collective-autobiographical acts of memory, group identities are created, the experience of time is culturally shaped, and shared systems of values and norms are established. Collective-autobiographical remembering is often described with terms such as 'remembrance' or 'commemoration'. The Assmanns' 'Cultural Memory' with its normative and formative myths, and the 'communicative memory' with its shared fabrication of narratives about the recent past are typical examples of this memory system. Nora's *lieux de mémoire*, on the other hand, are located below the level of autobiographical narrativization; they represent a kind of 'collective-episodic memory' which is not transformed into coherent stories (or 'master narratives'), but is instead condensed into a multitude of particular 'sites of memory'.

With the term 'collective-semantic memory' I denote processes of the social organization and storage of knowledge. This form of memory does *not* address the experience of time. Research on the collective-semantic memory typically looks at the symbolic representation of cultural knowledge, organizing principles, media and technologies of storage. The Assmanns' 'stored memory' and the 'cultural archive' as well as wisdom and common sense are part of the collective-semantic memory. On the social and media level, both autobiographical and semantic memories are the result of ongoing processes of negotiation.

Naturally, just as is the case with individual memory, we have also to assume an overlap and permeation of semantic and autobiographical memory on the level of the social. Collective systems of knowledge, for example, are culture-specific phenomena; they have emerged from historical experience and can be relevant to cultural identity (especially when the community is confronted with alternative systems of knowledge). Conversely, the creation of collective-autobiographical memories always takes place against the backdrop of existing cultural semantics. And, finally, memories of a common past can become identity-neutral knowledge when the events in question are no longer conceived of as an identity-related 'usable past'. This differentiation between semantic and autobiographical systems of collective memory can help answer the difficult question regarding the status of history in memory culture. In the model proposed here, the symbolic form 'history' (with historiography as its main medium) exhibits strongly 'autobiographical' aspects when it is clearly related to the group or society in which it originated, when it transmits concepts of identity, values and norms, and has affective elements. In contrast, we are dealing with historiography operating according to the collective-semantic system – and thus belonging more to the area of 'knowing' rather than 'remembering' – when it transmits identity-neutral knowledge (for example, about foreign cultures or about one's own group, but in the latter case in a way that does not suggest an identificatory reading). One must consider, though, that 'autobiographical and identity-creating' or 'semantic-scholarly' functions of media of cultural memory are never based exclusively on intrinsic characteristics, but are first and foremost created by their users (the members of a mnemonic community) and can thus vary in different contexts.

The term 'collective-procedural memory' is meant to accommodate phenomena such as the uncontrolled recurrence of bodies of knowledge and forms of expression. This includes, for example, the effect of Aby Warburg's 'pathos formulas'. 'Collective-procedural memory' would also describe an awareness of the past which – for example in Harald Welzer's (2001) understanding of 'social memory' – is expressed in non-intended acts of memory. The existence of cultural stereotypes and value hierarchies is likewise less an effect of the conscious efforts of a society to pass on certain versions of the past and bodies of knowledge, and more a result of a continuation *en passant*. Collective-procedural memory is thus the implicit, non-intentional side of the explicit forms of collective memory (semantic and autobiographical); it refers to ways of dealing with the past which are not conscious or capable of becoming conscious on the social level. As collective phenomena, however, acts of procedural memory are always tied to symbolic forms of expression, in media or patterns of social behaviour (Figure IV.3).

There is no collective memory without individual actualization. This is also the case in distinguishing systems of memory. What statements can thus be made about the representation of the aforementioned collective memory systems in the organic memory?

- Collective-autobiographical information ('*our* past') is represented in the individual memory as strongly affective contents of the semantic memory. However, the events of a more recent past that the rememberer has witnessed him- or herself (the 'communicative memory') can also be represented as episodic memories ('how I experienced the fall of the Berlin Wall'; 'how my family and I heard about the attacks on September 11, 2001').
- Collective-semantic information, on the other hand, encompasses the relatively neutrally experienced contents of the semantic memory (for example, historical facts about the Roman Empire as they are taught in school).

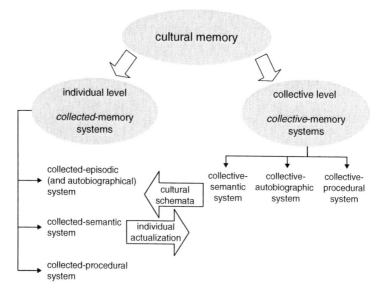

Figure IV.3 Systems and modes of cultural memory

- Collective-procedural phenomena, finally, can potentially be conscious knowledge in some individuals (for example, those who reflect critically on national stereotypes or everyday rituals of their society). But collective-procedural memory emerges and exists on the basis of its contents generally belonging to the non-conscious repertoire of individuals' knowledge and abilities. It rests in our culture-specific schemata and scripts.

In summary, one can say that groups and societies (with the help of symbolic forms, media, and institutions) refer to the past in different ways: They relate to past events in a constructive, evaluative and self-referential manner, in a way that is similar to individual *remembering* (collective-autobiographical system). They administer the past and its relics in a manner that seems in some ways to correspond to the individual *knowing that* (collective-semantic system). Finally, they are influenced by past events and traditional procedures, which remind one of the individual *knowing how* (collective-procedural system). The contents of these three social systems of memory are, in turn, represented in various ways within different cognitive systems of the individual's memory.

IV.4 Related concepts: Collective identity and cultural experience

In the course of the discussions about cultural memory, concepts of 'cultural experience' and 'collective identity' have also received a great deal of attention. The memory theories of Halbwachs, Nora and Assmann place collective identity front and centre. Jan Assmann understands 'concretion of identity' to be a central characteristic of the Cultural Memory. Therefore, he studies the 'connective structure' of societies which is constituted through shared remembering (J. Assmann 1992, 16 and 39). Yet ideas of collective identity have also received strong criticism, and rightfully so. One of the most polemical responses has been that by Lutz Niethammer (2000), directed towards the 'uncanny boom' of concepts of collective identity. Cooper and Brubaker (2000) suggest looking 'beyond identity' and discarding the term as an analytical category of social sciences altogether. And Jürgen Straub (2002, 69) expressly underlines: 'Every casual transposition of the concept of personal identity onto collectives must ... be rejected, every discourse about concrete "collective identities" must immediately be subjected to a "critique of ideology."' Straub distinguishes thus between a 'normative' and a 'reconstructive' type of reference to collective identity:

> Whereas the first, with respect to the (putative) members of the collective, (merely) pretends or presents, directs or suggests, or even imposes, common features, a historical continuity and practical coherence 'binding' once and for all, the second type describes the subjects' praxis as well as the self-understanding and world-understanding in order to arrive at a description of the collective identity in terms of a reconstructive and interpretative science of society and culture. (Straub 2002, 69)

Jan Assmann (1992, 132) clearly deals with the reconstructive (or descriptive) type when he defines the concept of collective identity as follows: 'With the terms *collective* or *we-identity* we describe the image that a group constructs of itself, and with which members of the group identify themselves.' Collective identity develops in a dynamic with concepts of alterity. Identity 'is a *plurale tantum* and presupposes other identities. Without multeity [there is] no unity, without otherness no uniqueness' (ibid., 135f.). The 'we-consciousness' of sociocultural formations is in no small part fed by shared remembering. Following Halbwachs, who observed the emphasis that collective memory places on similarities and continuities, Jan Assmann notes that 'concretion of identity' means that 'external differences are emphasized, and the internal ones in contrast played down' (ibid., 40).

Kwame A. Appiah (2005, 69) defines the structure of social identity in the following way: 'Where a classification of people as Ls is associated with a *social conception* of Ls, some people *identify* as Ls, and people are sometimes *treated* as Ls, we have a paradigm of a social identity that matters for ethical and political life.'

However, we should be careful not to overlook 'the recognition that identities are robustly plural' (Sen 2006, 19). Plurality here means not only that in every society a variety of sociocultural formations, memories and identities coexist, but also that each individual is a member of a variety of (mnemonic) collectives (Amartya Sen describes himself as 'an Asian, an Indian citizen, a Bengali with Bangladeshi ancestry, an American or British resident, ... a strong believer in secularism and democracy, a man, a feminist, a heterosexual, a defender of gay and lesbian rights'; ibid.). Through such multiple memberships, the individual becomes an intersection of (or, to use Halbwachs's term, a 'viewpoint on') various collective identities. On the level of the individual, collective identity thus denotes nothing other than the 'collective aspects of subjectivity that emerge from the individual's belonging to certain groups, which may define themselves through gender, culture, ethnicity or nation' (Friese 2002, 2).

In respect of the causes and manifestations of collective identity, one can distinguish different theories of identity by explanation types. For Jan Assmann, for example, collective identity is not just a matter of living in a shared symbolic world of meaning ('basic structure'), but also of becoming aware of this ('reflexive structure'): 'A collective identity is ... societal belonging that has become reflexive. Cultural identity is thus the reflexive participation in or the commitment to a culture' (J. Assmann 1992, 134). Benedict Anderson (1983) also emphasizes, through his concept of 'imagined communities', the conscious aspects of collective identity. Every member has a mental image of his or her community: 'In the minds of each lives the image of their communion' (Anderson 1983, 6). Jürgen Straub, in contrast, argues that we 'need not assume that such agreement is merely and in every case "reflexive" in the sense of "conscious" or even "rationally accessible." It should rather be conceived as often tacit knowledge, latent and everyday, that consistently structures and guides the thoughts, feelings, desires, and actions of the collective's members' (Straub 2002, 72). This interpretation coincides with Anthony Easthope's (1999, 4) definition of national identity as an 'unconscious structure' and of nation 'as a particular discursive formation' (ibid., 6). Such diverse accentuations in the research landscape result from the way different memory systems are involved in the making of collective identities. Collective identity is a phenomenon of both the explicit and the implicit systems of cultural memory: It can be consciously coded, but also at times unconsciously expressed, for example through discursive formations, mentalities, and patterns of thought and action. As a result, the existing, primarily descriptive theories of collective identity are not mutually exclusive but rather complementary. (For a cognitive psychology perspective on collective identity, see Mack and Hirst 2008.)

Current research has also shown the terms 'memory' and 'experience' to be close neighbours. Nikolaus Buschmann and Horst Carl (2001, 9) observe that 'the concept of experience in current methodological discussions within the humanities is more and more taking on the status of a key cultural studies concept'. Both concepts, experience and memory, draw on each other and are often used synonymously. It is often difficult to ascertain where the history of experience stops and the history of memory begins. What is needed is a theoretical specification of the notoriously complex concept of experience, which includes aspects such as perception, memory, interpretation and tradition.

Recent work in the history of experience emphasizes its collective and temporal dimensions. Fundamental concepts for the study of cultural experience have been developed in the framework of Berger and Luckmann's (1966) sociology of knowledge as well as in Reinhart Koselleck's (2004) work on historical semantics. Koselleck distinguishes between a society's 'space of experience' and its 'horizon of expectation'. 'Experience is present past, whose events have been incorporated and can be remembered' (ibid., 259); expectation, on the other hand, is 'the future made present' (ibid.). Without experience, there is no expectation; and without expectations we cannot make experiences. It is the tension between these two categories of thinking which produces what Koselleck calls 'historical time'.

Experience is now understood as a product of complex social processes of construction. One result of this constructionist understanding of experience is that the focus of research is no longer directed towards demarcating a border between individual and society or between 'authentic experience' and later 'intentional reinterpretation'. Instead, questions are asked about the interpretative contexts which pre-form experience but which can also be modified by them; about the temporal structure of experience, that is, about processes of consolidation or the recombination of cultural semantics; about specifics of (mass-)mediations which allow for 'second-hand' experiences; and, finally, about the practical relevance of experience in guiding future action (see Buschmann and Carl 2001).

Research on cultural experience is closely tied up with memory studies where the possibilities and limits of 'bearing witness' in an age of war, genocide, and terror are addressed. Trauma and the 'crises of witnessing' (Laub and Felman, see chapter III.1.2), which the violent history of the twentieth century has brought to the fore, raise the question of how extreme experience can (or cannot) be narrated and framed. In this context, Ernst van Alphen has forcefully argued that experience is not direct and unmediated, but 'depends of factors that are fundamentally discursive':

> Experience and memory are enabled, shaped and structured according to the parameters of available discourses ... Experiences are not only collectively shared because they are grounded on cultural discourses; this shared background also makes experience and memory 'sharable.' The discourse that made them possible is also the discourse in which we can convey them to other humans. Our experiences and memories are therefore not isolating us from others; they enable interrelatedness – culture. (van Alphen 1999, 36f.)

In the model proposed here, cultural memory provides the mental, material and social structures within which experience is embedded, constructed, interpreted and passed on. Memory is a kind of switchboard which organizes experience both prospectively and retrospectively: *Prospectively*, cultural memory is the source of schemata which already pre-form experience, that is, which decide what will even enter the individual's consciousness and how this information will be further processed. Memory as an apparatus of selection and schematization is thus the very condition for gaining experiences. But it is only *retrospectively*, through cultural remembering, that we create experience as an interpretation of events that guides future action (see also Middleton and Brown 2005).

V
Media and Memory

V.1   Media and the construction of memory

Cultural memory is unthinkable without media. It would be inconceivable without the role that media play on both levels – the individual and the collective. On the individual level, the sociocultural shaping of organic memories rests to a significant extent on mediation: memory talk between a mother and her child, oral communication within a family, the significance of photographs for media-based (re-)constructions of our childhoods, the influence of mass media and its schemata on way we code life experience. Even more so, memory on the collective level – that is, the construction and circulation of knowledge and versions of a common past in sociocultural contexts – is only possible with the aid of media: through orality and literacy as age-old media for the storing of foundational myths for later generations; through print, radio, television and the Internet for the diffusion of versions of a common past in wide circles of society; and, finally, through symbolically charged media such as monuments which serve as occasions for collective, often ritualized remembering.

Thus not only do media have a constitutive relevance for both levels of memory; they also represent an interface connecting the two areas. Since Halbwachs and Warburg, a basic assumption of cultural memory studies has been that memory is neither an entity abstracted from the individual nor a result of biological mechanisms such as heredity (see chapter II). It is for precisely the reason that we must understand media and mediation as a kind of switchboard at work between the individual and the collective dimension of remembering. Personal memories can only gain social relevance through media representation and distribution. This is particularly obvious in the case of eyewitnesses: Only through interviews or the publication of letters do their experiences become an element of cultural memory ('externalization'). Conversely, the individual only gains access to socially shared knowledge and images of the past through communication and media reception ('internalization').

In light of this inherent mediality of memory, it is no surprise that cultural memory research is often simultaneously media research. However, just like memory, media do not simply reflect reality, but instead offer constructions of the past. Media are not simply neutral carriers of information about the past. What they appear to encode – versions of past events and persons, cultural values and norms, concepts of collective identity – they are in fact first creating. In addition, specific modes of remembering are closely linked to available media technologies. For example, the detailed histories of nineteenth-century historiographers had no counterpart outside the medium of the book. The elaborate national histories of authors such as Jules Michelet or Leopold von Ranke are not to be found in the oral tradition, nor in historical paintings or rituals. History in this form simply did not exist in other media or indeed at all in a reality outside the media. Solely the medium of the book exhibited the capacity to present an enormous multitude of memory-relevant information in a temporal-causal order – and thus to construct national history in the detailed form that the scholarly historiographical method developed in the nineteenth century required.

This power of media to create realities has been emphasized in media theory from its very beginnings. Sybille Krämer (1998, 14f.) offers a remarkably clear summary of the cultural significance of media:

> Media do not simply convey messages, but instead develop a force which shapes the modalities of our thinking, perceiving, remembering, and communicating. ... 'Mediality' expresses the idea that our relationship to the world (and with this all of our activities and experiences) is shaped by (and the world is made accessible through) the possibilities for distinction which media open up, and the limitations which they thereby impose.

Whatever we know about the world, we know through media and in dependence on media. The images of the past which circulate in memory culture are thus not extrinsic to media. They are media constructs. This does not make them counterfeit or unreal; mediality represents instead the very condition for the emergence of cultural memory.

The implications of such a constructionist insight into the ineluctable mediality of our reality have been formulated within different media theories. The communications theorist James W. Carey emphasizes that 'Technology, the hardest of material artifacts, is thoroughly cultural from the outset: an expression and creation of the very outlooks and aspirations we pretend it merely demonstrates' (Carey 1992, 9). The sociologist Niklas Luhmann writes in his *The Reality of Mass Media* (2000b, 6): 'The theory of operational constructionism does not lead to a "loss of world", it does not deny that reality exists. However, it assumes that the world is not an object but rather a horizon, in the phenomenological sense. It is, in other words, inaccessible.' And the philosopher Martin Seel (1998, 255) explains: 'It does not ... follow from the internal connection of mediality and reality that reality is for all intents and purposes a media construction. It simply follows that it is media constructions through which reality is given or accessible. Reality is not given *as* media construction, but instead is given solely *by virtue of* media construction.'

In his now classic study *Understanding Media* (1964), Marshall McLuhan introduced the famous phrase 'the medium is the message' into the discourse of media theory, emphasizing that 'the personal and social consequences of any medium ... result from the new scale that is introduced into our affairs by extension of ourselves' (ibid., 8). Each medium transforms social reality; this is, for McLuhan, its message. Media of memory, too, which can be understood as 'extensions' of our organic memories, bring about consequences in that they shape cultural remembrance in accordance to their specific means and measures. In this sense, 'the medium is the memory.'

When we consider the medial construction of reality, we are dealing with two aspects, which Sybille Krämer, referring to the media theories put forward by Luhmann and McLuhan, condenses in the notion of the 'medium as trace and apparatus':

> The medium is to the message what the unintended trace is to the intentionally used sign. ... The meaning-making role of media must thus be thought of as the trace of something absent; this sheds light on why the role of media usually remains hidden. The medium is not simply the message; rather the trace of the medium is retained in the message. (Krämer 1998, 81)

> Media technology as apparatus ... educes artificial worlds, it opens up experiences, and makes possible processes which without the

apparatuses would not be simply attenuated, but which would not exist at all. Not improved performance but rather world-creation is the productive meaning of media technologies. (ibid., 85)

Working from Krämer's notion of the medium as trace and apparatus, we can distinguish two distinct aspects of the role media play in processes of cultural remembrance: (1) Media are not neutral carriers or containers of memory. In all media-supported acts of remembering a 'trace' of the specific memory medium that was used will be retained. On both the individual and the collective levels, we are therefore dealing not only with a fundamental media-dependence of remembering, but also with the fact that 'the medium is the memory' in that it shapes our acts of remembering in ways of which we are often not even aware. (2) As 'apparatuses', media of memory such as monuments, books, paintings or the Internet go far beyond the task of expanding the individual human memory through the externalization of information: They create media worlds of cultural memory according to their specific capacities and limitations – worlds that a memory community would not know without them.

V.2 The history of memory as the history of media

Because of the complex intertwinings of media and cultural memory – media first create memory culture; the trace of the medium is retained in the memory – histories of memory are often written as histories of its changing media. In this chapter, we will introduce three exponents of memory studies who have illuminated the historical depth of the relationship between medium and memory: the historian Jacques Le Goff; the interdisciplinary working group 'Archaeology of Literary Communication', led by Aleida and Jan Assmann; and Elena Esposito, who studies memory from the perspective of social systems theory.

In *History and Memory* (1992; orig.: *Storia e memoria* 1977ff.), Jacques Le Goff distinguishes five phases in the history of memory. He takes his cue from the writings of André Leroi-Gourham, who claimed that: 'The history of collective memory can be divided into five periods: oral transmission, written transmission with tables or indices, simple file cards, mechanical writing, and electronic sequencing' (Leroi-Gourhan, quoted in Le Goff, 54). Building on this, Le Goff then analyses:

1. the 'ethnic memory' in societies without writing, the so-called primitive societies;

2. the 'rise of memory, from orality to writing, from prehistory to antiquity;'
3. medieval memory 'in equilibrium' between orality and writing;
4. the 'progress of written and figured memory from the Renaissance to the present;'
5. the 'contemporary revolutions in memory'. (Le Goff 1992, 51–99)

The contents of memory in cultures without writing, which are dependent upon orality as a medium, are, according to Le Goff, first ideologically charged myths of origin which are evoked in rituals and endow collective identity, second genealogies of ruling families, and third technical and practical knowledge. Memory specialists (priests, shamans, court historians) are trained for the work of remembering. What they produce at occasions for remembrance as the contents of a community's memory, however, is not an exact, verbatim replica of earlier acts of remembering. Often, they recall only the deep structures of the memory tales, their narrative patterns. According to Le Goff (who refers to the studies of Jack Goody), oral societies thus exhibit a greater freedom in remembering than do literate societies. Their memory is more creative and dynamic than it is reproductive.

With the development of writing – and thus the medium of literacy – in the ancient world, two different forms of memory emerged, both of which were closely tied to the exigencies of urban societies: first commemoration based on inscriptions (for example, on monuments or gravestones), and second the document, which brought with it the ability to store information. In the Christian Middle Ages, oral and literate memory were in an equilibrium, and were indeed closely interwoven. The transmission of knowledge was still tightly linked with oral practices and techniques, and handwritten texts tended to be memorized.

It was the printing press that revolutionized memory in Europe – a process which started in the Renaissance. The distribution of printed books resulted in the slow but steady decline of the mnemotechnics inherited from ancient rhetorics. The 'discovery of history' around 1800 led to the creation of archives, museums and libraries. The plethora of media retained in these storehouses of memory required that institutions be created which trained specialists to preserve and study their inventory.

At the end of the nineteenth century, photography emerged as a further central medium of memory, one that suggested authenticity and – as it provided a portrait gallery in the family album – also 'democratized' memory. With the invention of the computer and the advent of 'electronic memory', the current 'revolution of memory' is finally reached. The electronic media have also had, as is pointed out by Le Goff, an important 'metaphorical' impact on memory culture, as organic and social remembering is now thought of in terms of computer analogies. (For a comprehensive history of memory written along the lines of media evolution and the different metaphors of memory that new media engendered, see Draaisma 2000.)

A more rigorous media theory perspective on the history of memory was provided by the German interdisciplinary working group 'Archaeology of Literary Communication', founded in the mid-1970s. The shared goal of its members (which included Aleida and Jan Assmann, Konrad Ehlich, Burkhard Gladigow, Christof Hardmeier, Dietrich Harth, Tonio Hölscher and Uvo Hölscher) was the historicization of media theories such as had been developed by the Toronto School (Harold Innis and Marshall McLuhan) and (in the German-speaking world) by F.A. Kittler, as well as of the poststructuralist 'philosophies of writing' of Michel Foucault, Jacques Lacan and Jacques Derrida. The working group defined 'literature' as written transmission, and thus exhibited a very broad understanding of the term. In a critical dialogue with the research done in the fields of philology and cultural anthropology on the relationship of orality and literacy (Milman Parry, Eric A. Havelock, Walter Ong, Jack Goody and Jan Vansina), the group considered what various media could contribute in the framework of a 'temporal extension': in cases in which the sender and the receiver of a message are many years, perhaps centuries apart. This is what Konrad Ehlich, in the first publication of the working group, *Schrift und Gedächtnis* (1983; 'Writing and Memory'), called 'expanded communication':

> The expansion of communication necessitates facilities for intermediate storage. The system of communication must develop a form of external storage, into which messages can be transferred, as well as forms of transfer (coding), storage and retrieval. This calls for institutional frameworks, specialists and normally also systems of notation external to the body, such as knotted strings, *tchuringas*, counting stones and finally writing. (Ehlich 1983, 203)

A central thesis of the Assmanns' theory is that orality and literacy are associated with two fundamentally different organizational forms of such expanded communication, which they called the Cultural Memory (see chapter II.4). In other words, the form of the Cultural Memory is due in significant measure to the available media in a society. In oral societies, the functional memory and the stored memory necessarily concur, in the absence of external, material carriers of memory. Media and remembering subjects are not divorced from each other. Oral memory is characterized by what J.A. Barnes has called a 'structural amnesia': everything not immediately needed must be forgotten. In literate societies, on the other hand, a stored memory may develop, since through the outsourcing of information to media more and different things can be retained than are actualized at any given moment.

Elena Esposito's outline of the history of memory in *Soziales Vergessen* (2002, 'Social Forgetting') distinguishes itself from the examples above as it was not developed on the basis of hermeneutic-semiotic theories of culture, but is instead based on the premises of Niklas Luhmann's systems theory. According to Esposito, the memory of a society comes by its specific form as a result of dynamic interactions between: (1) the forms of differentiation of society (according to Luhmann these can be segmentary, stratified, or functional); and (2) the available technologies of communication. Esposito distinguishes between four phases of the history of memory:

1. *Prophetic memory*: ancient civilizations; main metaphor: memory as 'wax';
2. *Rhetorical memory*: ancient and medieval societies; main metaphor: memory as 'storage';
3. The *memory of culture*: modern era; main metaphor: memory as 'archive' or 'mirror';
4. *Procedural memory*: post-modern period; main metaphor: memory as 'network' (see Esposito 2002, 41–3).

Esposito argues that 'the memory of a society depends on the available technologies of communication ... of the individual society: these influence its forms, range, and interpretation' (ibid., 10). Changes in media technologies therefore play a decisive role in the transitions from one form of social memory to another. New technologies of communication which engendered major memorial transformations are, according to Esposito, '(alphabetical and non-alphabetical) writing, the printing press ... and finally the computer' (ibid., 38).

Despite all its internal heterogeneity, cultural memory studies can be grasped as a field that 'focuses on the central question of the media of storage, communication, dissemination, and interpretation. The history of memory is, in this perspective, the history of its media' (J. Assmann in his afterword to Esposito 2002, 414). Different historiographies of media and cultural memory may present different kinds of periodization. However, the most significant ruptures in the history of mediated remembering appear to be the transitions from orality to writing, from writing to the printing press, and from the printing press to the digital age. Changes in media technology, society, politics and cultural memory are all very closely related. Yet this relationship must not be thought of as monocausal; it is not a one-way street. Media revolutions can change forms of collective remembering (as the invention of writing may have led to the development of a cultural stored memory), but specific challenges to memory culture can also lead to the emergence, acceptance and dissemination of new media technologies. For example, the new technology of the printing press developed fully over the course of the eighteenth century, as the middle classes emerged, with their desire to participate in public memory-making.

V.3 Medium of memory: A compact concept

The theories and histories of memory introduced thus far have profitably applied the concept of 'media', yet a closer look at the relationship of medium and memory exposes an unanswered, fundamental question: What exactly is a 'medium of memory'? What might first appear to be intuitively evident becomes distinctly more complicated when considering concrete processes of cultural remembrance: Media phenomena appear on various levels within cultural memory, and their manifestations and functions are quite diverse. Furthermore, complex social processes seem to be involved in the coding of a medium as a 'medium of memory'.

Understanding the logic of media of memory therefore requires looking at mediality from many different angles. This is not an easy task, as media studies itself proves to be an extremely heterogeneous research landscape with a multitude of often apparently incompatible theories, methods and concepts (see Hartley et al. 2002; Wardrip-Fruin and Montfort 2003). Cultural memory studies has a twofold interest in media: First, it seeks to understand the significance of fundamental forms of mediality for memory. This kind of research is based on an understanding of 'the medium' as an entity that, quite literally, 'mediates' between two or more phenomena – in our case, for example, between the individual and collective level of memory. At the same time, what is at stake is the question about the mnemonic impact of 'the media' as systems of social and increasingly global (mass) communication. Studying media from a cultural memory studies perspective therefore implies a conceptual balancing act between quite distant areas of current media research.

In an effort to tackle the problem of defining the term 'medium', in his writings on media culture the German theorist Siegfried J. Schmidt has proposed suggestions for what he calls an 'integrative concept'. He notes that 'medium' is indeed a multifarious term, which is used, both in everyday and in scholarly discourses, in very different ways. In order to disentangle the major denotations of the term, he distinguishes among four components:

> I conceive of the 'medium' ... as a compact concept which integrates four dimensions and areas of effect: 1. communication instruments (such as language and pictures); 2. technological devices (such as Internet technology on the side of receivers and producers); 3. the social dimensions of such devices (such as publishing houses or television stations); and 4. media offers which result from the coalescence of these components and can only be interpreted in relation to this context of production. (Schmidt 2008, 198f.)

Such a multi-level or multi-component model is even more important for an understanding of 'media of memory'. Studying media from a mnemohistorical perspective usually means considering rather different factors – such as instruments of communication (for example, writing), media technologies (for example, printing), the institutionalization within social systems (for example, canonization), and specific media offers (for example, a new edition of Homer's *Odyssey*). It is only in the interplay of such a range of distinct media and social phenomena that a 'medium of memory' is constituted.

What follows is an attempt to understand the 'medium of memory' as a compact concept. This involves both an adoption of Schmidt's model as well as its modification to speak to the concerns of cultural memory studies. Which factors are actually involved in the creation of a medium of memory? And on what levels are these factors located? Media of memory have a material as well as a social dimension (for mental factors see ch V.4.2). In a first step, therefore, I will define 'communication instruments', 'media technologies' and 'objectivations' as the principal material components of memory media. In a second step I will consider the social dimension, namely the different uses that memory media are put to by social communities.

V.3.1 Material dimension

1 Communication instruments: Externalization, inter- and transmediality of memory

Means of communication such as oral speech, writing, images or sound are instruments which make externalizations from individual minds to media possible in the first place, and thus create the very condition for the creation of cultural memory. Because communication instruments can be used in many different media technologies, this opens up possibilities for comparative research – for example, the study of how certain transmedial 'memory images' circulate among painting, photography, film, television, and the Internet; or of the intermediality of memory, for example, the interplay of text and image (this has been studied extensively in relation to W.G. Sebald's novels).

2 Media technologies: Storage and dissemination of memory

Media technologies allow for the dissemination, from a spatial point of view, and the storage, from a temporal point of view, of the contents of cultural memory. Instruments of communication such as writing, whether carved in stone, printed on paper, or published on the Internet, reach smaller or larger memory communities and prove to be storable for different lengths of time. Media technologies, however, are far from being neutral containers for memory semioses. Their specific materiality, their potentials and limits contribute to the character of the message (see chapter V.1).

Today, memory research is interested in the impact on cultural remembrance of significant changes in media technology. The Vietnam Veterans Memorial in Washington, DC ('The Wall'), for example, a stone monument commemorating the Americans who were killed in the Vietnam War, found a place on the Internet in the form of 'My Virtual Wall'. This change of medium and the novel possibilities offered by the technology of the World Wide Web also changed the practice of memory. For example, since every user of the Virtual Wall has the opportunity to customize his or her own homepage, this results in a strongly personalized mode of remembering (see the case study by Angela Sumner in Erll/Nünning 2004).

3 Media offers: Material objectivations and aesthetic forms of mediated memory

Homer's *Iliad*, medieval manuscripts, the British Museum, soldiers' letters from the trenches of the First World War, Picasso's *Guernica* (1937), and pictures in a family album are cultural objectivations which can turn into media of memory. They can, for example, serve as canonized media of national memory; as components of the stored memory they may await actualization in an archive; in the framework of the communicative memories they can transmit the specific everyday experience of a recent past and prompt communication between generations. But no matter what their specific role may be, media products must always be understood as no more than an 'offer' to a mnemonic community. This offer can be accepted, but the media product can also be ignored or used in other than memorial ways.

It is in particular art and literary studies which scrutinize specific objectivations of cultural memory. At the same time, these are the disciplines which emphasize what Fredric Jameson (1981) has called the 'content of form'. In fact, as Stuart Hall maintains, 'a "raw" historical event cannot, in that form, be transmitted' (1980, 129). Incorporating genres, metaphors and narrative structures would therefore seem to be indispensable especially for a conception of media of memory. To give just one example: There are certain forms which are preferred in coding contents of the Cultural Memory. In western cultures, the forms of 'tragedy' and 'epic' have mediated foundational memory for many centuries. In the case of John Milton's *Paradise Lost* (1667/74), the message is therefore not solely the media components 'writing' and 'printed book', the canonization process in English society, and the concrete work itself, but first and foremost its form, its epic structure. Forms are generally transmedial phenomena; as such they can migrate across media. However, forms are always tied to concrete media offers; they can only be materialized in cultural objectivations.

V.3.2   Social dimension

Not only does media communication have a material aspect; it is also inherently a social process. Stuart Hall emphasizes that while the '"message form" is the necessary "form of appearance" of the event in its passage from source to receiver', it must also 'be integrated into the social relations of the communication process as a whole, of which it forms only a part' (Hall 1980, 129). Social processes are important in any discussion of media, and even more so in the field of cultural remembrance. The three aforementioned material components (communication instruments, media technologies, media offers) are important analytical categories for the study of media and memory. From their specific constellations we can draw conclusions about possible 'memory effects' and mnemonic functions of media. The three material components engender a 'functional *potential*'; what we say about this potential remains purely hypothetical. The actual transition from a 'medial phenomenon' to a 'medium of memory', however, always comes to pass within the social dimension. This transition often rests on forms of institutionalization and always on the use, the function-alization of a medium *as* a medium of memory, by individuals, social groups, and societies.

4 The social use of media

Ever since Maurice Halbwachs, the social dimension of memory has been a central concern of memory studies. Memory is (re-)constructed in social contexts and it is the 'social frameworks of memory' (in the literal sense) which decide – consciously or unconsciously – which media to avail themselves of in this constructive process. The social institutional-ization of memory media finds its strongest manifestation in the frame-work of national, ideological, ethnic or religious memory. The media which are meant to convey official versions of the past require action in the social dimension in order to ensure their transmission: canoni-zation, the establishment of archives, the creation of school curricula, and so on. This is why, according to Jan Assmann, 'organization' – the institutionalization of memory and the specialization of its carriers – is a constitutive characteristic of the Cultural Memory.

Whether in the framework of highly institutionalized forms of national and religious remembrance or the less stable and more fluc-tuating everyday reference to the past, say, within a family – the term 'medium of memory' is only appropriate in the case of a corresponding mnemonic functionalization. The sociohistorical context not only con-tributes in great measure to the effects of media on cultural memory. It also even decides on their definition as such in the first place: Because media must be *used* as media of memory, the memory-making role must be *attributed* to them by specific people, at a specific time and place.

Two fundamental aspects of the mnemonic functionalization must be distinguished, which largely correspond to Stuart Hall's (1980) notion of 'encoding' and 'decoding':

- *Production-side functionalization:* A typical example is the Assmanns' 'cultural text' (see chapter VI.3.1), in which messages for posterity are encoded. Egyptian pyramids, national historiography of the nine-teenth century, the 'Memorial to the Murdered Jews of Europe' in Berlin – in all of these examples, we are dealing with production-side (and prospective) functionalizations of media of memory: Architects and historians who create as well as ruling classes and democratic societies which commission media of memory *intend* for these media to elicit processes of remembering in the future.

- *Reception-side functionalization:* A medium of memory exists when people think it does. As soon as it is perceived and used as such, a medium turns into a medium of memory – even if it was never intended to be one. Samuel Pepys's journal, written in England in the seventeenth century, in code and (in light of its juicy details) likely not intended for a broad public, or the relics of everyday life in the GDR that are presented in the German 'Ostalgia' ('Ost' [East] and 'nostalgia')-shows on television are retrospectively assigned the status of 'medium of memory'. Particularly in this area of the reception-side (and retrospective) functionalization, a broad understanding of the mediality of cultural memory must be applied: Here, everything is a medium of memory which is understood as 'transmitting something' from or about the past. In this way, everyday objects and even elements of the natural world can become media of memory. This recipient-side functionalization is not necessarily intentional; often it is only noticed in retrospect that certain phenomena evidently served in a certain epoch as media of memory. However, the question of what attributes of the phenomenon could suggest such a functionalization leads back to the first, the material, dimension of memory media, that is, to the analysis of the functional potential of their specific materiality.

The 'compact concept' shows that a medium of memory is not a given, but instead comes into being through a complex interplay of various material and social factors. Furthermore, this interplay takes place in specific contexts of remembrance; it is therefore historically and culturally variable. Media of memory always materialize against the backdrop of existing configurations of memory. Spaces of experience and horizons of expectation, structures of knowledge, memory practices, challenges and contested memories shape the production, transmission and reception of memory media. Whenever media are studied as parts of memory culture, they must be removed from a generalizing, ahistorical view, and seen in relationship to very specific cultural processes.

To sum up, media of memory construct versions of a past reality. The materiality of the medium is every bit as much involved in these constructions as is the social dimension: The producers and recipients of a medium of memory actively perform the work of construction – both in the decision as to which phenomena will be ascribed the qualities of memory media, as well as in the encoding and decoding of that which is (to be) remembered. Media and their users create and shape memory, and they always do so in very specific cultural and historical contexts. Whether and which versions of past events, persons, values or concepts of identity are constructed through a medium of memory depends to no small extent on the conditions prevailing within that memory culture.

V.4   Functions of media of memory

V.4.1   On the collective level: Storage, circulation, cue

As we have seen, media of memory come to life in the social world. Once they have emerged, which functions can they perform in mnemonic communities? In what follows, I will differentiate between three functional aspects of memory media on the collective level: storage, circulation and cue. This is a purely heuristic distinction. In fact, only in rare cases will one single functional aspect characterize a particular medium exclusively. On the contrary, the memory media which are most effective are usually those which simultaneously exhibit features of each of the three functions.

The storage function refers to media's task of storing contents of memory and making them available *across time*. This is the classic function of memory media, and also that which has been the subject of the most research to date (see chapter V.2). As we have seen, the capacity and temporal range of storage techniques is highly variable. But this is not their only contingency. Since storage media 'travel' through time, the danger of the collapse of collective codes is particularly significant. In respect of memory culture, systems of writing that can no longer be deciphered, or monuments whose symbolism can no longer be decoded, are dead material.

From the storage function we can distinguish, second, the circulation function of media of memory. Media enable cultural communication not only across time, but also *across space*. Circulation media can synchronize large memory communities in which face-to-face communication is no longer possible, and disseminate versions of a common past. This function has been performed by the printing press since the early modern period, by newspapers in the eighteenth and nineteenth centuries, and by television and the Internet in our times. Circulation media of memory are often part of popular culture (such as movies and historical novels). And in the era of globalization, they are increasingly mass media and new media, disseminating their messages across the globe in 'real time'.

To this point in the analysis, the distinction of two basic functions that media can fulfil – storage and circulation – follows the differentiation between 'time-biased' and 'space-biased' media made by Harold A. Innis in *The Bias of Communication* (1951). However, when dealing with cultural memory, the dimensions of time and space are not the only criteria to distinguish the storage from the circulation function. In addition, especially canonized storage media, such as monuments or epics, tend to refer not only to the versions of the past which they encode but also to themselves. Effective storage media, such as the Bible, Shakespeare's Histories, or the Arc de Triomphe, are usually simultaneously medium *and* content of cultural memory – media which 'remember something' and are themselves remembered.

This twofold nature of time-biased storage media is less often observed in the case of space-biased circulation media. On the contrary, these tend to communicate versions of the past, while maintaining the illusion of transparency. The images of the past that are conveyed by pamphlets, newspaper articles, television documentaries, popular movies and websites are usually more effective the less attention is drawn to their 'mediatedness'. Circulation media are moreover closely tied to the moment in which they appear, to specific ideas, problems and challenges of a mnemonic community; and they thus often fulfil additional didactic and ideological functions. Since their effectiveness is exhausted with the synchronous dissemination of information about the past and they are quickly replaced with more current media offers, circulation media seldom develop any further dimension as contents of cultural memory – or if they do so, then that may be a sign that they have shifted to the area of memory culture's storage media. (This seems the case with certain popular representations of the Holocaust, such as the 1978 television miniseries of the same name.)

Any discussion of storage and circulation media implies an understanding of communication in the tradition of Shannon and Weaver (1949). In their information theory, they introduced the concepts of 'sender, message, transmission, noise, channel, receiver and reception' as well as those of 'encoding and decoding'. The phenomena which communities avail themselves of as media of memory, however, do not always necessarily lead back to a 'sender' or feature a 'message' which has been 'encoded'. This hints at a third functional aspect of media of memory, one which only comes into view when the insights of psychological research are considered. Individual memory processes are set in motion by cues. These cues can be intrapsychic in nature (for example, associations, other memories), but they can also belong to the material and social context of remembering (for example, pictures, texts, other people and parts of conversation). On the social level, too, media can cue collective remembering.

This last function of media – to trigger collective remembrance – is performed above all by particular locations or landscapes (the White Cliffs of Dover, the Rhine, the Eiffel Tower, the Twin Towers) which the mnemonic community associates with specific narratives about the past. Many of Pierre Nora's sites of memory seem to be first and foremost *cues* for acts of cultural remembrance. As 'media cues' feature neither a sender nor a semiotic code, they cannot be actualized outside the context of the memory culture. Thus, social agreement – or: convention – is of central importance for the effectiveness of media which fulfil a pure cuing function. It is often the narratives *surrounding* such media (such as oral stories, historiography or novels) which determine their meaning.

Nonetheless, what is recalled in individual minds as a response to these media cues – and this also applies to storage and circulation media – is by no means homogeneous. The thoughts and memories inspired by the Tomb of the Unknown Soldier in Westminster Abbey will vary based on an individual's experience of war, his or her knowledge, and ideological persuasion. In memory culture there may be a shared core of media cues, which are used again and again to trigger memories, but the resulting mental images of the past are by no means uniform (see Table V.1).

V.4.2 On the individual level: The media frameworks of remembering

On the collective level, media store, circulate and cue collective remembrance. Now we will take a look at the individual level: What role do media play for what has been termed the *collected memory*, for the socially shaped individual remembering? The media worlds we live in exert a significant influence on our perceptions and memories. In fact, the cultural dimension of individual memory derives not purely from social contexts (as maintained by Halbwachs), but to a large degree from media environments. Collected memory must be understood as fundamentally a 'mediated memory.' This notion was introduced by Lev S. Vygotskij (see 1978, 38) in the field of developmental psychology in order to stress the degree to which our memories, from early childhood onwards, are mediated by social contexts, external aids and internal cues. Drawing on Vygotskij's work, James V. Wertsch emphasizes that 'remembering is a form of mediated action ... inherently situated in a

Table V.1 Three functions of media of memory

	Storage medium	Circulation medium	Media cue
Function	stores contents of cultural memory	disseminates/ circulates contents of cultural memory	triggers cultural recall
Type of mediality	sender/receiver, semiotic code, medium of communication	sender/receiver, semiotic code, medium of communication	sender and semiotic code are not necessary (not necessarily a 'medium' in the definition of information theory)
	often both a remembering medium *and* a remembered content of the Cultural Memory	often popular mass media	dimension as medium of memory develops with the help of surrounding media
Directions of research, for example	research on the canon and the archive	research on memory in the mass media/ in popular culture	Pierre Nora's *lieux de memoire*

sociocultural context' (2002, 13). And indeed, our parents' and grand-parents' oral stories, old photographs, but also movies, television series, and novels shape not only our images of the past we did not experience, but even – often via media schemata – our most intimate autobiographical memories. In this sense, we can speak, modifying Halbwachs's term, of the *cadres médiaux de la mémoire*, the media frameworks of individual remembering.

Halbwachs himself offers some examples for the influence of the media frameworks of memory. In *La mémoire collective*, he relates the anecdote of a 'walk through London': A person visiting the metropolis for the first time is touring the city's landmarks. The way in which he or she perceives these new sights, his or her thoughts and feelings are for Halbwachs by no means of purely individual origin. On the contrary: Halbwachs wants to illustrate with this example that perception and memory are shaped by *cadres sociaux*, social frameworks of reference, and that these frameworks originate in the communication and interaction of social groups. The perception of London, in Halbwachs's anecdote, is to a significant degree influenced by other people with whom the tourist forms social groups: Conversations with the architect, the historian, the painter, or the businessman each draw the viewer's attention to different facets of the overwhelming abundance of impressions. These people do not even have to be physically present – the memory of what they had said, of reading their books, of studying their plans, or looking at their pictures is enough.

> Passing before Westminster, I thought about my historian friend's comments (or, what amounts to the same thing, what I have read in history books). Crossing a bridge, I noticed the effects of perspective that were pointed out by my painter friend (or struck me in a picture or engraving). (Halbwachs 1980, 23)

What these examples all have in common – architecture, oral speech, writing, images –, but what Halbwachs never explicitly acknowledges, is that they are all media through which the person taking the walk through London establishes a connection to social groups. Media make it possible to 'momentarily adopt' a collective 'viewpoint' (ibid., 24): 'In each of these moments I cannot say that I was alone, that I reflected alone, because I had put myself in thought into this or that group ...' (ibid., 23) Through media, the individual gains access both to group-specific knowledge, such as dates and facts, as well as to social 'currents of thought and experience' (ibid., 64). In short, media are the interface between individual minds and what Halbwachs introduces here as the 'collective frameworks of memory' (ibid.).

In the development of his theory of collective memory, Halbwachs thus conceived of the role of media from the very beginning. For Halbwachs the sociologist, however, media are merely the vehicle facilitating the unimpeded access to a more comprehensive social dimension of memory. Such an understanding of media as neutral transmitters of information must certainly be rethought from a constructionist media studies perspective as it has been developed by Havelock, McLuhan and others since the 1950s: The media frameworks of remembering generate media-specific individual memories.

Media frameworks of memory enable and shape the remembering and interpreting of different types of experience – both one's own and also second-hand accounts. Media representations already pre-form our perception and then re-shape our memories along certain paths. What Halbwachs (ibid., 38) writes about social currents of thought also applies to the functioning of *cadres médiaux*: A media framework is 'ordinarily as invisible as the atmosphere we breathe. In normal life its existence is recognized only when it is resisted.' This is precisely the basis for the memory-making power of media. Exhibits in museums, history books, historical films, everyday stories, and monuments form a mediated mnemonic horizon, the constructed nature of which becomes generally only obvious when we realize contradictions or when we consciously take on an observer's point of view. (For more about literature as a media framework of remembering, see chapter VI.3.3.)

V.5   Concepts of media memory studies

Since the turn of the millennium we have witnessed the rapid development of a host of new concepts in memory studies which address media, specifically mass media and the new media. The reasons for this are arguably to be found in the ever-increasing and accelerating, worldwide dissemination of images and narratives about the past through mass media such as television, and in the triumphal march of the computer and the Internet – both of which now shape the everyday experience of most people, at least in the western world. Andreas Huyssen describes the impact of today's global media circulation on cultural memory in the following way:

> Print and image media contribute liberally to the vertiginous swirl of memory discourses that circulate globally and locally. We read about Chinese and Korean comfort women and the rape of Nanjing; we hear about the 'stolen generation' in Australia and the killing and kidnapping of children during the dirty war in Argentina; we read about Truth and Reconciliation Commissions in South Africa and Guatemala; and we have become witnesses to an ever-growing number of public apologies by politicians for misdeeds of the past. Certainly, the voraciousness of the media and their appetite for recycling seems to be the sine qua non of local memory discourses crossing borders, entering into a network of cross-national comparisons, and creating what one might call a global culture of memory. (Huyssen 2003, 95)

New technologies and applications, such as digital photography, Picasa, YouTube and Facebook, are rapidly becoming increasingly relevant for the formation of memories. In many ways, they seem to have become the primary site of the workings of Halbwachs's *cadres sociaux*. At the same time, what Anna Reading (2009) terms 'globital memory' – globalized and digitized memory – challenges old conceptions of the 'archive', which in its new, computerized and Internet-based forms, seems more like a collaborative enterprise 'from below' than the apparatus of power that Foucault, Derrida and Agamben have theorized (see Garde-Hansen, Hoskins and Reading 2009).

In order to address these more recent developments in the representation of history, Andrew Hoskins has introduced the term 'new memory'. He holds that our relation to the past must be 'considered in terms of its *mediation* and *remediation* in the global present' (Hoskins 2001, 334; for the notion of remediation see chapter V.5.3). The 'new media ecologies' which, according to Hoskins (2009), have come to the fore with the 'connective turn' are characterized by the 'abundance, ubiquity, and accessibility of communication networks' (ibid., 2) and by the 'fluidity, reproducibility, and transferability of digital data' (ibid., 20). Although it remains to be seen whether the 'new media' of our present age (Gitelman 2006 correctly points out that all media were once new) have really brought about a qualitative change in cultural memory that radically distinguishes it from all former epochs, what is certainly true is that the age of mass and digital media has sensitized us to the fact that there is no such thing as a pure, pre-media memory, or: the other way round, that all memory, individual and social, is mediated memory. Thus, 'new memory' can be described as a highly media-reflexive stage in the history of memory culture.

V.5.1 Conceiving of mediated memory

How has such mediated memory been conceived of in memory studies? Of fundamental importance is Marita Sturken's notion of *Tangled Memories* (1997). Studying how the Vietnam War and the AIDS epidemic were turned into elements of cultural memory by means of television, movies and other popular media, Sturken brings out the complex entanglements of memory and media. She emphasizes the active and memory-productive role of media: 'Cultural memory is produced through objects, images, and representations. These are technologies of memory, not vessels of memory in which memory passively resides' (ibid., 9). Focussing more on the role of media for individual remembering, Susannah Radstone and Katharine Hodgkin maintain, in their edited volume on *Memory Cultures* (2006, 12f.), that one of media's mnemonic functions consists in 'propping the subject'. Studying memory props therefore uncovers 'the ways in which the specific representational modes of particular media may sustain memory rather than simply contribute to its atrophy or debasement'. A contribution to the volume by Stephan Feuchtwang, for example, shows how the false autobiography

by Binjamin Wilkomirski became a '"memory prop" … for those seek-
ing recognition of their own *actual* Holocaust sufferings.' José van Dijck
(2007, 21) goes even further in revealing the inherent mediatedness of
all memory. She insists on the co-construction or the 'mutual shaping
of memory and media' and defines the term 'mediated memories' as
follows: '*Mediated memories are the activities and objects we produce and
appropriate by means of media technologies, for creating and re-creating a
sense of the past, present, and future of ourselves in relation to others.*'

Addressing the experiential dimension of mediated memory, Alison
Landsberg (2004) introduced the notion of prosthetic memory. Landsberg
studies the age of mass culture, with a particular focus on the effects
that representations of slavery and the Holocaust in literature, cinema
and museum exhibits have on memory. She argues that what makes
mass media so powerful in memory culture is that they allow us to 'take
on' other people's and groups' experiences and memories 'like an artificial limb' (ibid., 20). With this reference to Marshall McLuhan's (1964)
notion of media as the 'extensions of man', Landsberg updates classic
media theory within the horizon of memory studies. Using the metaphor of 'prosthesis', of memory-as-a-limb, she emphasizes the bodily,
experiential, sensuous and affective dimension of media memories and
she indicates the interchangeability of commodified memories in the
age of mass media. Landsberg defines prosthetic memory as follows:

> *Prosthetic memory* emerges at the interface of a person and a historical
> narrative of the past, at an experiential site, such as a movie thea-
> tre or a museum. In this moment of contact, an experience occurs
> through which the person sutures himself or herself into a larger
> history … In the process the person does not simply apprehend a
> historical narrative but takes on a more personal, deeply felt memory
> of a past event through which he or she did not live. The resulting
> prosthetic memory has the ability to shape the person's subjectivity
> and politics. (ibid., 2)

One striking feature of Landsberg's work is its ethical, utopian moment.
Prosthetic memory is characterized by its 'ability … to produce empathy
and social responsibility as well as political alliances that transcend race,
class, and gender' (ibid., 21). This specific kind of mediated memory
means 'inhabit[ing] other people's memories *as* other people's memories … thereby respecting and recognizing difference' (ibid., 24). Rather
than proliferating culture-pessimistic views of the 'end of memory'
(Nora), contributions such as Landsberg's offer a deeper scrutiny and

highlight also the enabling aspects of new media ecologies in relation to cultural memory.

V.5.2 Visual media: Photography, film and memory

Next to various forms of written documents, it is mainly visual media which have received attention in memory studies (research in auditory media is just coming to the fore; see Bithell 2006; Bijsterveld and van Dijck 2009). The scope of visual culture's involvement in the construction of cultural memory cannot be overrated. It ranges, as Barbie Zelizer's collection on *Visual Culture and the Holocaust* (2001) shows, from graphic novels, the visual arts, television, video, film, museum artefacts and photographs all the way to tattooed bodies and the Web. The sheer power of images for memory was articulated by Walter Benjamin, in his *Arcades* project, when he claimed that 'history decays into images, not into stories' ('Geschichte zerfällt in Bilder, nicht in Geschichten') (1999, N 11, 4; 476). Acknowledging the significance of images for memory also means a challenge to the narrativist paradigm that has prevailed in memory studies so far, since 'memory' consists for most scholars in the *stories* that are told about the past (see chapter III.3.2). This chapter focuses on the two visual media which are the best-researched in memory studies: photography and film.

Studying photography as a medium of memory means a double challenge: Photographs are commonly held to 'bear witness' to the past; at the same time, they often turn out to be staged. As Jens Ruchatz (2008) maintains, we have to realize that photography is usually both 'externalization' *and* 'trace' of memory. It is the active construction of an image of the past *and* an indexical sign, that is, the result of something that took place in front of the camera at the very point in time that the shutter opened. Because of its indexical quality, photography has always been – and arguably still is, even in times of digital photography – assigned the status of a 'record of the past'. For most people, a photograph appears to have a unique connection to past reality. It seems to say, as Roland Barthes (1980) famously claimed, 'cela a été là' – it has been there ('trace').

Nevertheless, the constructed nature ('externalization') especially of documentary photography has long been exposed, perhaps most powerfully in Susan Sontag's reflections on war photography, *Regarding the Pain of Others* (2003 [2004]). Sontag contemplates that 'what is odd is not that so many of the iconic news photos of the past, including some of the best-remembered pictures from the Second World War, appear to have been staged. It is that we are surprised to learn they were staged, and always disappointed' (ibid., 49). The mnemonic value of photography does not seem to correlate with its truth-value. In her book on *Holocaust Memory through the Camera's Eye* (1998), Barbie Zelizer therefore asks from a memory studies perspective 'how images function as vehicles of collective memory' (ibid., 2) and discusses the stakes involved in 'using photography to bear witness to war atrocity' (ibid., 10).

In more ways than one, a photograph is a sign for the past. In fact, all three dimensions of the sign according to Charles Peirce are relevant when viewing photography from a memory studies perspective: As an 'index', a photograph is causally linked to the past – and thus often understood as a powerful trace, document or witness of history and ascribed a specific truth-value. As an 'icon' it re-presents the visual shape of past events and existents. And as a 'symbol' it stands for the meaning of the past. Photographs which prove to be powerful media of memory usually lend themselves to a realization of all three dimensions. For example, Robert Capa's photographs of the Spanish Civil War were long seen as infallible documents of war (although, in fact, many of them were staged). Viewers also turned them into iconic representations: still today, Capa's images determine 'the look' of the Spanish Civil War. And, finally, they stand symbolically for war's atrocities and victims. However, because of the arbitrary relation between signifier and signified, by which the symbol is characterized, the mnemonic meaning of a photographic image is not inherent, but the result of convention. In different social contexts, the meaning of an image can change considerably. For example, in fundamentalist Islamic circles the burning Twin Towers of '9/11' may be seen as a symbol of triumph, whereas in most parts of the western world the image stands for catastrophe and victimhood. Also over time, symbolic meanings of photographic images will be de- and reascribed.

Apart from the fact that photography – like all media of memory – constructs versions of a past reality rather than reflects it, what is striking about this particular medium (in contrast to most written or filmic media) is that it is essentially non-narrative. Taken by itself, a photographic image does not tell a story. It can depict what Gotthold Ephraim Lessing in *Laokoon* (1766) termed a 'pregnant moment'. It can provide an *occasion* for narration or cue a story in the observer's mind. What photography needs in order to function as a medium of memory is narrative contextualization, either by captions that come with it or by stories that surround or emerge from it. Studies which conceive of photography as a medium of memory therefore tend to stress its social embeddedness and intermedial relations.

Focussing on private photography, Annette Kuhn and Kirsten Emiko McAllister (2006, 1), for example, propose to examine pictures '*in situ*'. In their collection of essays fittingly called *Locating Memory*, they set out to 'literally locate – *place* – the images in the social world, bringing them "to life"' (ibid.). Similarly, in *Family Frames* (1997), Marianne Hirsch has concentrated on family pictures and emphasized that they depend on 'a narrative act of adoption that transforms rectangular images of cardboard into telling details connecting lives and stories across continents and generations' (ibid., xii). Indeed, an old family portrait that we find at a flea market 'tells us' little or nothing. For the foreign observer, it has at best a vague function as a medium of memory; for example, the stance and clothing might be interpreted as typical expressions of a past era. A great-granddaughter who knows the family stories, in contrast, will be able to actualize the photograph as a media cue, which then triggers much richer memories of past times. This transgenerational dimension of photographic memory is one of Hirsch's major concerns. She introduces the term 'postmemory' in order to explain how traumatic experiences of parents and grandparents are transmitted through photography and narrative to children and grandchildren. For her, photographs are 'the medium connecting first- and second-generation remembrance, memory and postmemory' (ibid., 23).

Research on historical film has traditionally addressed the difficult divide between, on the one hand, the historian's claim to be the sole provider of (methodologically sound) representations of the past in the apposite medium of historiography and, on the other hand, the incomparably wider appeal and impact of filmic versions of history – fictional, semi- and non-fictional (see Rosenstone 1995; Sobchack 1996; Landy 2001). Film stands out as a medium with a distinctly double mnemonic dimension. Film appears, firstly, as a (fictional) re-presentation of history ('historical film') and, secondly, as an archival source ('historical footage'). We find combinations of these two aspects in documentaries, and their increasing blurring in 'docufictions', with their mixture of historical footage and fictional re-enactments of past events.

An early, rather critical stance on the question of film and popular memory was taken by Michael Foucault. In an interview of 1974, he contended that in the 'fight' over memory, cheap books, television and cinema function as 'apparatuses … *reprogramming* popular memory', which – he thinks – was formerly coded by the people themselves in oral stories or songs. He goes on to assert that 'if one controls people's memory, one controls their dynamism … their experience, their knowledge' (Foucault 1975 [1974], 25). More recent contributions to the field seem to agree that indeed we cannot overemphasize the power of popular culture and its mass media to mould our images of the past (see Lipsitz 1990; Sturken 1997; Landsberg 2004). However, they also show that mass culture and the possibilities for remembrance it offers can be enabling for individuals and social groups, while at the same time the active role of audiences in appropriating media of popular memory puts them well beyond simple mind control.

Arguably, the most impressive popular versions of the past can be encountered in the cinema of cultural memory – which produces and disseminates what I call 'memory films'. These films fall into two broad categories: Movies such as *Blade Runner* (1982), *Total Recall* (1990) and *Memento* (2000) address concepts of memory, and problematize and imaginatively realize acts of individual and collective remembering. They are thus memory-reflexive films. *Apocalypse Now* (1978), *Schindler's List* (1993) or *Saving Private Ryan* (1998), on the other hand, tell us little or nothing about the workings of memory, but they have led to the powerful global dissemination of images of the past. These are memory-productive films. Addressing this latter category, Paul Grainge emphasizes in his seminal study *Memory and Popular Film* (2003, 4) that it is specifically Hollywood which 'has functioned strategically in the articulation and codification of the cultural past', nationally as well as transnationally. A movie like *Schindler's List* can certainly be criticized as part of the 'Holocaust industry' (Norman Finkelstein). But we must also acknowledge – and find ways to study – what Grainge (ibid.) calls 'the nature of popular film and its function as a approbate or "authentic" memory text'.

The actual study of memory films can proceed from the different dimensions of the medium. We can take on technological, aesthetic and/ or social perspectives. From a technological point of view, one can address, for example, the different mnemonic qualities of analogue and digital filmmaking or the significance of filmic remediation (see chapter V.5.3). But there are also certain formal and aesthetic strategies which contribute to memory-effects in film. Anton Kaes (1992) has drawn attention to the fact that, through certain aesthetic structures, historical films often enable their viewers to 'experience' the past. I have argued elsewhere that it is indeed a combination of 'experientiality' and 'saturation with the past' which lies at the basis of most memory-productive films – and that both effects are created by technological and aesthetic means (in Erll and Wodianka 2008, 139–69). But while aesthetic strategies may be responsible for marking a movie as a medium of memory, they can only endow it with a *potential* for mnemonic effects. This potential has to be *realized* within situative, social and institutional frameworks. Put simply, in order to become a memory film, a movie must be viewed *as* a memory film. Films that are not watched may well provide the most intriguing images of the past or perspectives on the workings of memory, yet they will not have any effect in memory culture.

What seems to be essential for the cinema of cultural memory is a certain kind of context, in which films are prepared and received as memory-relevant media. Scrutinizing the social practices surrounding memory films from *All Quiet on the Western Front* (1930) to *Das Leben der Anderen* (*The Lives of Others*, 2004) it becomes clear that what turns mere 'movies *about* memory/the past' into veritable memory films is often to be found not *in* the movies themselves, but instead in what has been established *around* them. A tight network of different media representations prepares the ground for memory films, leads reception along certain paths, opens up and channels public discussion, and thus endows movies with their mnemonic meaning. Reviews in national and international newspapers and movie magazines, special features on TV, carefully targeted marketing strategies, merchandise, DVD versions (including 'making of' segments, interviews with producers and actors, historical background information, and so on), awards, political speeches, academic controversies, the publication of 'a book about' or 'a book based on' the film, and, last but not least, the didactic formats which turn movies into teaching units in classrooms – all of these advertisements, comments, discussions, and controversies constitute the 'pluri-media networks', or constellations, of memory (Erll and Wodianka 2008) which channel a movie's reception and potentially turn it into a memory film, that is, a medium reflecting or producing memory in specific social contexts. Good examples of how different mnemonic contexts may turn the same movie into very different memory films can be found in the case studies collected by Loshitzky (1997) on the reception of *Schindler's List* in Britain, France, Germany, Israel, the Netherlands, and the USA, as well as in van der Knaap's (2006) work on the international reception of Alain Resnais's *Nuit et Brouillard* (*Night and Fog*, 1955).

While movies still seem to provide the grand narratives of popular memory, television exerts its memory-making power by virtue of its constant presence. In *Television Histories* (2001, 1f.), Gary R. Edgerton contends that 'television is the principal means by which most people learn about history today'. Specifically addressing 'history TV' (as we find it on history channels), he reminds us that screening the past is, above all, 'big business'. The format of history TV follows certain rules.

It is, for example, subject to 'the twin dictates of *narrative* and *biography*'. Television moreover has a tendency to personalize history (whereas historiography has long tended to regard larger historical structures and processes); it creates '*intimacy* and *immediacy*', which involves viewers in the historical matters represented.

TV events sometimes prove to be landmarks and turning points in the development of societal – and indeed global – memory discourses. One case in point is the American TV miniseries *Holocaust* (1978) which initiated – or at least served as a catalyst for – a new phase of engagement with the Shoah worldwide (see Shandler 1999). However, television audiences are not passive consumers of a pre-set agenda of televised history. In his investigations of the role of TV for German collective memory, Wulf Kansteiner (2006, 109–80) draws on audience research and contends that – through consumption practice – viewers are an active force when it comes to the question of which parts of the past are represented, where, when, and how: 'The consumers' influence on television policy and programming can be described as a veto power' (ibid., 135).

News coverage is another television format which bears on cultural memory, screening not the past, but present events and thus encoding them for future memory. News footage is the raw material of filmic memory, fulfilling – just like news photography – the functions of a document while being the result of a highly selective and constructive media representation. In *Televising War* (2004), Andrew Hoskins studies the Gulf War of 1991 as the first 'TV video war' (ibid., 16) and draws attention to the fact that 'television and particularly television news produce a new and apparently reliable stream of historical consciousness of today's events'. He contends, however, that television news coverage can effect a '*collapse* of memory', because televising the Gulf War and other warlike events such as '9/11' actually 'prevents memory through its satiation and overload of images, yet at the same time crystallizes memory of events around scenes that it obsesses over' (ibid., 5f.; see also Hoskins and O'Loughlin 2007; on news magazines as a medium of cultural memory Kitch 2000).

V.5.3   Diachronic dynamics: Remediation – premediation

In his reflections about 'new memory', Andrew Hoskins maintains that memories 'should not be considered as fixed representations of the past in the present, but, rather, they exist across a continuum of time'. Therefore, 'the process – the way in which memory has "lived" across this time in many different forms – needs to be addressed' (2001, 335).

One possibility of tackling this task is making use of the concept of 'remediation' which David Bolter and Richard Grusin have developed in their eponymous edited volume *Remediation: Understanding New Media* (1999). With its subtitle, Bolter and Grusin, too, refer to Marshall McLuhan's now classic text of media theory. They do so in order to underline their ambition of uncovering the logic of new media – and, interestingly, this turns out to be essentially a memory-logic. The term 'remediation,' according to Bolter and Grusin, refers to 'the formal logic by which new media refashion prior media forms' (ibid., 273). 'Each act of mediation depends on other acts of mediation. Media are continually commenting on, reproducing, and replacing each other, and this process is integral to media' (ibid., 55). Studying remediation means paying attention to the diachronic dimension that underlies each (new) media technology, to the fact that media are constantly 'borrowing from, paying homage to, critiquing, and refashioning their predecessors' (Grusin 2004, 17). Remediation is therefore a concept which refers to what might be called 'the memory of media', following Renate Lachmann's description of intertextuality as 'the memory of literature' (see chapter III.2.2). (For the equally important focus on the 'oblivion of media', or 'neglected, abandoned and trashed media technologies', and an inquiry into the mechanisms involved in the fading and persistence of media, see Acland 2007: xixf.)

What Bolter and Grusin (1999, 5) have called the 'double logic of remediation' – its oscillation between 'immediacy' and 'hypermediacy', transparency and opacity, between creating 'the experience of the real' and 'the experience of the medium' – is also visible in the operations of mnemonic media. On the one hand, most media of memory strive for ever greater immediacy. Their function is to provide a seemingly transparent 'window' on the past, to make us forget the presence of the medium and instead present us with the illusion of an unmediated memory. On the other hand, this effect is – paradoxically – usually achieved by hypermediacy, that is, the recycling and multiplication of media: Internet platforms of remembrance such as www.YadVashem.org offer online photo archives, written testimonies and virtual museum tours, thus combining many different media to provide access to the past and occasions for remembrance. The relatively new TV genre of 'docufiction' attempts to present viewers with a window on the past by combining documentary media with witness interviews and fictional re-enactments. Many war movies and history films employ what may be called a remediation-as-reality-effect: Historical documentary material (such as war photography and filmic footage) is incorporated into new movies. Such an integration of older media, which are commonly held to have 'witnessed' the past, into a new medium produces an *effet de réel*. The fiction film suddenly seems indexically linked to the historical events it depicts. Hypermediacy thus serves to create immediacy; remediation is used to endow media representations of the past with an aura of authenticity.

With the concept of remediation we are able not only to fathom the evolution of media technology as a mnemonic process or to highlight the double logic of media of collective memory. Refashioned into a distinct concept of memory studies, it has also helped to describe the diachronic and intermedial dynamics that underlie the very production of cultural memory (see Erll and Rigney's *Mediation, Remediation and the Dynamics of Cultural Memory*, 2009). As a concept of memory studies, remediation has therefore been defined as the ongoing transcription of a 'memory matter' into different media (ibid.). Memory matter – those images and narratives of the past which circulate in a given social context and may even converge into sites of memory – is a transmedial phenomenon; it is not tied to one specific medium. Contents of cultural memory can therefore be represented across the spectrum of available media: in handwritten manuscripts and printed newspaper articles, in historiographical books and in novels, in drawings, paintings and photographs, in movies and on websites. This is exactly what can be observed when studying the history of memory sites such as 'Odysseus', 'The Fall of the Roman Empire', 'The French Revolution' or 'Anne Frank'. What is culturally remembered about an ancient myth, a revolution, a hero (or any other story or image) usually refers not so much to what one might cautiously call the 'original' or the 'actual' events, but instead to a palimpsestic structure of existent media representations. Repeated representation, over decades and centuries, in different media, is exactly what creates a powerful site of memory.

Remediation tends to solidify cultural memory, creating and stabilizing certain narratives and icons of the past. Such stabilizing effects of remediation can be examined, for example, in the emergence of '9/11' as a global site of memory. The burning Twin Towers quickly crystallized into the one iconic image of the event, and this icon has been remediated ever since: in television news, movies, comic strips, on websites and so on. But such iconization-through-remediation is not restricted to visual media. Another example connected with '9/11' is the icon of the 'falling man', which stands for those people who were trapped by the fire on the upper floors of the World Trade Center and decided to jump rather than die in the flames. The first representation of the 'falling man' was a photograph taken by Richard Drew. It shows a man falling into certain death, his body upside down and in eerie symmetry with the façade of the WTC's North Tower. The image appeared in newspapers, on TV, and in the Internet, but it was also remediated in narrative form: among others, in a magazine story, a TV documentary and finally in Don DeLillo's novel *Falling Man* (2007). These remediations feature different semiotic systems and media technologies, they tell different stories and convey even contradictory meanings, but at the same time they all contribute to the stabilization of the 'falling man' as an icon of '9/11'.

But why is *one* image of '9/11' remediated time and again and turned into a mnemonic icon, while virtually thousands of other visual representations are left to oblivion? One reason for such choices is the (media) cultural resonance of a given representation. The 'falling man' seems to resonate with Biblical accounts of the Fall of Man, but also with, say, John Milton's classic account of angels falling from heaven in *Paradise Lost* (1667). Moreover, its clear black-and-white structure echoes a modernist aesthetics, ironically the very device of creating order in a world perceived as falling apart. These are but two examples of the workings of 'premediation', the companion term to remediation, which draws attention to the processes of mediated memory that are at work even *before* the choice for representing a matter in a certain fashion is made (for similar concepts see Grusin 2004, 2010; Thrift 2004). Premediation means that existent media circulating in a given context provide schemata for future experience – its anticipation, representation and remembrance. In this way, for example, representations of the colonial wars premediated the First World War; and the images and narratives of the First World War, in turn, were used as models for understanding the Second World War. But not only depictions of earlier, yet somehow comparable events shape our understanding of later events. Media which belong to even more remote cultural spheres, such as art, mythology, religion or law, can exert great power as premediators, too. John Bunyan's *The Pilgrim's Progress* (1678), with its 'Valley of the Shadow and Death' episode, premediated many journals and letters written during the First World War. (At the same time it was itself a remediation of the Bible.) And the American understanding and representation of '9/11' was clearly premediated by disaster movies, the crusader narrative as well as Biblical stories. Premediation therefore refers to cultural practices of looking, naming, and narrating. It is the effect of *and* the starting point for mediated memories.

It is the twin dynamics of premediation and remediation – the medial preformation and re-shaping of mnemonic images and narratives – which links each individual representation of the past with the history of mediated cultural memory. Pre- and remediation are basic processes of cultural memory. Their functions are manifold: first and foremost, they make the past intelligible; at the same time, they can endow media representations with the aura of authenticity; and, finally, they play a decisive role in stabilizing certain mnemonic contents into powerful sites of memory. The field of research into such complex intermedial processes of memory has only just opened up. However, with its general interest in the 'travel' of representation across time, space, and cultures – and thus with transmedial and transcultural memory – the study of pre- and remediation must be located in the tradition of one of the founding fathers of memory studies, Aby Warburg (see chapter II.2).

VI
Literature as a Medium of Cultural Memory

As a medium of cultural memory literature is omnipresent: The lyrical poem, the dime novel, the historical novel, fantasy fiction, romantic comedies, war movies, soap operas and digital stories – literature manifested in all genres and media technologies, both popular and 'trivial' literature as well as canonized and 'high' literature have served – and continue to serve – as media of memory. They fulfil a multitude of mnemonic functions, such as the imaginative creation of past life-worlds, the transmission of images of history, the negotiation of competing memories, and the reflection about processes and problems of cultural memory. Literature permeates and resonates in memory culture. But at what points exactly do cultural memory and its symbol system 'literature' intersect? How are literary media distinguished from non-literary media of memory? How do literary representations of memory refer to mnemonic contexts and how do those contexts, in turn, refer to literature? How does a literary text become a medium of memory? What mnemonic functions is it then able to fulfil? And which methodological tools can we use to study literature's impact in memory culture?

VI.1   Literature as a symbolic form of cultural memory

Literature is an independent 'symbolic form' (Ernst Cassirer, 1994) of cultural memory. It is a specific 'way of worldmaking' (Nelson Goodman, 1978) and that includes, in our perspective, also 'memory-making' (see chapter IV.2). Literature stands alongside other symbolic forms, or symbol systems, including history, myth, religion, law, and science. What are the specific characteristics of literature as a symbolic form? And how are those features related to cultural memory?

The effect of literature in memory culture rests on its similarities *and* differences to processes of remembering and forgetting. First of all, literature and memory exhibit several noticeable similarities. These include the forming of condensed 'memory figures' and a tendency towards creating meaning through narrativization and genre patterns. Form-giving operations such as these lie at the basis of both literature's and memory's world-making. Second, literature is characterized by significant differences to other symbol systems of cultural memory, such as history, religion, and myth. It is at least since the development of the modern system of art in the eighteenth century that literary texts have been equipped with particular privileges and restrictions, and from these results their specific contribution to memory culture.

VI.1.1   Literature and memory: Intersections

Memory proceeds selectively. From the abundance of events, processes, persons, and media of the past, it is only possible to remember very few elements. As Ernst Cassirer noted, every act of remembering is a 'creative and constructive process. It is not enough to pick up isolated data of our past experience; we must really *re-collect* them, we must organize and synthesize them, and assemble them into a focus of thought' (Cassirer 1944, 51). The selected elements must be formed in a particular manner to become an object of memory. Such formative processes can be detected in many media and practices of memory; they are also – and in fact primarily – found in literature. In the following I will highlight three central intersections between literature and memory. These are, first, 'condensation', which is important for the creation and transmission of ideas about the past; second, 'narration' as a ubiquitous structure for creating meaning; and, third, the use of 'genres' as culturally available formats to represent past events and experience.

(a) Condensation

With 'condensation' we look at what is arguably *the* main characteristic of literature. In German, the term *Gedicht* (poem) even maintains a linguistic connection to *Verdichtung* (condensation). One of the major effects of literary forms, such as metaphor, allegory, symbolism, and intertextuality, is the bringing together and superimposition of various semantic fields in a very small space.

In memory studies, 'condensation' has come to mean, at least since Sigmund Freud's *Traumdeutung* (1900; *The Interpretation of Dreams*), the compression of several complex ideas, feelings or images into a single, fused or composite object. The result is over-determination: many different associations about the past can converge in one condensed mnemonic object; and therefore the object will lend itself to different interpretations. For example, the date '9 November' brings together several German memories: the opening of the Berlin Wall, the November Revolution of 1918, the Munich 'Beer Hall putsch' by Hitler in 1923, and the *Reichspogromnacht* in 1938. In a palimpsest-like structure, different events and different meanings converge into the memory of Germany's highly ambivalent past.

The idea of condensation can be found not only in psychoanalytical approaches to memory. It has also been at the heart of ancient and medieval *ars memoriae* (see III.2.1); and it is clearly present in the more recent theories of cultural remembrance, from Aby Warburg's 'pathos formula', to Maurice Halbwachs's 'idée étoffée', E.R. Curtius's 'topos', Pierre Nora's *lieu de mémoire*, and to Jan Assmann's *Erinnerungsfigur* (memory figure). Ann Rigney (2005) has shown how different memories tend to 'converge and coalesce' into a single site of memory. And finally, condensation is also at the basis of those global icons, 'transnational symbols', and 'floating signifiers' which move across time and space (see chapter III.1.6).

Just like literary works, and because both are the result of condensation, cultural memories require active reception, interpretation. The memory of 'Versailles', to give just one example, assumed rather different meanings in its various contexts: before and after the First World War, in France and in Germany, among pacifists and revanchists. 'Reading' memory is what social groups continually, and often contestingly, do. If we want to reconstruct such interpretive practices – and thus gain insight into the dynamics of cultural memory –, then one way to proceed is by looking at the various narratives, which unfold condensed mnemonic objects into meaningful stories.

(b) Narration

Cultural memory rests on narrative processes. To be more precise, every conscious remembering of past events and experience – individual and collective – is accompanied by strategies which are also fundamental for literary narrative. In analysing literary works, proponents of structuralist narratology make a fundamental distinction between the paradigmatic aspect of the selection of narrative elements and the syntagmatic aspect of their combination. Such a differentiation can also prove useful in looking at memory: Both individual and collective memory are only capable of taking up a limited amount of information. From the abundance of impressions, dates, or facts, only a few elements can be selected to be encoded and remembered. In this way, that which is important (for the present) is distinguished from that which seems insignificant. The chosen elements, however, only become meaningful through the process of combination, which constructs temporal and causal orders. The individual elements are assigned a place in the course of events, and thereby also assume a specific meaning. In sum, large parts of cultural memory seem to be configured in much the same structure, namely narrative, that we encounter in large parts of literature. (Though it must also be emphasized that neither *all* of literature nor *all* of memory is inherently narrative. Visual, olfactory, and unconscious memories seem essentially non-narrative, although one could argue that they become conscious and meaningful through narrativization.)

The 'most narrative' of all our individual memory systems is auto-biographical memory. From the mass of disparate lifetime events, we retrospectively select some experiences, and turn them – through the use of narrative structures – into coherent, meaningful life stories (see chapter III.3.2). Aleida Assmann transfers these insights to the level of the Cultural Memory: Nations, ethnic and religious groups create narratives ('myths') which tell the story of their origins and distinctiveness. Mnemonic communities tend to remember only those 'elements which are tied into the configuration of the story' (A. Assmann 1999, 135). Just like the narratives of autobiographical memory, the story – or 'master narrative' – of the Cultural Memory rests on the 'process of selection, connection, and the creation of meaning' (ibid., 137).

Narrative structures play a significant role in every memory culture. We find them in the life stories and anecdotes that are listened to oral historians; and in the patterns of oral tradition on which anthropologists focus. The main function of narrative in culture is, according to Jörn Rüsen, 'temporal orientation', the linking of past, present and future in a meaningful way (see III.1.1; see Ricoeur's theory of time and narrative in chapter VI.2). The narrativization of historical occurrences and pre-narrative experience first allows their interpretation. Even the profoundly condensed, and arguably non-narrative, *lieux de mémoire* are generally entwined with and accompanied by stories, which circulate in social contexts and endow those sites with their changing meanings. The world of cultural memory is a world of narrative. (But this does *not* mean that it is a world of 'fiction,' fictionality is one of the privileges of the symbol system of literature; see chapter VI.1.2.)

(c) Genre

Genres are conventionalized formats we use to encode events and experience; and repertoires of genre conventions are themselves contents of memory. They belong to the body of cultural knowledge which individuals acquire through socialization and enculturation. We automatically draw on genre schemata (retained in our semantic memory) when we read literary texts – so that, for example, we expect death at the end of a tragedy, and a wedding at the end of a comedy. But genre schemata are also an essential component of autobiographical memory. The *Bildungsroman*, the adventure novel, and the spiritual autobiography, for instance, provide models of individual of development, which rememberers tend to fall back on when they want to explain the course of their lives (see Brockmeier 2001). Such genre memories are also an inherent part of the historical imagination (see Olick 1999b). Using nineteenth-century historiography as an example, Hayden White (*Metahistory*, 1973) has shown to what extent the choice of plot structure already pre-forms the meaning given to an historical event. The encoding of selected elements into opening, transitional, or closing motifs and their emplotment according to what Northrop Frye (1957) has identified as the archetypical narrative forms of romance, comedy, tragedy, and satire are various strategies of historical explanation, which White moreover associates with specific ideological implications: anarchist, radical, conservative and liberal.

Because literature is the site on which genre patterns manifest themselves most visibly (and in a socially sanctioned way), it is of pivotal importance for the circulation of memory genres. Literature takes up existing patterns, shapes and transforms them, and feeds them back into memory culture. Around 1800, for example, the process of a person's intellectual and social maturation found expression in the new literary genre of the *Bildungsroman*; and in turn, its typical plot structure of development became a powerful and persistent cultural model for the understanding an individual's coming-of-age. Other literary genres have primarily been used to encode the Cultural Memory. The epic, for example, was long a core pattern when it came to explaining the origin and uniqueness of an ethnic group. In nineteenth-century Europe, the historical novel became a dominant memory genre which represented the course of history and helped shape national identities. Pierre Nora (2001) has shown that at the same time statesmen's memoirs were used to exemplify French identity and values.

Genres are also a method of dealing with challenges that is faced by a memory culture. In uncommon, difficult, or dangerous circumstances it is especially traditional and strongly conventionalized genres which writers draw upon in order to provide familiar and meaningful patterns of representation for experiences that would otherwise be hard to interpret. For example, in late-nineteenth-century British fictions of empire, the genre patterns of romance provided a ready format for dealing with colonial anxieties. In poems and novels remembering the First World War, it was – of all genres – the pastoral which authors fell back on to convey the traumatic experience of the trenches, provide images of peace, and reconnect with tradition (Fussell 1975). By the same token, the emergence of new genres can also be understood as an answer to mnemonic challenges. At the end of the twentieth century, the postmodern insight into the constructed nature of history and identity found suitable expression in the genre of historiographic metafiction (see Nünning 1997).

VI.1.2 Literature and other symbolic forms: Differences

Because literary and mnemonic processes have many resemblances, literature seems ideally suited to be a medium of cultural memory. And yet literary works should not be considered as being simply equivalent to media of other symbolic forms that play a role in the making of cultural memory – such as chronicles, historiography, legal texts, religious writings, and mythic tales. In the construction of memory, the symbolic form of literature displays distinctive characteristics. In the following, we offer four brief descriptions of these characteristics: fictional privileges and restrictions, interdiscursivity, polyvalence, and the 'reversible figure' of production/reflection.

(a) Fictional privileges and restrictions

One of the most important differences between literature and other symbolic forms results from the fictional status of literary works which Wolfgang Iser conceives of as the result of 'fictionalizing acts' (see Iser, *The Fictive and the Imaginary*, 1993). According to Iser's phenomenological and anthropological theory of literature, every fictional representation rests on two forms of boundary-crossing: Elements of external 'reality' are repeated in the literary text, but not simply for their own sake. In the context of the fictional world, the repeated reality becomes a sign and takes on other meanings. On the other hand, the 'imaginary' – which according to Iser 'tends to manifest itself in a somewhat diffuse manner, in fleeting impressions that defy our attempts to pin it down in a concrete and stabilized form' (ibid., 3) – is given form through its representation in the medium of fiction, thereby achieving a determinacy which it did not previously possess. We are thus dealing here with 'two distinct processes. ... Reproduced reality is made to point to a "reality" beyond itself, while the imaginary is lured into form.' The result is that 'extratextual reality merges into the imaginary, and the imaginary merges into reality' (ibid.) Through this interplay between the real and the imaginary, fictional texts restructure cultural perception. In modern societies, an unwritten social compact restricts access to the realm of the imaginary to the symbol system of literature. Imaginary elements do also, it is true, find their way into the memory created by religious, and probably also historiographic writings. However, it is only in the literary text that they are simultaneously marked and accepted *as* imaginary.

As Ansgar Nünning (1997) has shown, literature's power in culture rests on a number of 'fictional privileges'. Fictive narrators, the representation of consciousness, the integration of unproven and even counterfactual elements into the representation of the past, and the imagination of alternative realities belong to the privileges enjoyed by the symbolic form of literature. It is these privileges that allow us to distinguish between historical fiction and historiography on the level of the text. But according to the 'logic of literature' (Hamburger 1957), the fictional status of literary works and their resultant depragmatization will also lead to certain restrictions, such as a severely limited claim to referentiality, adherence to facts, and objectivity (see Cohn 1999). Literary representations of the past are distinct from historiography in this aspect. They are also distinct from autobiographies and memoirs – however 'literary' in style those may be. Having said this, it must also be conceded that in the social sphere these distinctions are by far not as clear-cut as in literary theory. It is especially in connection with cultural remembrance that we find rather complicated performances of what Philippe Lejeune (1975) has called the 'autobiographical pact'.

(b) Interdiscursivity

As Mikhail M. Bakhtin (1981) showed as early as the 1920s, literary works are characterized by their 'heteroglossia.' They represent varying idioms and discourses and bring them together in the space of a single text. Bakhtin emphasizes that 'all languages of heteroglossia ... are specific points of view on the world, forms for conceptualizing the world in words, ... each characterized by its own objects, meanings, and values. As such they may all be juxtaposed to one another, mutually supplement one another, contradict one another, and be interrelated dialogically' (Bakhtin 1981, 291f.). By representing different ways of speaking about the past (and of memory), literature gives voice to the epistemological and ideological positions connected with these languages. In this way, literary works can display and juxtapose divergent and contested memories and create mnemonic multiperspectivity. In a world of increasingly specialized – and separated – discourses (such as those of history, theology, economy, and law), literature thus also acts as a 'reintegrative interdiscourse' (Link 1988), as a medium which brings together, and re-connects, in a single space the manifold discrete parlances about the past

(c) Polyvalence

In the medium of literature, the condensation and over-determination which are at the basis of every process of remembering are augmented in such a way that literary representations of the past usually display a semantic complexity foreign to other media of cultural memory. Highly ambiguous versions of memory are therefore reserved for the symbolic form of literature (see Eco 1989; on 'polyvalence' as a literary convention, see Schmidt 1992). Aesthetic theories postulate that art's affective potential and power derive from its very complexity. This pertains also to literature's specific role in memory culture.

(d) Production/reflection of memory

A specific feature of literature, and indeed of art in general, is its ability to offer (as systems theory would formulate it) first- *and* second-order observations of the world simultaneously (see Luhmann 2000a). On the one hand, literary works construct versions of the past: affirmative and subversive, traditional and new ones. On the other hand, they make exactly this process of construction observable, and thus also criticizable. Literary works are memory-productive *and* memory-reflexive, and often, like a reversible figure, simultaneously. There are varying ratios of memory-productivity and memory-reflexivity in literature, which may be characteristic of certain periods or genres. (The history of the historical novel proves a good example of those changing ratios.)

All of the distinctive characteristics of literature discussed here must be seen as 'conventions of the modern system of literature' (see Schmidt 1992). They may take on a different shape in earlier historical times or in non-western contexts. Bearing these limitations in mind, it can nevertheless be maintained that much of modern western literature's specific contribution to cultural memory seems to have rested on the interplay between literature's *similarities* with mnemonic processes on the one hand, and its *differences* to competing media of memory on the other. Certainly, literature is only *one* way of memory-making among many. It shares methods with everyday storytelling, historiography, and even with monuments. Yet at the same time, literature, because of its unique characteristics, offers representations of the past which are significantly different to those of other symbol systems. Literature can inject new and distinct elements into memory culture.

VI.2   Literary text and mnemonic context: Mimesis

How does literature construct versions of the past? Which different processes must be considered when one speaks of the 'literary creation of cultural memory'? What is the relationship of literary text and the sociocultural contexts of remembering and forgetting? One model which can help to illustrate these complex interrelations between literature and cultural memory is that developed by Paul Ricoeur in his philosophical treatise on time and narrative *Temps et Récit* (1983–5; *Time and Narrative*, 1984–6). Ricoeur proceeds from the presupposition that 'time becomes human time to the extent that it is organized after the manner of a narrative; narrative, in turn, is meaningful to the extent that it portrays the features of temporal experience' (1984, 3). To illustrate the dynamics of fictional narrative in the making of human time he introduces the model of a 'circle of mimesis,' Ricoeur refers to the classical concept of mimesis that goes back to Aristotle, but he differentiates among three levels of representation, which he terms $mimesis_1$, $mimesis_2$ and $mimesis_3$. For Ricoeur, literary world-making rests on a dynamic transformation process – on the interaction among the 'prefiguration' of the text, that is, its reference to the already existent extratextual world ($mimesis_1$); the 'textual' configuration, with its major operation of emplotment, which creates a fictional world ($mimesis_2$); and the 'refiguration' by the reader ($mimesis_3$). In this approach, literature appears as an active, constructive process, in which cultural systems of meaning, narrative operations, and reception participate equally, and in which reality is not merely reflected, but in fact 'poetically refigured' (xi) and 'iconically augmented' (81). Text and contexts, the symbolic order of extratextual reality and the fictional worlds created within the medium of literature, enter into a relationship of mutual influence and change.

Slightly reformulating Ricoeur's tripartite model for the purpose of conceiving of literature as a medium of cultural memory, we can distinguish among three aspects of mnemonic mimesis:

1. the prefiguration of a literary text by memory culture,
2. the literary configuration of new memory narratives, and

3. their refiguration in the frameworks of different mnemonic communities.

VI.2.1 Mnemonic prefiguration: Drawing on the reality of memory culture

Ricoeur points out that our experience of reality is symbolically pre-formed, or prefigured. Cultural practice establishes a 'conceptual net-work' that makes 'practical understanding' possible (1984, 55). Cultures create symbolic orders which include, among other aspects, value hierarchies and an understanding of temporal processes. Within this complex, symbolically mediated 'world of action', our experiences are characterized by their 'prenarrative quality' (74). Ricoeur emphasizes that every literary text is related to this extra-literary world. The idea of mimesis₁ brings home the fact that 'whatever the innovative force of poetic composition ... may be, the composition of the plot is grounded in a pre-understanding of the world of action, its meaningful structures, its symbolic resources, and its temporal character' (54).

Looking at mnemonic prefiguration means focusing attention on those areas of pre-understanding that concern cultural memory. It is in the 'textual repertoire', to use Wolfgang Iser's term, that the literary text's prefiguration becomes palpable: The structure of its paradigmatic axis of selection indicates from which cultural fields the text draws its elements. Literature can refer to the material dimension of memory culture (for example, historiography, memorials, memory movies, and discourses about the past); to its social dimension (for example, commemorative rituals, different mnemonic communities and institu-tions); and to its mental dimension (for example, values and norms, stereotypes and other powerful schemata for representing the past). It appropriates elements from these dimensions through intertextual, intermedial, and interdiscursive references.

Literature fills a niche in memory culture, because like arguably no other symbol system, it is characterized by its ability – and indeed tendency – to refer to the forgotten and repressed as well as the unnoticed, unconscious, and unintentional aspects of our dealings with the past. It is thus already on the level of mimesis₁, through the references that constitute the tex-tual repertoire, that literature actualizes elements which previously were not – or could not be – perceived, articulated, and remembered in the social sphere. Through the operation of selection, literature can create new, surprising, and otherwise inaccessible archives of cultural memory: Elements from various memory systems and things remembered and for-gotten by different groups are brought together in the literary text.

VI.2.2 Literary configuration: The creation of fictional memory narratives

With the term mimesis$_2$ Ricoeur (1984, 53) describes 'the concrete process by which the textual configuration mediates between the prefiguration of the practical field and its refiguration through the reception of the work'. Elements chosen within the framework of mimesis$_1$ are connected syntagmatically and moulded into a specific story. While in the extratextual world elements of the conceptual network may exist 'in a relation of intersignification' (55), in the literary text they we find them arranged, or emplotted, in a certain temporal and causal order. Within the narrative structure of the literary text, every element has its place and thus also gains its meaning. 'This passage from the paradigmatic to the syntagmatic constitutes the transition from mimesis$_1$ to mimesis$_2$. It is the work of the configurating activity' (66). It is also the passage into fiction; with their configuration into a story the ontological status of the chosen elements changes: 'With mimesis$_2$ opens the kingdom of the *as if* (64). Literary mimesis is therefore not simply a *re-presentation* of reality; in fact, configuration is an active, constructive process, a *creation* of reality, so that the term 'poiesis' seems a more fitting description (66).

Ricoeur emphasizes the 'emplotment's mediating role in the mimetic process'. Mimesis$_2$ is the site where '*a prefigured time ... becomes a refigured time through the mediation of a configured time*' (54; emphasis in the original). The level of configuration is thus the key to literature's role as a medium of cultural memory. It is here that literary works bring together, reshape and restructure real and imaginary practices of remembering and forgetting. With their transition into the literary text, elements of cultural memory are separated from their original contexts and can be combined and arranged in novel ways, into new and different memory narratives.

Not only emplotment is to be counted among the configurating activities taking place on the level on mimesis$_2$. Other literary forms also contribute in great measure to the creation of fictional memory narratives: Narrative voice, perspective, and focalization, literary chronotopoi (time-space combinations), metaphors, and symbols, to name just some particularly significant examples, are strategies involved in the performance, or staging, of cultural memory *in* literature (see also VI.2.4).

VI.2.3 Collective refiguration: Effects of literature in memory culture

According to Ricoeur, the act of reading brings about the transition between mimesis$_2$ and mimesis$_3$ and closes the mimetic circle. Mimesis$_3$

'marks the intersection of the world of the text and the world of the hearer or reader' (1984, 71). In the act of reading fiction enters into a renewed connection with the world of action. What results is not only the reader's actualization of that which is represented in literature, but at the same time the 'iconic augmentation' (81) of reality. 'It is only in reading that the dynamism of configuration completes its course. And it is beyond reading, in effective action, instructed by the works handed down, that the configuration of the text is transformed into refiguration' (Ricoeur 1988, 159). The meaning(s) ascribed by readers thus affect not only their understanding of the text. Literary works can also change perceptions of reality and in the end – through the readers' actions, which can be influenced by literary models – also cultural practice and thereby reality itself.

One of the first 'actions' to result from the refiguration of literature as a medium of memory is temporal orientation: With their narrative structure, literary stories shape our understanding of the sequence and meaning of events, and of the relation between past, present and future. Literature moulds memory culture thus through its structure and forms, but of course, and more obviously so, also through its contents: Representations of historical events (such as wars and revolutions) and characters (such as kings and explorers), of myths and imagined memories *can* have an impact on readers and *can* re-enter, via mimesis$_3$, the world of action, shaping, for example, perception, knowledge and everyday communication, leading to political action – or prefiguring further representation (and this is how the circle of mnemonic mimesis continues to revolve).

With a view to literature's effects on the collective level of memory, mimesis$_3$ should, however, be conceived of as *collective* refiguration, as socially shared ways of reading. There are two conditions for literary works to affect cultural memory: They must be received *as* media of memory; and they must be read in a broad swathe across society. Clues to such an 'effective presence' of literary texts in memory culture are provided by public debates as well as bestseller lists, forms of institutionalization such as their being added to school or university curricula, and the use of literary quotes in everyday speech. Social institutions may attempt to monitor, force or curtail the collective refiguration of literary texts – for example, by canonization. Political intervention, such as censorship and state-sponsored publications, must be taken into account. But economic factors, publishing and marketing strategies also play a crucial role. As far as the appropriation and interpretation of literary works is concerned, we must start from the premise of the existence of mnemonic 'interpretive communities' (see Fish 1980). Social groups agree or disagree on possible refigurations and on the value of a literary text for cultural memory. In all of these social processes, power is a factor that cannot be underestimated: Literary texts offer possible interpretations of the past and develop a number of – partly affirmative, partly subversive – narrative potentials. How these potentials are actualized in the social arena is a matter of negotiation and contestation.

From a media studies perspective, a literary work's prefiguration and refiguration can be observed in the ways it has been premediated and remediated. Refiguration manifests itself in remediating activities such as intertextuality and different forms of intermedial references (film adaptation, digitalization, and so on). A literary text's premediation is more difficult to pin down, but clues as to the media schemata which might have prefigured the text can be found by looking at earlier media representations which display, for example, similar narrative patterns and rhetoric strategies.

To sum up, literary narratives mediate between pre-existing memory culture on the one hand and its potential restructuring on the other. Connected with this mediation process is an exchange in two directions. First, the exchange between cultural memory and the literary text on the level of mimesis$_1$: The literary text makes reference to contents, forms, media, and practices of memory. Second, the exchange takes

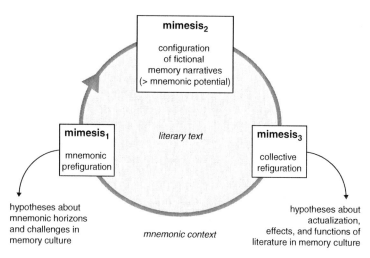

Figure VI.1 The three levels of the mimesis of cultural memory

place in the opposite direction: On the level of mimesis$_3$, (collective) reception may lead to an 'iconic augmentation' of memory culture, and shape perception, representation, and action (see also Figure VI.1).

VI.2.4   A narratology of cultural memory?

Ricoeur emphasizes that for those interested in a semiotic analysis of the text, it is solely mimesis$_2$, its configuration, which is accessible. He points out that 'a science of the text can be established only upon the abstraction of mimesis$_2$, and may consider only the internal laws of a work of literature, without any regard for the two sides of the text' (1984, 53). What can narratology, as a science of the narrative text, contribute to understanding literature's mnemonic dimension? What are the possibilities, limits, and pitfalls of a narratology of cultural memory?

From a narratological perspective, the totality of the 'internal laws' of the literary text can be termed its 'narrative potential'. Roy Sommer (2000, 328) defines the narrative potential of fictional texts as 'an assumption substantiated by the text regarding the possible effects of the narrative strategies which structure and organize its content and are thus essential for its meaning'. The narrative potential is thus a purely textual feature; it must be distinguished from actual historical realizations, effects and functions of a literary text. Reformulated in the terms of Ricoeur's model: An analysis of the narrative potential allows us to draw *hypotheses* about both the text's refiguration, its realization, effects, and functions in culture (mimesis$_3$), as well as about its prefiguration, the horizons within which it is produced and the challenges it answers to (mimesis$_1$). Such hypotheses will of course never pinpoint the actual pre- and refigurations of a literary text. But in combination with sound historical knowledge, they promise insight into the work that literature does in culture. Starting from these premises, we can speak of the mnemonic potential of a literary text, which materializes on the level mimesis$_2$ and which can provide clues as to the pre- and refiguration of the text in memory culture.

As a contribution to a narratology of cultural memory, and using war novels as well as (post-)colonial fiction as examples, I have introduced elsewhere the notion of the 'rhetoric of collective memory' (see Erll 2003, 2004, 2006), which describes such mnemonic potentials for literature to transmit versions of a socially shared past. I define the rhetoric of collective memory as an ensemble of narrative forms which provokes the naturalization of a literary text as a medium of memory. I distinguish among various modes of this rhetoric.

Different modes of remembering are closely linked to different modes of (narrative) representation (see chapter IV.2). Changes in the form of representation may effect changes in the kind of memory we retain of the past. In the following I will give some examples of how such mnemonic modes are constituted in the medium of literary narrative. It is, however, never one formal characteristic alone which is responsible for the emergence of a certain mode; instead we have to look at whole clusters of narrative features, whose interplay may contribute to a certain memory effect. It is, of course, impossible to predict how stories will be interpreted by actual readers; but certain kinds of narrative representations seem to bear an affinity to different modes of remembering, and thus one may risk some hypotheses on the *potential* memorial power, or effects, of literary forms.

Literary works represent the past in varying combinations of experiential, monumental, antagonistic, historicizing, and reflexive modes. Some of the narrative forms involved in establishing different mnemonic modes are narrative voice (such as personal, authorial and communal voice; see Lanser 1992), forms of unreliable narration, internal focalization, circumstantial realism, metaphors of memory, and literary chronotopoi. The following three examples show how different modes can be constituted in the literary text:

- Experiential mode: This mode is constituted by literary forms which represent the past as lived-through experience. Experiential modes evoke the 'living memory' of contemporary history, generational or family memories (that is, those forms of cultural remembering which the Assmanns subsume under the 'communicative memory'). In contrast, monumental modes envisage the past as mythical (that is, as part of the 'Cultural Memory'); and historicizing modes convey literary events and persons as if they were objects of scholarly historiography. Texts in which the experiential mode predominates tend to stage communicative memory's main source: the episodic-autobiographical memories of witnesses. Typical forms of this mode of literary remembering are the 'personal voice' generated by first-person narration; addressing the reader in the intimate way typical of face-to-face communication; the use of the more immediate present tense; lengthy passages focalised by an 'experiencing I' in order to convey embodied, seemingly immediate experience; circumstantial realism, a very detailed presentation of everyday life in the past (the *effet de réel* turns into an *effet de mémoire*); and, finally, the representation of everyday ways of speaking (sociolects, slang, and so on) to convey the linguistic specificity and fluidity of a near past. Travel literature often operates with such features of the experiential mode. So do war novels presenting 'the soldiers' tale' (Hynes 1997), that is, views 'from below'. And much Holocaust fiction resorts to strong experiential modes (but also shows, reflexively, the limits of experience and its representation).

- Antagonistic mode: Literary forms which help to promote one version of the past and reject another constitute an antagonistic mode. This mode of remembering tends to infuse literary works which represent identity-groups and their versions of the past, for example, feminist or postcolonial writing. We also find it in imperial fictions and in politically oriented *littérature engagée*. Negative stereotyping is the most obvious technique of establishing an antagonistic mode. More elaborate is the resort to biased perspective structures: Only the memories of a certain group are presented as true, while those versions articulated by members of conflicting memory cultures are deconstructed as false. 'We'-narration may underscore this claim.

- Reflexive mode: As already mentioned in chapter VI.1.2, literature always allows its readers both a first- and a second-order observation. It gives us the illusion of glimpsing the past and is, often simultaneously, a major medium of critical reflection upon such processes of representation. Literature is a medium which simultaneously builds and observes memory. Prominent reflexive modes are constituted by narrative forms which draw attention to processes and problems of remembering, for instance by explicit narratorial comments on the workings of memory, metaphors of memory, the juxtaposition of different versions of the past (narrated or focalized), and also by highly experimental narrative forms (like the inversion of chronology in the novels by Kurt Vonnegut and Martin Amis). Most of present-day historiographic metafiction features strong reflexive modes.

Such an alliance of narratology and cultural memory studies is made possible through the assumption that literary forms are 'semanticized' (Nünning 1997): They are not simply 'vessels' to hold content, but carry meaning themselves. However, memory culture also follows what Meir Sternberg (1982, 148) has termed the 'Proteus Principle': 'in different contexts ... the same form may fulfil different functions *and* different forms the same function'. An unequivocal correlation between literary form and mnemonic function is thus impossible; this is a relation which is never stable. For example, first-person narration can convey the authenticity of the eyewitness in one literary text, yet undermine the reliability of the narrated past in the other. Just as forms of cultural remembering change from one historical period to the next and from one cultural context to the other, so too do the forms of their representation. Moreover, literary memory narratives are not confined to the written medium. They can also manifest themselves in oral, visual, and digital media. Narrative is a transmedial phenomenon (Ryan 2004); and the stories of cultural memory therefore travel not only across time and space, but also 'across media', from novels to drama to movies to TV series and to the Internet. What we need, then, is not universal recipes, but instead flexible categories of a context-sensitive narratology, which takes into consideration the historically and culturally variable contents, forms, media, practices, and ideologies of cultural memory, and orients its narratological analysis accordingly (for more on a cultural narratology, see Erll 2005; on political narratology, Bal 2004).

In the field of literary studies – which redefines itself more and more as part of 'media culture studies' and shows interdisciplinary leanings towards cultural history, cultural sociology, and media theory – a narratology of cultural memory is only *one* option, *one* methodological tool. For the study of literature as a part of memory culture, it is ideally combined with other, contextualizing approaches, which accompany and enrich the text-centred analysis. Such wider social and media perspectives will be presented in the following section, which addresses the question of how literary works can become effective media of cultural memory.

VI.3 Literature as a medium of collective and individual memory

As we know from Aby Warburg, all media of cultural memory need to be *actualized*, charged with meaning, in order to unfold their mnemonic potential and to have an effective presence within the social sphere. This is also the case for literary works. Literature as a medium of cultural memory is therefore first and foremost a phenomenon of reception. When we study literary works and ask what functions they fulfil in memory culture, we must start from the premise of their appropriation through readers, from the aspect of refiguration.

On the collective level, literary works can fulfil all three functions of media of cultural memory (see chapter V.4). Literature is a storage medium and a circulation medium. Both aspects will be discussed in the following by using the concepts of 'cultural texts', 'collective texts', and 'literary afterlives'. Literature can moreover serve as a media cue, for example when during each year devoted to Shakespeare, Goethe or Cervantes the mentioning of those authors and their works is used to awaken ideas of a 'great' tradition and national identity among people across a broad spectrum of society – even if the texts in question were never even read by many of those same people. On the individual level, our '*collected* memory', literature exerts great influence as a media framework of remembering. Literary stories and their patterns are represented in our semantic and episodic memory systems. They shape knowledge, life experience, and autobiographical remembering.

VI.3.1   Literature as a storage medium: Cultural texts

The importance of literature as a medium of collective memory has always been at stake in discussions about the literary canon (see chapter III.2.3). One influential approach to canonization was developed by Aleida and Jan Assmann, who coined the term 'cultural texts'. Because this concept can help us understand how literary works are turned into storage media of cultural memory, the 'cultural text' will be discussed in the following and then serve as a starting point for further reflections on literature as a medium of memory.

Jan and Aleida Assmann introduced the 'cultural text' as a prototypical instance of the Cultural Memory's 'reusable texts' (see chapter II.4). However, it is important to note that the term neither refers exclusively to literature, nor is it restricted to written media. An oral tale, a legal document, a holy scripture, or a political tract can, depending on certain circumstances, all be assigned the status of 'cultural text'. This tendency to level the differences between objectivations of various symbol systems and media technologies comes as a result of the Assmanns' definition of 'text', which they understand, following the linguist Konrad Ehlich, as 'retrieved communication' (J. Assmann 2006, 103; see chapter V.2). Defining text in this way means that it is 'not the written form that is decisive, but the act of storage and transmission'. What constitutes a text is thus its separation from the immediate speech situation. Communication via texts means that 'the *immediate* situation of copresence is replaced by the *"expanded* context"'. Texts are 'speech acts' in expanded contexts; they connect producers and receivers of a message across spatial and temporal borders (ibid.). Defined in this way, texts can indeed take shape in different media and symbol systems. There are, for example, 'oral texts', such as orally transmitted myths; but 'not every utterance is a text' (104).

What Aleida and Jan Assmann refer to as '*cultural* texts' is a 'potentiation' of such texts. Cultural texts 'possess' a special normative and formative authority for a society as a whole' (J. Assmann 2006, 104). Cultural texts, too, are media-unspecific and manifest themselves in oral, visual, and written media. An oral narrative, a painting, a ritual, or a legal document can take on the function of the cultural text. No matter what media are used to store and transmit the cultural texts of a society, according to Aleida and Jan Assmann's theory, they are all functionally equivalent; they all produce cultural identity and coherence: 'Everything can become a sign that represents community. It is not the medium that matters, but rather the symbolic function and the structure of the sign' (J. Assmann 1992, 139).

What can we say about the workings of literature as a cultural text? How can a piece of literature be transformed into such a normative and formative medium? These questions are answered in Aleida Assmann's essay 'Was sind kulturelle Texte?' (1995, 'What are cultural texts?'). She emphasizes that the 'cultural text' is not a literary genre that could be identified by the text's inherent characteristics. It is instead a framework of reception. Assmann differentiates between two 'reception frameworks ..., within which texts are constituted either as "literary" or as "cultural"' (ibid., 234). The two frames are characterized by 'differing approaches to potentially identical texts'. The particular reading, or actualization, thus cannot be deduced from any text-internal features. It is in fact based on the 'decisionist act' of the reader, who assigns to the text either the status 'cultural' or the status 'literary' (ibid.).

From the multitude of literary works which a society produces and preserves, only a few are chosen and attributed a 'cultural', and this means for Aleida Assmann: canonical status. This attribution fundamentally changes the way these texts are perceived. Once they enter into the core area of the Cultural Memory, literary texts are turned into normative and formative texts and thereby gain additional semantic and pragmatic dimensions: They now seem to embody – and are used to transmit – cultural, national or religious identity as well as shared values and norms. By establishing a 'canon of religious, national, or educational texts' (ibid., 241), societies describe themselves.

Aleida Assmann emphasizes that cultural texts are made to differ from literary texts through an entirely different reading practice. Instead of solitary reception, aesthetic distance, and the desire for novelty, the reception of cultural texts is characterized by 'reverence, repeated study, solemnity' (ibid., 242). This type of reading is guided by the reader's certainty that he or she is, through the act of reading, part of a mnemonic community. Unconditional identification with what is supposed to be the text's message; a desire to acquire – through reading – knowledge about cultural origins, identity, values and norms; and the search for truth are further characteristics of the specific reading practice connected with the cultural text. Given this definition it is little surprising that Aleida Assmann sees the Bible as the 'paradigmatic cultural text' (ibid., 237).

Reading a literary work as a cultural text seems to imply both a retrospective reduction in literary ambiguity *and* an enrichment in cultural meaning. The publication of a piece of writing as a literary text marks it as a *version* of reality, one which is by no means unambiguous or normative, but rather marked as fictional, and which therefore lends itself to different interpretations. This is certainly a convention, but at least since the development of the modern system of art in the eighteenth century it has become standard practice. The prerequisite for a literary text to be read as a cultural text, however, is that it must be simultaneously simplified and over-determined. The polyvalence of the literary text dissipates and gives way to a uniform message; and its original historical situatedness is lost to view. With the loss of its 'literary' and 'historical' characteristics, however, it gains 'cultural' depth: The cultural text is now taken to impart a 'binding, ineluctable, and timeless truth' (ibid., 242).

The cultural text is a storage medium, or, to be more exact: It is through the reception framework of 'cultural texts' that literary texts are turned into storage media of the Cultural Memory. For centuries, the works of Homer, Virgil, Ovid, Dante, Shakespeare, Milton, and Bunyan have been a core component of enculturation, in school or religious education. They were medium *and* object of the Cultural Memory at the same time: media which 'remember something' about a community's past and are themselves remembered as canonical works. They thus fulfilled the typical double function of storage media of cultural memory (see chapter V.4.1).

VI.3.2   Literature as a circulation medium: Collective texts and literary afterlives

But what about all those other literary texts which are not canonized, not conceived of as a vital component of 'a culture'? In order to fully grasp and do justice to the role of literature in the social production of memory, we must distance ourselves from the assumption that only so-called high literature is read in association with the Cultural Memory. (On the contrary, often it is precisely 'popular' or even 'trivial' literature which makes use of its mythical and symbolic resources, as the example of fantasy fiction clearly shows.) Literary works of all origins and qualities can produce and transmit images of the past – within the framework of the Cultural Memory as well as within communicative memory. The concept of 'collective texts' is therefore meant to describe literature's function as a circulation medium that disseminates and shapes cultural memory. As in the case of the Assmanns' 'cultural texts', the 'collective text', too, is first and foremost a phenomenon of reception. But in contrast to the cultural text, the concept of the collective text points to a way of reading in which literary works are actualized not so much as precious *objects* to be remembered themselves, but rather as *vehicles* for envisioning the past. Collective texts create, circulate, and shape contents of cultural memory.

Examples of collective texts abound: Historical novels, such as Walter Scott's *Waverley* (1814), provided large audiences with a sense of the course of history; war novels such as Erich Maria Remarque's *All Quiet on the Western Front* (1929) seemed to take their readership back to the battle; romances such as Jane Austen's *Pride and Prejudice* (1813) or Margaret Mitchell's *Gone With the Wind* (1936) had the power to shape images of the lifeworld in past periods and regions; Gabriel García Márquez's *One Hundred Years of Solitude* (1967) and Salman Rushdie's *Midnight's Children* (1981) inspired an imagination of South American and Indian history in worldwide audiences. All of these are instances of the circulation of literature through global media cultures, often in translation, thus constituting what one might call a 'world literature of memory' (see Damrosch 2003). Most examples are, moreover, cases in which textual and filmic versions of the same story have provided mutual mnemonic support. Because narratives of memory tend to travel across media, the collective text, too, is a transmedial phenomenon.

But how does the phenomenon of the collective texts come about? Paradoxically, one important condition for literary works to have such an influence on cultural memory is that readers ascribe to them some kind of referentiality. Wolfgang Braungart (1996, 149) is thus correct when he argues that 'The disempowering of the text through the awareness of its fictional status has evidently not yet been completely achieved. This is not exclusively a problem of the "logic of fiction," nor of the (onto-)logical status of fiction, and cannot be explained solely by recourse to narrative form and narrative time, but must also take into account reading habits and desires.' Literary theory might well be able to show that and how fictional worlds differ from non-fictional representations. And this basic research is indeed necessary if we want to gain insight into the specific forms of expression and the epistemological possibilities of literary texts; and to counteract all-too-simple poststructuralist positions which claims that all facts are fiction and every narration about the past is literature. A look at the actual reading strategies of empirical interpretive communities, however, seems to justify the assumption that the ontological gap between fiction and reality postulated in theory is smoothly overcome in practice, and that literary works clearly shape our ideas about past realities.

Literature is frequently produced and received in rather pragmatic ways, and often enough with a referentializing and disambiguating eye. The ideological, didactic, and normative functions of historical novels, war literature, and children's books and also their 'this is the way it was' tone are one example. Yet this does not render obsolete the borders between the symbol systems. Readers do not confuse an historical novel with historiography, or an elegy with a memorial service. Indeed, in contrast, one can see what a sensitive topic the transition between symbol systems in fact is in mnemonic practice when one considers the social performance, the way that readers deal with, autobiography or autobiographical writing. As soon as the 'literarization' of a lived life crosses the line to fictionalization, such texts are as a rule no longer accepted by readers as autobiographical. The 'Wilkomirski Case', the heated discussion about the autobiography of an ostensible Holocaust survivor (*Fragments*, 1995) which – along with the persona of the author – soon turned out to be fictive, has been one of the best examples for the impenetrable lines which the social sphere draws between different symbol systems, despite all the similarities and overlaps.

The power of literature as a circulation medium of cultural memory must therefore be founded on a downright paradoxical reading practice. Literary works are perceived *as* literature, and that means (according to the specific characteristics of that symbol system) as polyvalent and interdiscursive forms of representation, which can also integrate imagined elements into their versions of the past. Yet *simultaneously* they are ascribed a certain kind of referentiality. This referentializing movement in the reading process, however, does not seem to be directed towards the pre-narrative reality of past events (as is the case when reading historiographical texts), but rather towards the horizons of meaning that are produced by cultural memory – and thus to a 'reality' which is already profoundly symbolically condensed, narratively structured, and transformed by genre patterns. What is at stake when reading literature as collective texts is thus 'truth' according to memory. Collective texts have to 'fit', have to be able to resonate with a memory culture's horizons of meaning, its (narrative) schemata, and its existing images of the past. These are the grounds on which 'mnemonic authenticity' is generated. And this is why Scott's visions of the past could exert such great influence in the historicist nineteenth century; Remarque's narrative of young men at war in a time bristling with generational antagonism; Rushdie's magic realist image of Indian history in the post-modern age; and Wilkomirski's forged autobiography in an age used to 'fragmented' patterns in Holocaust-representation.

Collective texts emerge from, intervene in, and can only be under-stood in conjunction with the 'plurimedia networks' of cultural memory (see chapter V.5.2). To give one example: Around the millen-nium, the topic of flight and expulsion of Germans from the eastern territories at the end of the Second World War was slowly (re-)emerging as a topic of social discourse in Germany – pervading political discus-sions, newspaper commentaries, and TV programmes. Günter Grass's novella *Crabwalk* (2002) moved into this burgeoning mnemonic field, gave shape and articulated much of that which until then might have seemed shapeless and disconnected, and was consequently awarded the status of 'taboo-breaker' by the German press. As Kirsten Prinz has argued with a view to the heated discussions following the publication of Grass's novella: 'The border between fiction and non-fiction becomes functional here: With its limited claim to referentiality and depragma-tization, literary works can put certain versions of the past to the test; the social and political relevance of which is then determined in non-fictional, say journalistic, discourse' (Prinz 2004, 193).

While the concept of 'collective texts' directs attention to such synchronic networks and the circulation of cultural memory through literature, the study of 'literary afterlives' (which is reminiscent of Aby Warburg's research on art's afterlife) opens up a diachronic perspective. Historical approaches to the 'life' and ongoing impact of literature in memory culture are gaining increasing currency in memory studies. There are, for example, studies on the 'afterlives' of Walter Scott's nov-els (Rigney 2004, 2011), on more than 300 years of Bunyan's *Pilgrim's Progress* and its worldwide transmission (Hofmeyr 2004), and on the afterlives of anticolonial prophecy in South African literature and other media (Wenzel 2009). Such research addresses the basic process of mem-ory culture: that of continuation and actualization. And it testifies to what Ann Rigney (2010, 17) has identified as the 'specificity of the arts as media of collective remembrance', namely their 'temporally convo-luted combination of "monumentality"' (that is, their persistence) and 'malleability' (that is, their 'openness to appropriation by others').

In reconstructing the 'social life' (*sensu* Appadurai 1986) or 'cultural biography' of a literary text we may ask how – across long periods of time – it was received, discussed, used, canonized, forgotten, censored, and re-used. What is it that confers repeatedly upon some literary works a new lease of life in changing social contexts, whereas others are forgotten and relegated to the archive? These questions may be addressed from social, medial, and textual viewpoints – and the phenomenon of literary afterlives will arguably be tackled best by a balanced combination of all three.

The social perspective emphasizes the active appropriations of a literary text by social actors. How do changing social formations – with their specific views of history and present challenges, their interests and expectations, discourses and reading practices – receive and re-actualize literature? How do the responses to the same literary work change from generation to generation? For example, as is shown by Jesseka Batteau (2009), the social performance and public reputation of iconic Dutch authors, such as Gerard Reve, changed greatly over the past decades along with the transformations of Dutch society, and this in turn also altered the images of the religious past that their works convey.

Looking at 'literary afterlives' from a media culture perspective means directing the focus to the intermedial networks, which maintain and sustain the continuing impact of certain stories: intertextual and intermedial references, rewriting and adaptation, forms of commentary and cross-reference. Using the concepts of premediation and remediation I have shown elsewhere (Erll 2007, 2009b) how the narratives and iconic images of the 'Revolt of 1857' (a colonial war in Northern India against British rule) were pre-formed by stories and images of similar earlier events (such as the 'Black Hole of Calcutta' of 1756), then remediated in colonial and postcolonial contexts across the spectrum of available media technologies (from newspaper articles to novels, photography, film, and the Internet), in order to turn, finally, into premediators of other stories and events (such as the Amritsar massacre of 1919, nostalgic postimperial novels of the 1950s, or current debates about terrorism).

In a more text-centred perspective, we may ask if there are certain properties of literary works which make them more 'actualizable' than others, which effect that the works lend themselves to rereading, rewriting, remediating, and continued discussion. For example, studying the long and rich afterlife of Walter Scott's *Ivanhoe* (1819), Ann Rigney (2010, 215f.) has shown that the novel's continuing appeal can be attributed to a combination of two (seemingly contradictory) characteristics of its plot: More than any other novel by Walter Scott, *Ivanhoe* is both 'highly schematic' *and* highly 'ambivalent'. On the one hand, it offers a basic narrative paradigm that can be used as a model 'for dealing with *other* events'; on the other hand, it keeps readers puzzled and engaged by its 'de-stabilizing tension between the outcome of the story and its emotional economy'. (On women's rewriting, see also Plate 2010.)

What the 'cultural texts', 'collective texts' and 'literary afterlives' all have in common is that they are *approaches* to studying literature as a medium of cultural memory; they mean taking on a certain perspective on literary texts – and often, one and the same text may potentially be regarded through all three lenses. However, each lens raises different questions and will yield different answers. While the 'cultural-texts approach' looks at literary works as storage media, and asks about the social institutions involved in the preservation and interpretation of canonical, holy, or classical texts, the 'collective-texts approach' is more interested in (often popular) literature's interventions in current memory-debates, in its lively depiction of the past, and in the ways in which it thus shapes collective images of history. The 'afterlives approach', finally, transfers these concerns to the diachronic dimension. It means asking about the continuing impact of some literary works, how they manage to 'live on' and remain in use and meaningful to readers; and it means addressing the complex social, textual and intermedial processes involved in this dynamics. To round out the discussion of literature as a mediator of memory, the following chapter will complement the approaches delineated so far with psychological perspectives on the relation of literature and individual memory.

VI.3.3   Literature as a media framework of memory

How can literature be conceived of as a medium of individual memory? On the one hand, literature is a part of everybody's semantic memory. We remember the characters and plots of the novels we have read and the movies we have watched. Such individual actualization is a necessary condition for the kind of socially shared reading practices described above with the concepts of 'cultural texts' and 'collective texts' (and, of course, it can be at odds with socially dominant readings). On the other hand – and perhaps more disturbingly – literature is also a medium which shapes episodic memory: the way we recall our life experience.

To understand literature's significance for episodic remembering, let us turn, once more, to Maurice Halbwachs's anecdote of a 'walk through London' (see chapter V.4.2). Halbwachs not only emphasizes the role that different social frameworks and media play for his perception of the city; he also hints at the importance of literary models: 'Many impressions during my first visit to London – St. Paul's, Mansion

House, the Strand, or the Inns of Court – reminded me of Dickens' novels read in childhood' (Halbwachs 1980, 23f.). The complex inter-relations of literature and memory emerge clearly here: The perception of the London cityscape reminds the visitor of a literary work, and the past readings, in turn, pre-form his appreciation of the city. Because Halbwachs is interested in social frameworks, he concludes, 'so I took my walk with Dickens' (ibid.). Like the architect or the painter, there-fore, the (then long-deceased) author of a novel can form a social group with the rememberer and serve as a virtual communication partner in the socially shared production of individual memory.

A literary scholar might find Halbwachs's statements too imprecise, or perhaps even wrong. And, of course, the representations of London in *Bleak House* (1852), *Great Expectations* (1860/61) or *Oliver Twist* (1837/38) are not exact and verifiable representations of the metropolis such as we would expect to find in historical treatises or maps. Dickens's novels are *fictional* texts, which do not mimetically reproduce London's reality, but which instead create poietic models of the city. It is equally unwar-ranted to ascribe to the real author Charles Dickens the description of the location, the fictive events that take place there, or their meaning. Narratology maintains that fictional worlds are mediated by fictive nar-rative instances (which may be extremely unreliable). But how can fic-tive depictions, conveyed by an equally fictive narrator, influence a real situation? For Halbwachs, literature obviously functions as a medium from which social frames of reference can be derived. Literature is a *cadre médial*. The reading of literary texts would appear to shape the individual memory as much as social interaction within groups or com-munication through other, non-fictional media.

And indeed, much recent research has shown that literature plays a central role in the perception and remembering of individual life experi-ence. It is a medium which already pre-forms our encounter with reality; and then helps re-shape experience into our most personal memories. In her book *An Intimate History of Killing* (1999, 28), Joanna Bourke provides a series of examples for the efficacy of literary and filmic rep-resentations of war. She reports, for example, that during the invasion of Grenada in 1983 American soldiers played Wagnerian operas, thus imitating Colonel Kilgore (Robert Duvall) – a protagonist from the war movie *Apocalypse Now* (1979) who flew his helicopter attacks to the soundtrack of the 'The Ride of the Valkyries'. Here we find life imitat-ing literature, as Oscar Wilde would have it. And also in less dramatic situations of everyday life, literature has an – often inconspicuous – presence, for example, when we suffer under the burden of our work like 'Sisyphus', search for a suitable partner like Elizabeth Bennet, migrate, get lost and in danger like Odysseus, feel jealous like Othello, or appreciate a field of spring flowers like Wordsworth's persona. The screenwriters' guru Robert McKee (1997, 62) emphasizes the influence of literary structures on the way we think about ourselves and our lives: 'Most human beings believe that ... they are the single and active protagonists of their own existence; that their existence operates through continuous time within a consistent, casually interconnected reality; that inside this reality events happen for explainable and meaningful reasons.' In Mark Turner's (1996) words, we all possess a fundamentally 'literary mind'.

The key to literature's influence on individual memory lies in its circulation of cultural schemata – and arguably, it is no coincidence that Bartlett's fundamental work on cultural schemata was done by using literary narratives an example (see chapter III.3.1). Today, it is in particular literature communicated through mass media which plays an important role as a source of such schemata. From movies and TV series to radio-plays and Internet role play games – literary media assimilate, embody, alter, and transmit patterns for encoding experience. They thus reinforce existing structures of cultural schematization, but also generate new ones; they pre-form experience (of war and revolution, but also of graduation and marriage) and guide recall into certain paths.

The function of literature as a media framework of memory and as generator of cultural schemata has also been studied in the fields of social psychology and the neurosciences. Harald Welzer (2002), for example, conducted interviews with veterans of the Second World War and realized that literary models taken from popular war movies (ibid., 179f.) and prose fiction (from the *Odyssey* to Karl May and the Grimms' fairy tales; ibid., 186) serve as templates for autobiographical remembering. Welzer considers it 'rather probable that we have all added to our life stories elements and episodes which other – fictional or real – people have experienced and not we ourselves' (ibid., 169). He argues that fiction in particular provides 'tested models for stories which have been proved successful, with which one can captivate and excite one's listeners' (ibid., 186). Our accessing of already existing stories, however, does not seem to occur consciously. On the contrary, as a rule, the interviewees considered their memories to be a quite precise representation of their past experience. In fact, the feeling that our autobiographical memories are authentic tends to be supported by the very elements taken from literary texts. By using literary structures, we overwrite the incoherent events of the past in such a way that they follow one another in a plausible manner, and thus appear particularly authentic, quite logical, and thus 'real'.

One thought-provoking insight into the relation between literature, memory, and our ideas of authenticity has been gained in the field of neuroscientific research. Welzer mentions 'that the neuronal processing pathways for visual perception and for imagined contents overlap to such an extent that even when remembering purely imaginary events, people can vividly see them "before their eyes"' (ibid., 39). This would perhaps explain why the condensed images created through literary texts can sometimes not be distinguished in our memory from that which we have actually experienced personally. However that may be, from a memory studies perspective, literature clearly proves to be 'part of a social, cultural, and historical intertextual web, a distributed memory' (ibid., 187).

Conceiving of 'literature as a medium of cultural memory' requires a rigorous contextualization of literary works. It means envisioning literature as a part of memory culture, entangled in its social, medial, and mental dimensions. It also calls for a nuanced view, and to some extent entails a modification, of basic assumptions made by traditional literary theory, for example, regarding the clear separability between text and context, literature's (non-)referentiality, actual reading practices (which are in dire need of rigorous study), or the alleged stability and unchangeability of literary works. What is at stake here is the realization that the literary production of cultural memory is an ongoing process, characterized by a dynamic interplay between text and context, the individual and the collective, the social and the medial.

VII
Afterword: Whither Memory Studies

Looking back on the history of memory studies, at least two distinct phases are discernible: A first phase in the 1920s and 1930s, with Maurice Halbwachs, Aby Warburg, Walter Benjamin, Frederic Bartlett, Karl Mannheim and others as protagonists; and a second phase starting roughly in the mid-1980s, with Pierre Nora's work on *lieux de mémoire* as its most prominent manifestation. After those two phases, the first characterized by pioneering research that extended across a broad spectrum of academic disciplines, the second equally open to a range of different perspectives on memory, yet more thematically focused on national remembrance and traumatic events – will there be a third phase of memory studies? Or will the field merely consolidate and continue in the mode established since the mid-1980s?

The question is 'Whither memory studies?' In a recent article entitled 'A Looming Crash or a Soft Landing', Gavriel D. Rosenfeld (2009) articulates one now rather common idea among memory studies' critics about the future prospects of the field, namely that after more than two decades' intensive work done on the Holocaust and the unearthing of historical injustices all across the globe – from the Aboriginals' 'stolen generation' to apartheid – we have now arrived at a point of saturation with 'memory'. Instead of continuing to deal with memory and the past, such critics argue, we should start looking at the present and future. Rosenfeld considers '9/11' as the tipping point and beginning of the demise of memory studies and sums up: 'In such a world, the study of memory ... may increasingly appear to be a luxury that a new era of crisis can ill afford' (ibid., 147).

I would rather claim the opposite: Today (and whether this is more an era of crisis than any other age is also open to debate) we cannot afford the luxury of *not* studying memory. If we want to understand '9/11', the actions of Islamic terrorists, or the re-actions of the West, we must naturally look at certain mental, discursive, and habitual paradigms that were formed in long historical processes – via cultural memory, as it were. We must try to understand the different ways in which people handle time, and this refers not only to their 'working through the past', but also includes their understanding of the present and visions for the future. If we want to get our heads around current wars in Afghanistan, Iraq, and on the African continent, the rise of China and India, global warming (ibid.) – and especially around the ways that people make sense of these experiences and from there begin to deal with them (or fail to do so) – then we have to acknowledge that many of the 'hard facts' of what we encounter as 'economy', 'power politics', or 'environmental issues' are at least partly the result of 'soft factors', of cultural processes grounded in cultural memory.

However, the prerequisite for using memory studies as a tool to either address the pressing questions of our age or to do innovative and challenging work on historical constellations is freeing the field from restrictive definitions. Memory studies is not reducible to 'commemoration studies', 'national remembrance studies', 'Holocaust studies', or 'trauma studies' – although it comprises these research areas and draws on the methodologies developed in them. I have argued in this book that memory studies is interested in the entire spectrum of possible interrelations between past, present, and future as they take shape in sociocultural contexts. It is only such a broad definition of the field that will enable its further development and prevent it from repetition and a certain predictability of its findings. With the opening up of memory studies' horizon we can lay the foundation for future memory research that addresses the social, medial, and mental dynamics at work whenever people deal with, or are influenced by, the past and from there address their present reality and future prospects.

What are, then, promising roads for memory studies to take while it leaves behind the narrowing self-definitions, thematic restrictions, and methodological nationalism that were characteristic of its second phase and enters its third phase? Conceiving of memory as process and movement, rather than as a phenomenon that is fixed in time and space, might challenge and help to rethink some fundamental categories of memory studies – among them Halbwachs' *cadres sociaux*, the 'memory site', and the idea of culture. A transcultural perspective on memory will help to address not only 'memory in a global age', but also those mnemonic dynamics which were not apparent under the 'national paradigm' predominant in memory studies since the 1980s. It might,

for example, be a fruitful approach for research on historical constellations of cultural remembering. So far, much of memory studies rests on
seminal works that were written with a view to the 'modern memory'
of the nineteenth and twentieth centuries. As a by-product, the field's
key assumptions and methodologies seem to be geared to memory in
the age of nation-states, in the rivalry with academic history, and in
an era of rapid media evolution. Even if we do not subscribe to naïve
dichotomies between pre-modern and modern memory, we are still
a long way from comprehensive and satisfying answers to questions
about the historical differences, continuities, and changes in cultural
remembering.

Fundamental research on cultural remembering would also have to
include generating in-depth knowledge about memory's inherent mediatedness. Collaboration between media theory, sociology, psychology,
and the neurosciences could further our understanding of the role that
media play in the construction, passing on, and dissemination of powerful cultural schemata. It could show how such schemata 'premediate'
thinking, feeling, and action – and thus provide insights into the unintentional, implicit side of cultural memory, which seems to impinge on
politics more strongly the less people are aware of it. Moreover, further
work on memory and new media could show if and how the digital age
conflates – or generates new relations between – individual and collective levels of remembering. Research on 'global (new) media cultures'
might show how altered relations of time and space change the ways in
which memory 'travels'. However, it is, again, only through more historical work, the scrutiny of ancient, medieval, and early modern memory, that we can answer the question if remembering in the 'modern',
'global', or 'digital age' is really (as often postulated) different in nature
to earlier mnemonic constellations, or merely different in degree.

Memory does not necessarily (and indeed, not even first of all) mean
tradition, preservation, inertia. On the contrary, research on the dynamics of cultural remembering has clearly brought to light that memory
is fluid, ever-changing, even while it appears to remain the same. Due
to its capacity to relate past, present, and future – envisioning alternative trajectories through a recourse to the past, activating forgotten
knowledge in the present, making sense of the new by comparing it to
the old – memory is the very apparatus that enables change. Memory
studies is therefore not an exercise in nostalgia, but can be a method
to discover and reflect the mechanisms and potentialities of cultural
change and renewal. Most importantly, it helps us to realize when and
how the present and future are shaped by memory.

As far as the future of academia is concerned, the most promising and challenging fact about memory studies is that it is developing steadily into a true convergence field. Memory research has not only inspired new alliances between the humanities, social sciences, and natural sciences. Slowly but palpably, it is also bringing together the knowledge and approaches of scholars from very different parts of the world. This book, which is doubtless written from my German and literary and media studies perspective, has tried to take some further steps towards an international and interdisciplinary integration of memory studies. And I hope that, to quote Joseph Beuys, its 'reason lies in the future'.

References

Acland, Charles R. (2007) *Residual Media* (Minneapolis: University of Minnesota Press).

Adorno, Theodor W. (2010) *Guilt and Defense: On the Legacies of National Socialism in Postwar Germany,* ed., trans. and introd. Jeffrey K. Olick and Andrew J. Perrin (Cambridge, MA: Harvard University Press).

Agazzi, Elena and Vita Fortunati (eds.) (2007) *Memoria e saperi: percorsi transdisciplinari,* Universale Meltemi 32 (Roma: Meltemi).

Alexander, Jeffrey C. et al. (2004) *Cultural Trauma and Collective Identity* (Berkeley, CA: University of California Press).

Allen, Graham (2000) *Intertextuality,* New Critical Idiom (London: Routledge).

Althoff, Gerd, Johannes Fried and Patrick J. Geary (eds.) (2002) *Medieval Concepts of the Past: Ritual, Memory, Historiography,* Publications of the German Historical Institute Washington, DC (Cambridge: Cambridge University Press).

Amberber, Mengistu, (ed.) (2007) *The Language of Memory in a Crosslinguistic Perspective* (Amsterdam: John Benjamins).

Amin, Shahid (1995) *Event, Metaphor, Memory: Chauri Chaura, 1922–1992* (Berkeley: University of California Press).

Anderson, Benedict (1983) *Imagined Communities: Reflections on the Origin and Spread of Nationalism* (London: Verso).

Antze, Paul and Michael Lambek, (eds.) (1996) *Tense Past: Cultural Essays in Trauma and Memory* (New York: Routledge).

Appadurai, Arjun (1986) *The Social Life of Things: Commodities in Cultural Perspective* (Cambridge: Cambridge University Press).

Appiah, Kwame A. (2005) *The Ethics of Identity* (Princeton, NJ: Princeton University Press).

Arendt, Hannah (1951) *The Origins of Totalitarianism* (New York: Harcourt, Brace and Co).

Argenti, Nicolas and Katharina Schramm (2010) *Remembering Violence: Anthroplogical Perspectives on International Transmission* (New York: Berghahn Books).

Assmann, Aleida and Dietrich Harth (eds.) (1991) *Mnemosyne. Formen und Funktionen der kulturellen Erinnerung* (Frankfurt am Main: Fischer).

Assmann, Aleida and Jan Assmann (1994) 'Das Gestern im Heute. Medien und soziales Gedächtnis', in Klaus Merten, Siegfried J. Schmidt and Siegfried Weischenberg (eds.) *Die Wirklichkeit der Medien. Eine Einführung in die Kommunikationswissenschaft* (Opladen: Westdeutscher Verlag), 114–40.

Assmann, Aleida and Sebastian Conrad, (eds.) (2010) *Memory in a Global Age: Discourses, Practices and Trajectories* (Basingstoke: Palgrave Macmillan).

Assmann, Aleida (1991) 'Kultur als Lebenswelt und Monument', in Aleida Assmann and Dietrich Harth (eds.), *Kultur als Lebenswelt und Monument* (Frankfurt am Main: Fischer), 11–25.

Assmann, Aleida (1995) 'Was sind kulturelle Texte?', in Andreas Poltermann (ed.), *Literaturkanon – Medienereignis – kultureller Text. Formen interkultureller Kommunikation und Übersetzung* (Berlin: Erich Schmidt), 232–44.

Assmann, Aleida (1996a) 'Im Zwischenraum zwischen Geschichte und Gedächtnis: Bemerkungen zu Pierre Noras *Lieux de mémoire*' in Etienne François (ed.) *Lieux de mémoire, Erinnerungsorte. D'un modèle français à un projet allemand* (Berlin: Centre Marc Bloch), 19–27.

Assmann, Aleida (1996b) 'Texts, Traces, Trash: The Changing Media of Cultural Memory', *Representations*, 56, 123–34.

Assmann, Aleida (1999) *Erinnerungsräume: Formen und Wandlungen des kulturellen Gedächtnisses* (Munich: Beck).

Assmann, Aleida (2000) 'Individuelles und kollektives Gedächtnis – Formen, Funktionen und Medien', in Kurt Wettengl (ed.), *Das Gedächtnis der Kunst: Geschichte und Erinnerung in der Kunst der Gegenwart* (Ostfildern-Ruit: Hatje Cantz), 21–7.

Assmann, Aleida (2002) 'Gedächtnis als Leitbegriff der Kulturwissenschaften', in Lutz Musner and Gotthart Wunberg (eds.), *Kulturwissenschaften: Forschung – Praxis – Positionen* (Vienna: WUV), 27–45.

Assmann, Aleida (2004) 'Four Formats of Memory: From Individual to Collective Constructions of the Past' in Christian Emden and David Midgley (eds.) *Cultural Memory and Historical Consciousness in the German-Speaking World Since 1500* (Bern: Peter Lang), 19–37.

Assmann, Aleida (2006a) 'History, Memory, and the Genre of Testimony', *Poetics Today*, 27:2, 261–74.

Assmann, Aleida (2006b) 'The Battle of Memories in Shakespeare's Histories' in Christa Jansohn (ed.) *German Shakespeare Studies at the Turn of the Twenty-First Century* (Newark, DE: University of Delaware Press), 21–41.

Assmann, Aleida (2007) 'Europe: A Community of Memory? Twentieth Annual Lecture of the GHI', *GHI Bulletin*, 40, 11–25.

Assmann, Aleida (2008) 'Canon and Archive' in Astrid Erll, Ansgar Nünning (eds.) and Sarah B. Young (coll.), *Cultural Memory Studies: An International and Interdisciplinary Handbook* (Berlin and New York: de Gruyter), 97–107.

Assmann, Jan (1988) 'Kollektives Gedächtnis und kulturelle Identität' in Jan Assmann and Tonio Hölscher (eds.) *Kultur und Gedächtnis* (Frankfurt am Main: Suhrkamp), 9–19.

Assmann, Jan (1992) *Das kulturelle Gedächtnis: Schrift, Erinnerung und politische Identität in frühen Hochkulturen* (Munich: Beck).

Assmann, Jan (1995) 'Collective Memory and Cultural Identity', trans. John Czaplicka, *New German Critique*, 65, 125–33.

Assmann, Jan (1997) *Moses the Egyptian: The Memory of Egypt in Western Monotheism* (Cambridge, MA: Harvard University Press).

Assmann, Jan (2002) 'Das kulturelle Gedächtnis', *Erwägen, Wissen, Ethik* 13:2, 239–47.

Assmann, Jan (2006) *Religion and Cultural Memory: Ten Studies*, trans. Rodney Livingstone, Cultural Memory in the Present (Stanford, CA: Stanford University Press).

Assmann, Jan (2008) 'Communicative and Cultural Memory', in Astrid Erll, Ansgar Nünning (eds.) and Sarah B. Young (coll.), *Cultural Memory Studies: An International and Interdisciplinary Handbook* (Berlin/New York: de Gruyter), 109–18.

Augé, Marc (2004 [1998]) *Oblivion* (Minneapolis: University of Minnesota Press).

Avelar, Idelber (1999) *The Untimely Present: Postdictatorial Latin American Fiction and the Task of Mourning* (Durham: Duke University Press).

Bakhtin, Mikhail M. (1981) *The Dialogic Imagination: Four Essays*, trans. Michael Holquist (Austin: University of Texas Press).

Bal, Mieke (2004) *Political Narratology*, Critical Concepts in Literary and Cultural Studies (London: Routledge).

Bal, Mieke, Jonathan Crewe and Leo Spitzer, (eds.) (1999) *Acts of Memory: Cultural Recall in the Present* (Hanover and London: University Press of New England).

Bangerter, Adrian (2002) 'Kollektives Erinnern als Prozess und Handlung', *Erwägen, Wissen, Ethik* 13: 190–92.

Banner, Gillian (2000) *Holocaust Literature: Schulz, Levi, Spiegelman and the Memory of the Offence* (London: Vallentine Mitchell).

Barnes, John A. (1990 [1947]) 'Postscript. Structural Amnesia' in J.A.B., *Models and Interpretations: Selected Essays* (Cambridge: Cambridge University Press), 52–3.

Baronian, Marie-Aude, Stephan Besser and Yolande Jansen (eds.) (2007) *Diaspora and Memory: Figures of Displacement in Contemporary Literature, Arts and Politics* (Amsterdam: Rodopi).

Barthes, Roland (1980) *La chambre claire: note sur la photographie* (Paris: Gallimard).

Bartlett, Frederic C. (1932) *Remembering. A Study in Experimental and Social Psychology* (Cambridge: Cambridge University Press).

Batteau, Jesseka (2009) 'Literary Icons and the Religious Past in the Netherlands: Jan Wolkers and Gerard Reve', in Astrid Erll and Ann Rigney (eds.), *Mediation, Remediation, and the Dynamics of Cultural Memory* (Berlin and New York: de Gruyter), 229–44.

Bauman, Zygmunt (1989) *Modernity and the Holocaust* (Ithaca, NY: Cornell University Press).

Becker, Annette (2003) *Maurice Halbwachs: un intellectuel en guerres mondiales 1914–1945* (Paris: Viénot).

Bell, Terry and Dumisa B. Ntsebeza (2001) *Unfinished Business: South Africa, Apartheid & Truth* (Cape Town: Redworks).

Ben-Amos, Dan and Liliane Weissberg (eds.) (1999) *Cultural Memory and the Construction of Identity* (Detroit: Wayne State University Press).

Benjamin, Walter (1999) *The Arcades Project*, trans. Howard Eiland and Kevin McLaughlin (Cambridge, MA: Belknap Press).

Ben-Ze'ev, Efrat, Ruth Ginio and Jay. M. Winter (eds.) (2010) *Shadows of War: A Social History of Silence in the Twentieth Century* (Cambridge: Cambridge University Press).

Berger, Peter L. and Thomas Luckmann (1966) *The Social Construction of Reality: A Treatise in the Sociology of Knowledge* (Garden City, NY: Doubleday).

Bergson, Henri (1988) *Matter and Memory* (New York: Zone Books).

Berliner, David C. (2005) 'The Abuses of Memory: Reflections on the Memory Boom in Anthropology', *Anthropological Quarterly*, 78:1, 197–211.

Berndt, Frauke (2005) 'Topikforschung', in Astrid Erll and Ansgar Nünning (ed.), *Gedächtniskonzepte der Literaturwissenschaft* (Berlin/New York: de Gruyter), 31–52.

Bigsby, C. W. E. (2006) *Remembering and Imagining the Holocaust: The Chain of Memory*, Cambridge Studies in Modern Theatre (Cambridge: Cambridge University Press).

Bijsterveld, Karin and José van Dijck (eds.) (2009) *Sound Souvenirs: Audio Technologies, Memory and Cultural Practices* (Amsterdam: Amsterdam University Press).

Birke, Dorothee (2008) *Memory's Fragile Power Crises of Memory, Identity and Narrative in Contemporary British Novels* (Trier: WVT).

Bithell, Caroline, (ed.) (2006) *The Past in Music*, special issue of *Ethnomusicology Forum*, 15:1.

Blanchard, Pascal and Isabelle Veyrat-Masson (eds.) (2008) *Les guerres de mémoires: La France et son histoire* (Paris: La découverte).

Blanchard, Pascal, Marc Ferro and Isabelle Veyrat-Masson (eds.) (2008) *Les Guerres de mémoires dans le monde*, Hermès 52 (Paris: CNRS).

Bloch, Marc (1925) 'Mémoire collective, tradition et coutume', *Revue de Synthèse Historique* 40: 73–83.

Bloom, Harold (1973) *The Anxiety of Influence: A Theory of Poetry* (New York: Oxford University Press).

Bloom, Harold (1975) *A Map of Misreading* (New York: Oxford University Press).

Bloom, Harold (1994) *The Western Canon: The Books and School of the Ages* (New York: Riverhead).

Bloxham, Donald and Dirk A. Moses (eds.) (2010) *The Oxford Handbook of Genocide Studies* (Oxford: Oxford University Press).

Blustein, Jeffrey (2008) *The Moral Demands of Memory* (Cambridge: Cambridge University Press).

Bodnar, John (1992) *Remaking America: Public Memory, Commemoration, and Patriotism in the 20th Century* (Princeton, NJ: University of Princeton Press).

Bolter, Jay David and Richard Grusin (eds.) (1999) *Remediation: Understanding New Media* (Cambridge, MA: MIT Press).

Borgolte, Michael (2002) 'Memoria. Bilan intermédiaire d'un projet de recherche sur le Moyen Age', in Jean-Claude Schmitt and Otto Gerhard Oexle (eds.), *Les tendances actuelles de l'histoire du Moyen Age en France et en Allemagne. Actes des colloques de Sèvres (1997) et Göttingen (1998)* (Paris: Publications de la Sorbonne), 53–69.

Bourke, Joanna (1999) *An Intimate History of Killing. Face-to-face Killing in Twentieth-Century Warfare* (London: Granta Books).

Bowker, Geoffrey C. (2005) *Memory Practices in the Sciences*, Inside Technology (Cambridge, MA: MIT Press).

Boyer, M.C. (1994) *The City of Collective Memory: Its Historical Imagery and Architectural Entertainments* (Cambridge, MA: MIT Press).

Boyer, Pascal and James V. Wertsch (eds.) (2009) *Memory in Mind and Culture* (New York: Cambridge University Press).

Boym, Svetlana (2001) *The Future of Nostalgia* (New York: Basic Books).

Bozzoli, Belinda and Mmantho Nkotsoe (1991) *Women of Phokeng: Consciousness, Life Strategy, and Migrancy in South Africa, 1900–1983* (Portsmouth, NH: Heinemann) Social History of Africa.

Braungart, Wolfgang (1996) *Ritual und Literatur* (Tübingen: Niemeyer).

Brockmeier, Jens (2001) 'Retrospective Teleology: From the End to the Beginning', in Jens Brockmeier and Donal Carbaugh (eds), *Narrative and Identity: Studies in Autobiography, Self and Culture* (Amsterdam/Philadelphia: John Benjamins), 247–82.

Brockmeier, Jens (2002) 'Introduction: Searching for Cultural Memory', *Narrative and Cultural Memory*, special issue of *Culture & Psychology*, 8:1, 5–14.

Brockmeier, Jens and Donal Carbaugh (eds.) (2001) *Narrative and Identity: Studies in Autobiography, Self and Culture* (Amsterdam: John Benjamins).

Broszat, Martin and Saul Friedländer (1990) 'A Controversy about the Historicization of National Socialism', in Peter Baldwin (ed.), *Reworking the Past: Hitler, the Holocaust, and the Historians' Controversy* (Boston: Beacon), 102–43.

Bruce, Darryl (1985) 'The How and Why of Ecological Memory', *Journal of Experimental Psychology*, 114, 75–90.

Bruner, Jerome (1991) 'The Narrative Construction of Reality', *Critical Inquiry*, 18, 1–21.

Buchinger, Kirstin, Claire Gantet and Jakob Vogel, (eds.) (2009) *Europäische Erinnerungsräume. Zirkulationen zwischen Frankreich, Deutschland und Europa* (Frankfurt: Campus Verlag).

Bueren, Truus van and Andrea van Leerdam (eds.) (2005) *Care for the Here and the Hereafter. Memoria, Art and Ritual in the Middle Ages* (Turnhout, Belgium: Brepols).

Burke, Peter (1989) 'History as Social Memory' in Thomas Butler (ed.) *Memory: History, Culture and the Mind* (New York: Blackwell), 97–113.

Buschmann, Nikolaus and Horst Carl (eds.) (2001) *Die Erfahrung des Krieges: Erfahrungsgeschichtliche Perspektiven von der Französischen Revolution bis zum Zweiten Weltkrieg* (Paderborn et al.: Schöningh).

Butzer, Günter (2000) 'Meditation' in Gerd Ueding et al. (eds.), *Historisches Wörterbuch der Rhetorik* (Tübingen: Niemeyer), 1016–23.

Byatt, A.S. and Harriet Harvey Wood (2008) *Memory: An Anthology* (London: Chatto & Windus).

Carey, James W. (1992 [1989]) *Communication As Culture: Essays on Media and Society* (New York: Routledge).

Carrier, Peter (2000) 'Places, Politics and the Archiving of Contemporary Memory in Pierre Nora's *Les Lieux de mémoire*', in Susannah Radstone (ed.), *Memory and Methodology* (Oxford: Berg), 37–58.

Carruthers, Mary J. (1990) *The Book of Memory: A Study of Memory in Medieval Culture* (Cambridge: Cambridge University Press).

Carruthers, Mary J. and Jan M. Ziolkowski (2002) *The Medieval Craft of Memory: An Anthology of Texts and Pictures* (Philadelphia: University of Pennsylvania Press).

Caruth, Cathy (1996) *Unclaimed Experience: Trauma, Narrative, and History* (Baltimore: Johns Hopkins University Press).

Casement, William (1996) *The Great Canon Controversy: The Battle of the Books in Higher Education* (New Brunswick: Transaction).

Cassirer, Ernst (1944) *An Essay on Man: An Introduction to a Philosophy of Human Culture* (New Haven and London: Yale University Press).

Chamberlain, Mary and Paul Richard Thompson (1998) *Narrative and Genre*, Routledge Studies in Memory and Narrative 1 (London: Routledge).

Clark, Noel K. and Geoffrey M. Stephenson (1995) 'Social Remembering: Individual and Collaborative Memory for Social Information', *Review of Social Psychology* 6, 127–60.

Clifford, James (1992) 'Travelling Cultures', in Lawrence Grossberg, Cary Nelson and Paul A. Treichler (eds.), *Cultural Studies* (New York: Routledge), 96–116.

Cohen-Pfister, Laurel and Dagmar Wienröder-Skinner (eds.) (2006) *Victims and Perpetrators, 1933–1945: (Re)Presenting the Past in Post-Unification Culture*, Interdisciplinary German Cultural Studies 2 (Berlin and New York: de Gruyter).

Cohen, Stanley (2000) *States of Denial: Knowing about Atrocities and Suffering* (Cambridge: Polity).

Cohn, Dorrit (1999) *The Distinction of Fiction* (Baltimore: Johns Hopkins University Press).

Cohn, Samuel K. (1992) *The Cult of Remembrance and the Black Death: Six Renaissance Cities in Central Italy* (Baltimore: Johns Hopkins University Press).

Confino, Alon (2008) 'Memory and the History of Mentalities', in Astrid Erll, Ansgar Nünning (eds.) and Sara B. Young (coll.), *Cultural Memory Studies: An International and Interdisciplinary Handbook* (Berlin/New York: de Gruyter), 77–84.

Confino, Alon (1997) 'Collective Memory and Cultural History: Problems of Method', *American Historical Review*, 102:5, 1386–403.

Confino, Alon (2006) *Germany as a Culture of Remembrance: Promises and Limits of Writing History* (Chapel Hill, NC: University of North Carolina Press).

Connerton, Paul (1989) *How Societies Remember* (Cambridge: Cambridge University Press).

Connerton, Paul (2009) *How Modernity Forgets* (Cambridge: Cambridge University Press).

Coombes, Annie E. (2003) *History After Apartheid: Visual Culture and Public Memory in a Democratic South Africa* (Durham: Duke University Press).

Cooper, F. and Brubaker, R. (2000) 'Beyond Identity', *Theory and Society*, 29, 1–47.

Crane, Susan A. (1997) 'Writing the Individual Back into Collective Memory', *American Historical Review*, 105:5, 1372–85.

Crane, Susan A. (2000) *Museums and Memory* (Stanford, CA: Stanford University Press) Cultural Sitings.

Crownshaw, Rick (2010) *The Afterlife of Holocaust Memory in Literature and Culture* (Basingstoke: Palgrave Macmillan).

Crownshaw, Rick (ed.) (2011) *Transcultural Memory*, special issue of *Parallax* (in press).

Cubitt, Geoffrey (2007) *History and Memory: Historical Approaches* (Manchester: Manchester University Press).

Curtius, Ernst Robert (1953) *European Literature and the Latin Middle Ages*, trans. Willard R. Trask (New York: Pantheon Books) Bollingen Series 36. Originally published as *Europäische Literatur und lateinisches Mittelalter* (Bern: A. Francke, 1948).

D'haen, Theo and Patricia Krüs (eds.) (2000) *Colonizer and Colonized*, Literature as Cultural Memory 2 (Amsterdam: Rodopi).

D'Hulst, Lieven and John Milton (eds.) (2000) *Reconstructing Cultural Memory*: *Translation, Scripts, Literacy*, Literature as Cultural Memory 7 (Amsterdam: Rodopi).

Damasio, Antonio R. (1994) *Descartes's Error: Emotion, Reason, and the Human Brain* (New York: Putnam).

Damrosch, David (2003) *What Is World Literature?* (Princeton, NJ: Princeton University Press).

den Boer, Pim and Willem Frijhoff (eds.) (1993). *Lieux de mémoire et identités nationales* (Amsterdam: Amsterdam University Press).

Derrida, Jacques (1995) 'Archive Fever: A Freudian Impression', trans. Eric Prenowitz, *Diacritics*, 25:2, 9–63. Originally published as *Mal d'Archive* (Paris: Editions Galilée).

Diers, Michael (1995) 'Warburg and the Warburgian Tradition of Cultural History', trans. Thomas Girst and Dorothea von Moltke, *New German Critique*, 65, 59–73.

Dijck, José van. (2007) *Mediated Memories in the Digital Age* (Stanford, CA: Stanford University Press) Cultural Memory in the Present.

Diner, Dan (1986) 'Negative Symbiose: Deutsche und Juden nach Auschwitz' in Dan Diner (ed.) *Ist der Nationalsozialismus Geschichte? Zu Historisierung und Historikerstreit* (Frankfurt am Main: Fischer), 185–97.

Diner, Dan and Gotthart Wunberg, (eds.) (2007) *Restitution and Memory: Material Restoration in Europe* (New York: Berghahn).

Donald, Merlin (1991) *Origins of the Modern Mind* (Cambridge, MA: Harvard University Press).

Draaisma, D. (2000) *Metaphors of Memory: A History of Ideas About the Mind* (Cambridge: Cambridge University Press).

Eakin, Paul John (1999) *How Our Lives Become Stories: Making Selves* (Ithaca, NY: Cornell University Press).

Easthope, Antony (1999) *Englishness and National Culture* (London and New York: Routledge).

Ebbinghaus, Hermann (1885) *Über das Gedächtnis* (Leipzig: Duncker & Humblot).

Echterhoff, Gerald and Martin Saar (eds.) (2002) *Kontexte und Kulturen des Erinnerns. Maurice Halbwachs und das Paradigma des kollektiven Gedächtnisses* (Konstanz: UVK).

Echterhoff, Gerald and Jürgen Straub (2003–2004) 'Narrative Psychologie: Facetten eines Forschungsprogramms', *Handlung, Kultur, Interpretation*, Part 1 (2003), 12:2, 317–42; Part 2 (2004), 13:1, 151–86.

Echterhoff, Gerald, E. Tory Higgins and Stephan Groll (2005) 'Attitudes and Social Cognition – Audience-Tuning Effects on Memory: The Role of Shared Reality', *Journal of Personality and Social Psychology*, 89:3, 257.

Echterhoff, Gerald (2004) 'Das Außen des Erinnerns: Was vermittelt individuelles und kollektives Gedächtnis?' in Astrid Erll and Ansgar Nünning (eds.), Hanne Birk, Birgit Neumann and Patrick Schmidt (coll.), *Medien des kollektiven Gedächtnisses: Konstruktivität – Historizität – Kulturspezifität* (Berlin and New York: de Gruyter), 61–82.

Eco, Umberto (1988) 'An *Ars Oblivionalis*? Forget it!', *Publications of the Modern Language Association of America*, 103:1, 254–61.

Eco, Umberto (1989) *The Open Work* (Cambridge, MA: Harvard University Press).

Edelman, Gerald M. and Guilio Tonomi, *A Universe of Consciousness: How Matter Becomes Imagination* (New York: Basic Books).

Eder, Klaus and Willfried Spohn (eds.) (2005) *Collective Memory and European Identity: The Effects of Integration and Enlargement* (Aldershot: Ashgate).

Edgerton, Gary R. and Peter C. Rollins (2001) *Television Histories: Shaping Collective Memory in the Media Age* (Lexington: University Press of Kentucky).

Edmunds, June and Bryan S. Turner (eds.) (2002) *Generations, Culture and Society* (Buckingham: Open University Press).

Ehlich, Konrad (1983) 'Text und sprachliches Handeln. Die Entstehung von Texten aus dem Bedürfnis nach Überlieferung', in Aleida Assmann, Jan Assmann and Christof Hardmeier (eds.), *Schrift und Gedächtnis*, Archäologie der literarischen Kommunikation (Munich: Fink) 1, 24–43.

Eliot, T. S. (1975) 'Tradition and the Individual Talent. [1919]', in Frank Kermode (ed.), *Selected Prose of T.S. Eliot* (London: Faber and Faber), 37–44.

Elster, Jon (2004) *Closing the Books: Transitional Justice in Historical Perspective* (Cambridge: Cambridge University Press).

Ender, Evelyne (2005) *Architexts of Memory: Literature, Science, and Autobiography* (Ann Arbor, MI: University of Michigan Press).

Erdfelder, Edgar (2002) 'Auf dem Wege zu einer interdisziplinär verwendbaren Systematik des Gedächtnisses?', *Erwägen, Wissen, Ethik*, 13, 197–200.

Erll, Astrid (2003) *Gedächtnisromane: Literatur über den Ersten Weltkrieg als Medium englischer und deutscher Erinnerungskulturen in den 1920er Jahren* (Trier: WVT).

Erll, Astrid (2004) 'Reading Literature as Collective Texts: German and English War Novels of the 1920s as Media of Cultural and Communicative Memory', in Christoph Bode, Sebastian Domsch and Hans Sauer (eds), *Anglistentag München 2003. Proceedings* (Trier: WVT), 335–53.

Erll, Astrid (2005) 'Cultural-Studies Approaches to Narrative', in David Herman, Manfred Jahn and Marie-Laure Ryan (eds.), *The Routledge Encyclopaedia of Narrative Theory* (London: Routledge), 88–93.

Erll, Astrid (2006) 'Re-writing as Re-visioning: Modes of Representing the "Indian Mutiny" in British Literature, 1857 to 2000', in Astrid Erll and Ann Rigney (eds.), *Literature and the Production of Cultural Memory*, special issue of *EJES (European Journal of English Studies)*, 10:2, 163–85.

Erll, Astrid (2007) *Prämediation – Remediation. Repräsentationen des indischen Aufstands in imperialen und post-kolonialen Medienkulturen (von 1857 bis zur Gegenwart)* (Trier: WVT).

Erll, Astrid (2009a) 'Narrative and Cultural Memory', in Sandra Heinen and Roy Sommer (eds.), *Narratology in the Age of Interdisciplinary Narrative Research* (Berlin and New York: de Gruyter), 212–27.

Erll, Astrid (2009b) 'Remembering across Time, Space and Cultures: Premediation, Remediation and the "Indian Mutiny"', in Astrid Erll and Ann Rigney (eds.), *Mediation, Remediation, and the Dynamics of Cultural Memory* (Berlin and New York: de Gruyter), 109–38.

Erll, Astrid (2010) 'Regional Integration and (Trans)Cultural Memory', *Asia-Europe Journal*, 8:3, 305–15.

Erll, Astrid (2011) 'Travelling Memory', in Rick Crownshaw (ed.) *Transcultural Memory*, special issue of *Parallax*, 61.

Erll, Astrid and Ansgar Nünning (eds.) (2004) *Medien des kollektiven Gedächtnisses. Konstruktivität, Historizität, Kulturspezifität* (Berlin and New York: de Gruyter).

Erll, Astrid and Ansgar Nünning (eds.) (2005a) *Gedächtniskonzepte der Literaturwissenschaft*, Media and Cultural Memory/Medien und kulturelle Erinnerung 2 (Berlin and New York: de Gruyter).

Erll, Astrid and Ansgar Nünning (2005b) 'Where Literature and Memory Meet: Towards a Systematic Approach to the Concepts of Memory in Literary Studies', in Herbert Grabes (ed.), *Literature, Literary History, and Cultural Memory* (Tübingen: Narr) REAL: Yearbook of Research in English and American Literature 21, 265–98.

Erll, Astrid and Ansgar Nünning (eds.) (2008) *Cultural Memory Studies: An International and Interdisciplinary Handbook* Sara B. Young (coll.) (Berlin and New York: de Gruyter).

Erll, Astrid and Ann Rigney (eds.) (2006) *Literature and the Production of Cultural Memory*, special issue of *EJES (European Journal of English Studies)*, 10:2.

Erll, Astrid and Ann Rigney (eds.) (2009) *Mediation, Remediation, and the Dynamics of Cultural Memory*, Media and Cultural Memory/Medien und kulturelle Erinnerung 10 (Berlin and New York: de Gruyter).

Erll, Astrid and Stephanie Wodianka (eds.) (2008) *Film und kulturelle Erinnerung: Plurimediale Konstellationen*, Media and Cultural Memory/Medien und kulturelle Erinnerung 9 (Berlin and New York: de Gruyter).

Ernst, Wolfgang (2004) 'The Archive as Metaphor', *Open*, 7, 46–52.

Ernst, Wolfgang (2007) *Das Gesetz des Gedächtnisses: Medien und Archive am Ende (des 20. Jahrhunderts* (Berlin: Kulturverlag Kadmos).

Erstantrag des Sonderforschungsbereichs 434 'Erinnerungskulturen'. Gießen 1996, 9–23.

Esposito, Elena (2002) *Soziales Vergessen: Formen und Medien des Gedächtnisses der Gesellschaft* (Frankfurt am Main: Suhrkamp).

Esposito, Elena (2008) 'Social Forgetting: A Systems-Theory Approach', in Astrid Erll and Ansgar Nünning (eds.), Sara B. Young (coll.), *Cultural Memory Studies: An International and Interdisciplinary Handbook* (Berlin/New York: de Gruyter), 181–90.

Eyerman, Ron (2001) *Cultural Trauma: Slavery and the Formation of African American Identity* (Cambridge: Cambridge University Press).

Ezell, Margaret J. (1993) *Writing Women's Literary History* (Baltimore: Johns Hopkins University Press).

Fara, Patricia and Karalyn Patterson (eds.) (1998) *Memory: The Darwin College Lectures* (Cambridge: Cambridge University Press).

Favorini, Attilio (2008) *Memory in Play: From Aeschylus to Sam Shepard* (New York: Palgrave Macmillan).

Felman, Shoshana (1995) 'Education and Crisis, or the Vicissitudes of Teaching', in Cathy Caruth (ed.), *Trauma: Explorations in Memory* (Baltimore: Johns Hopkins University Press), 13–60.

Fentress, James and Chris Wickham (1992) *Social Memory* (Oxford: Blackwell).

Ferretti, Silvia (1989) *Cassirer, Panofsky, and Warburg: Symbol, Art, and History* (New Haven: Yale University Press).

Field, Sean, Renate Meyer and Felicity Swanson (eds.) (2007) *Imagining the City Memories and Cultures in Cape Town* (Cape Town: HSRC Press).

Figes, Orlando (2007) *The Whisperers: Private Life in Stalin's Russia* (London: Allen Lane).

Finkelstein, Norman G. (2000) *The Holocaust Industry: Reflection on the Exploitation of Jewish Suffering* (London: Verso).

Fish, Stanley (1980) *Is There a Text in This Class? The Authority of Interpretive Communities* (Cambridge, MA: Harvard University Press).

Fivush, Robyn (2008) 'Sociocultural Perspectives on Autobiographical Memory', in Mary Courage and Nelson Cowan (eds.), *The Development of Memory in Infancy and Childhood* (New York: Psychology Press), 283–302.

Fludernik, Monika (1996) *Towards a 'Natural' Narratology* (London: Routledge).

Foucault, Michel (1975) 'Film and Popular Memory: An Interview with Michel Foucault. 1974', *Radical Philosophy*, 11, 24–9.

Foucault, Michel (2002 [1972]) *The Archaeology of Knowledge*, trans. A. M. Sheridan Smith (London: Routledge Classics). Originally published as *L'archéologie du savoir* (Paris: Gallimard, 1969).

Foucault, Michel (1977) 'Nietzsche, Genealogy, History', in Donald F. Bouchard (ed.), *Language, Counter-Memory, Practice: Selected Essays and Interviews* (Ithaca, NY: Cornell University Press).

François, Etienne and Hagen Schulze (eds.) (2001) *Deutsche Erinnerungsorte*, 3 vols (Munich: Beck).

Frey, Indra Sengupta, (ed.) (2009) *Memory, History, and Colonialism: Engaging with Pierre Nora in Colonial and Postcolonial Contexts* (London: German Historical Institute) Bulletin of the German Historical Institute London.

Friedländer, Saul (ed.) (1992) *Probing the Limits of Representation: Nazism and the 'Final Solution'* (Cambridge, MA: Harvard University Press).

Friedländer, Saul (1993) *Memory, History, and the Extermination of the Jews of Europe* (Bloomington: Indiana University Press).

Friedman, Saul S. (1993) *Holocaust Literature: A Handbook of Critical, Historical, and Literary Writings* (Westport, CT: Greenwood Press).

Friese, Heidrun (ed.) (2002) *Identities: Time, Difference, and Boundaries*, Making Sense of History 2 (New York: Berghahn Books).

Frisch, Michael H. (1990) *A Shared Authority: Essays on the Craft and Meaning of Oral and Public History*, SUNY Series in Oral and Public History (Albany: State University of New York Press).

Fritzsche, Peter (2004) *Stranded in the Present: Modern Time and the Melancholy of History* (Cambridge, MA: Harvard University Press).

Frye, Northrop (1957) *Anatomy of Criticism: Four Essays* (Princeton, NJ and Oxford: Princeton University Press).

Funkenstein, Amos (1989) 'Collective Memory and Historical Consciousness', *History and Memory: Studies in the Representation of the Past*, 1:1, 5–26.

Fussell, Paul (1975) *The Great War and Modern Memory* (Oxford: Oxford University Press).

Garde-Hansen, Joanne Andrew Hoskins and Anna Reading (eds.) (2009) *Save As – Digital Memories* (Basingstoke: Palgrave Macmillan).

Geary, Patrick (1994) *Phantoms of Remembrance. Memory and Oblivion at the End of the First Millennium* (Princeton, NJ: Princeton University Press).

Gedi, Noa and Yigal Elam (1996) 'Collective Memory – What Is It?', *History & Memory: Studies in Representation of the Past*, 8:1, 30–50.

Gibbons, Joan (2007) *Contemporary Art and Memory: Images of Recollection and Remembrance* (London: I.B. Tauris).

Gillis, John R. (ed.) (1994) *Commemorations: The Politics of National Identity* (Princeton, NJ: Princeton University Press).

Gilroy, Paul (2004) *After Empire: Multiculture or Postcolonial Melancholia* (Abingdon: Routledge).

Gilroy, Paul (1993) *The Black Atlantic: Modernity and Double Consciousness* (Cambridge, MA: Harvard University Press).

Ginzburg, Carlo (1989 [1966]) 'From Aby Warburg to E. H. Gombrich: A Problem of Method', in *Clues, Myths, and the Historical Method* (Baltimore: Johns Hopkins University Press), 17–59.

Gitelman, Lisa (2006) *Always Already New: Media, History and the Data of Culture* (Cambridge, MA: MIT Press).

Gombrich, Ernst H. (1986 [1970]) *Aby Warburg: An Intellectual Biography* (Chicago: University of Chicago Press).

Goodman, Nelson (1978) *Ways of Worldmaking* (Indianapolis, IN: Hackett).

Goody, Jack (2000) *The Power of the Written Tradition* (Washington: Smithsonian Institution Press).

Gordon, Bruce and Peter Marshall (eds.) (2000) *The Place of the Dead: Death and Remembrance in Late Medieval and Early Modern Europe* (Cambridge: Cambridge University Press).

Grabes, Herbert (ed.) (2001) *Literary History/Cultural History: Forcefields and Tensions*, REAL: Yearbook of Research in English and American Literature 17 (Tübingen: Narr).

Grainge, Paul (ed.) (2003) *Memory and Popular Film*, Inside Popular Film (Manchester: Manchester University Press).

Graumann, Carl F. (1997) 'Zur Ökologie des Gedächtnisses', in Gerd Lüer and Uta Lass (eds.), *Erinnern und Behalten: Wege zur Erforschung des menschlichen Gedächtnisses* (Göttingen: Vandenhoeck & Ruprecht), 269–86.

Green, Anna (2004) 'Individual Remembering and "Collective Memory": Theoretical Presuppositions and Contemporary Debates', *Oral History*, 32:2, 35–44.

Greenwald, Anthony G. (1980) 'The Totalitarian Ego: Fabrication and Revision of Personal History', *American Psychologist*, 35, 603–18.

Gross, David (2000) *Lost Time: On Remembering and Forgetting in Late Modern Culture / David Gross* (Amherst: University of Massachusetts).

Grusin, Richard A. (2004) 'Premediation', *Criticism*, 46:1, 17–39.

Grusin, Richard A. (2010) *Premediation: Affect and Mediality After 9/11* (Basingstoke: Palgrave Macmillan).

Guha, Ranajit (1983) *Elementary Aspects of Peasant Insurgency in Colonial India* (Delhi: Oxford University Press).

Habermas, Jürgen (1988) 'Concerning the Public Use of History', *New German Critique* 44, 40–50.

Halbwachs, Maurice (1941) *La topographie légendaire des Évangiles en Terre Sainte: étude de mémoire collective* (Paris: Presses universitaires de France).

Halbwachs, Maurice (1980) *The Collective Memory*, trans. Francis J. Ditter, Jr. and Vida Yazdi Ditter (New York: Harper & Row).

Halbwachs, Maurice (1992) *On Collective Memory*, trans. Lewis Coser (Chicago: University of Chicago Press).

Halbwachs, Maurice (1994 [1925]) *Les cadres sociaux de la mémoire*, ed. by Gérard Namer (Paris: Albin Michel).

Halbwachs, Maurice (1997 [1950]) *La mémoire collective*, ed. by Gérard Namer (Paris: Albin Michel).

Hall, Stuart (1980 [1973]) 'Encoding/Decoding', in Stuart Hall, Dorothy Hobson, Andrew Lowe and Paul Willis (eds.), *Culture, Media, Language: Working Papers in Cultural Studies, 1972–79* (London: Hutchinson), 128–38.

Hamburger, Käte (1957) *The Logic of Literature*, trans. Marilynn J. Rose (Bloomington: Indiana University Press).

Hamilton, Carolyn et al. (eds.) (2002) *Refiguring the Archive* (Cape Town: David Philip).

Hamilton, Paula and Linda Shopes (eds.) (2008) *Oral History and Public Memories* (Philadelphia, PA: Temple University Press).

Hancock, Mary E. (2008) *The Politics of Heritage from Madras to Chennai* (Bloomington, IN: Indiana University Press).

Harth, Dietrich (ed.) (1991) *Die Erfindung des Gedächtnisses* (Frankfurt am Main: Keip).

Harth, Dietrich (2008) 'The Invention of Cultural Memory', in Astrid Erll and Ansgar Nünning, (eds.) and Sara B. Young (coll.), *Cultural Memory Studies. An International and Interdisciplinary Handbook* (Berlin and New York: de Gruyter), 85–96.

Hartley, John, Martin Montgomery, Ellie Rennie and Marc Brennan (2002) *Communication, Cultural and Media Studies: The Key Concepts* (London: Routledge).

Hartman, Geoffrey H. (ed.) (1994) *Holocaust Remembrance: The Shapes of Memory* (Oxford: Blackwell).

Havelock, Eric A. (1986) *The Muse Learns to Write: Reflections on Orality and Literacy from Antiquity to the Present* (New Haven and London: Yale University Press).

Haverkamp Anselm and Renate Lachmann (eds.) (1993) *Memoria: Vergessen und Erinnern* (Munich: Fink) Poetik und Hermeneutik 15.

Haverkamp, Anselm and Renate Lachmann (1991) *Raum—Bild—Schrift: Studien zur Mnemotechnik* (Frankfurt am Main: Suhrkamp).

Healy, Chris (2008) *Forgetting Aborigines* (Sydney: University of New South Wales Press).

Hebel, Udo J. (ed.) (2009) *Transnational American Memories* (Berlin and New York: de Gruyter).

Hebel, Udo (ed.) (2003) *Sites of Memory in American Literatures and Cultures* (Heidelberg: Winter).

Hervieu-Léger, Danièle (2000) *Religion as a Chain of Memory* (Cambridge: Polity Press) Originally published as *La religion pour mémoire*, Sciences humaines et religions (Paris: Éditions du Cerf, 1993).

Herzfeld, Michael (1991) *A Place in History: Social and Monumental Time in a Cretan Town*, Princeton Studies in Culture/Power/History (Princeton, NJ: Princeton University Press).

Hewison, Robert (1987) *The Heritage Industry: Britain in a Climate of Decline* (London: Methuen).

Hirsch, Marianne (1997) *Family Frames: Photography, Narrative, and Postmemory* (Cambridge, MA: Harvard University Press).

Hirsch, Marianne and Valerie Smith (eds.) (2002) *Gender and Cultural Memory*, special issue of *Signs*, 28:1.

Hobsbawm, Eric and Terence Ranger (eds.) (2005 [1983]) *The Invention of Tradition* (Cambridge: Cambridge University Press).

Hodgkin, Katharine and Susannah Radstone (eds.) (2006) *Memory Cultures: Memory, Subjectivity and Recognition*, Memory and Narrative Series (New Brunswick, NJ: Transaction). Originally published as *Regimes of Memory* (London: Routledge, 2003).

Hofmeyr, Isabel (1994) *We Spend Our Years As a Tale That Is Told: Oral Historical Narrative in a South African Chiefdom* (Portsmouth, NH: Heinemann) Social History of Africa.

Hofmeyr, Isabel (2004) *The Portable Bunyan: A Transnational History of the Pilgrim's Progress*, Translation/Transnation (Princeton, NJ: Princeton University Press).

Holsey, Bayo (2008) *Routes of Remembrance: Refashioning the Slave Trade in Ghana* (Chicago: University of Chicago Press).

Horstkotte, Silke (2009) *Nachbilder: Fotografie und Gedächtnis in der deutschen Gegenwartsliteratur* (Cologne: Böhlau).

Hoskins, Andrew and John Sutton (gen. eds.) (2009) *Memory Studies* (London: Palgrave Macmillan).

Hoskins, Andrew and Ben O'Loughlin (eds.) (2007) *Television and Terror: Conflicting Times and the Crisis of News Discourse* (Basingstoke: Palgrave Macmillan).

Hoskins, Andrew (gen. ed.) (2008–) *Memory Studies*. Available online at http://mss.sagepub.com.

Hoskins, Andrew (2001) 'New Memory: Mediating History', *Historical Journal of Film, Radio and Television*, 21:4, 333–46.

Hoskins, Andrew (2004) *Televising War: From Vietnam to Iraq* (London: Continuum).

Hoskins, Andrew (2009) 'The Mediatization of Memory: Media and the End of Collective Memory' (manuscript).

Houts, Elisabeth van (ed.) (2001) *Medieval Memories. Men, Women and the Past, 700–1300* (Harlow, UK: Longman).

Hungerford, Amy (2003) *The Holocaust of Texts: Genocide, Literature, and Personification* (Chicago: University of Chicago Press).

Hutton, Patrick (1987) 'The Art of Memory Reconceived: From Rhetoric to Psychoanalysis', *Journal of the History of Ideas*, 48:3, 371–92.

Hutton, Patrick (1993) *History as an Art of Memory* (Hanover, NH: University Press of New England).

Huyssen, Andreas (1995) *Twilight Memories: Marking Time in a Culture of Amnesia* (New York: Routledge).

Huyssen, Andreas (2003) *Present Pasts: Urban Palimpsests and the Politics of Memory* (Stanford, CA: Stanford University Press).

Hynes, Samuel L. (1997) *The Soldiers' Tale: Bearing Witness to Modern War* (New York: Penguin).

Ibsch, Elrud (ed.), Douwe Fokkema and Joachim von der Thüsen (coll.) (2000) *The Conscience of Humankind: Literature and Traumatic Experiences*, Literature as Cultural Memory 3 (Amsterdam: Rodopi).

Innis, Harold A. (1951) *The Bias of Communication* (Toronto: University of Toronto Press).

Irwin-Zarecka, Iwona (1994) *Frames of Remembrance: The Dynamics of Collective Memory* (New Brunswick, NJ: Transaction Publishers).

Iser, Wolfgang (1993) *The Fictive and the Imaginary: Charting Literary Anthropology* (Baltimore: John Hopkins University Press). Originally published as *Das Fiktive und das Imaginäre. Perspektiven literarischer Anthropologie* (Frankfurt am Main: Suhkamp, 1991).

Isnenghi, Mario (ed.) (1987–97) *I luoghi della memoria*, 3 vols (Rome: Laterza).

Jameson, Fredric (1981) *The Political Unconscious: Narrative as Socially Symbolic Act* (London: Methuen).

Jay, Gregory S. (1997) *American Literature and the Culture Wars* (Ithaca, NY: Cornell University Press).

Jehn, Peter (ed.) (1972) *Toposforschung: Eine Dokumentation* (Frankfurt am Main: Athenäum).

Jimerson, Randall C. (2009) *Archives Power: Memory, Accountability, and Social Justice* (Chicago: Society of American Archivists).

Jing, Jun (1996) *The Temple of Memories: History, Power, and Morality in a Chinese Village* (Stanford, CA: Stanford University Press).

Judt, Tony (1998) 'A la Recherche du Temps Perdu. Review of Pierre Nora, The Realms of Memory: The Construction of the French Past', *New York Review of Books*, 3, 51–8.

Kaes, Anton (1992) *From Hitler to Heimat: The Return of History as Film* (Cambridge, MA: Harvard University Press).

Kammen, Michael (1991) *The Mystic Chords of Memory: The Transformation of Tradition in American Culture* (New York).

Kammen, Michael (1995) 'Review of *Frames of Remembrance: The Dynamics of Collective Memory* by Iwona Irwin-Zarecka', *History and Theory*, 34:3, 245–62.

Kansteiner, Wulf (2002) 'Finding Meaning in Memory: A Methodological Critique of Collective Memory Studies', *History and Theory*, 41:2, 179–97.

Kansteiner, Wulf (2004) 'Genealogy of a Category Mistake: A Critical Intellectual History of the Cultural Trauma Metaphor', *Rethinking History*, 8, 193–221.

Kansteiner, Wulf (2006) *In Pursuit of German Memory: History, Television, and Politics After Auschwitz* (Athens, OH: Ohio University Press).

Kansteiner, Wulf and Harald Weilnböck (2008) 'Against the Concept of Cultural Trauma', in Astrid Erll and Ansgar Nünning (eds.) and Sara B. Young (coll.), *Cultural Memory Studies: An International and Interdisciplinary Handbook* (Berlin/ New York: de Gruyter), 229–40.

Kany, Roland (1987) *Mnemosyne als Programm: Geschichte, Erinnerung und die Andacht zum Unbedeutenden im Werk von Usener, Warburg und Benjamin* (Tübingen: Niemeyer).

Keppler, Angela (1994) *Tischgespräche: Über Formen kommunikativer Vergemeinschaftung in Familien* (Frankfurt am Main: Suhrkamp).

Kitch, Carolyn L. (2000) *Pages from the Past: History and Memory in American Magazines* (Chapel Hill: University of North Carolina Press).

Klein, Kerwin Lee (2000) 'On the Emergence of Memory in Historical Discourse', *Representations*, 69, 127–50.

Kmec, Sonja, Michael Margue, Benoît Majerus and Pit Péporté (eds.) (2008) *Lieux de mémoire au Luxembourg: usages du passé et construction nationale = Erinnerungsorte in Luxembourg: Umgang mit der Vergangenheit und Konstruktion der Nation* (Luxembourg: Éditions Saint-Paul).

Kolboom, Ingo and Sabine Alice Grzonka, (eds.) (2002) *Gedächtnisorte im anderen Amerika: Tradition und Moderne in Québec/Lieux de mémoire dans l'autre Amérique: Tradition et modernité au Québec* (Heidelberg: Synchron).

Koselleck, Reinhart (2004) *Futures Past: On the Semantics of Historical Time* trans. by Keith Tribe (New York: Columbia University Press). Originally published as *Vergangene Zukunft: Zur Semantik geschichtlicher Zeiten* (Frankfurt am Main: Suhrkamp, 1979).

Krämer, Sybille (ed.) (1998) *Medien – Computer – Realität. Wirklichkeitsvorstellungen und Neue Medien* (Frankfurt am Main: Suhrkamp).

Kristeva, Julia (1969) *Séméiôtiké: Recherches pour une sémanalyse* (Paris: Éditions du Seuil).

Kritz, Neil J. (ed.) (1995) *Transitional Justice: How Emerging Democracies Reckon with Former Regimes*, 3 vols (Washington, DC: United States Institute of Peace Press).

Kuhn, Annette and Kirsten Emiko McAllister (eds.) (2006) *Locating Memory: Photographic Acts* (New York: Berghahn Books) Remapping Cultural History 4.

Kunstforum International 128 (1994). Special issue *Zwischen Erinnern und Vergessen*.

Kurasawa, Fuyuki (2009) 'A Message in a Bottle', *Theory, Culture and Society*, 26:1, 92–111.

LaCapra, Dominick (1996) *Representing the Holocaust: History, Theory, Trauma* (London: Cornell University Press).

LaCapra, Dominick (1998) *History and Memory after Auschwitz* (Ithaca, NY: Cornell University Press).

Lachmann, Renate (1993) 'Kultursemiotischer Prospekt' in Anselm Haverkamp and Renate Lachmann (eds.) *Memoria: Vergessen und Erinnern, Poetik und Hermeneutik* 15 (Munich: Fink), xvii–xxvii.

Lachmann, Renate (1997) *Memory and Literature: Intertextuality in Russian Modernism*, Theory and History of Literature 87 (Minneapolis: University of Minnesota Press). Originally published as *Gedächtnis und Literatur: Intertextualität in der russischen Moderne* (Frankfurt am Main: Suhrkamp, 1990).

Lakoff, George and Mark Johnson (1980) *Metaphors We Live By* (Chicago: University of Chicago Press).

Lakoff, George and Mark Johnson (1999) *Philosophy in the Flesh: The Embodied Mind and Its Challenge to Western Thought* (New York: Basic Books).

Landsberg, Alison (2004) *Prosthetic Memory: The Transformation of American Remembrance in the Age of Mass Culture* (New York: Columbia University Press).

Landy, Marcia (2001) *The Historical Film: History and Memory in Media*, Rutgers Depth of Field Series (New Brunswick, NJ: Rutgers University Press).

Langer, Lawrence (1991) *Holocaust Testimonies: The Ruins of Memory* (New Haven, CT: Yale University Press).

Lanser, Susan Sniader (1992) *Fictions of Authority: Women Writers and Narrative Voice* (Ithaca, NY: Cornell University Press).

Laqueur, Walter (ed.) (2004) *Collective Memory*, special issue of *Journal of Contemporary History* 39:4.

Laub, Dori and Shoshana Felman (eds.) (1992) *Testimony: Crises of Witnessing in Literature, Pychoanalysis and History* (New York: Routledge).

LeDoux, Joseph E. (1996) *The Emotional Brain: The Mysterious Underpinnings of Emotional Life* (New York: Simon & Schuster).

Le Goff, Jacques (1992) *History and Memory*, trans. Steven Rendall and Elizabeth Claman (New York: Columbia University Press). Originally published as *Storia e memoria* (Turin: Giulio Einaudi 1977ff.).

Le Rider, Jacques, Moritz Czàky and Monika Sommer (eds.) (2002) *Transnationale Gedächtnisorte in Zentraleuropa* (Innsbruck: Studien-Verlag).

Le Rider, Jacques (2008) 'Mitteleuropa as a *lieu de mémoire*', in Astrid Erll and Ansgar Nünning (eds.) and Sara B. Young (coll.), *Cultural Memory Studies: An International and Interdisciplinary Handbook* (Berlin/New York: de Gruyter), 37–46.

Legg, Stephen (2005) 'Contesting and Surviving Memory: Space, Nation, and Nostalgia in *Les Lieux de Mémoire*', *Environment and Planning D: Society & Space*, 23:4, 481–504.

Lejeune, Philippe (1975) *Le pacte autobiographique* (Paris: Seuil).

Lennon, J.J. and Malcolm Foley (eds.) (2000) *Dark Tourism* (London: Continuum).

Levy, Daniel and Natan Sznaider (2006) *The Holocaust and Memory in the Global Age*, trans. Assenka Oksiloff, Politics, History, and Social Change (Philadelphia: Temple University Press). Originally published as *Erinnerung im globalen Zeitalter: Der Holocaust* (Frankfurt am Main: Suhrkamp, 2001).

Lewis, Bernard (1975) *History: Remembered, Recovered, Invented* (Princeton, NJ: Princeton University Press).

Leydesdorff, Selma, Luisa Passerini and Paul Thompson (eds.) (1996) *Gender and Memory* (Oxford: Oxford University Press).

Leys, Ruth (2000) *Trauma: A Genealogy* (Chicago: University of Chicago Press).

Link, Jürgen (1988) 'Literaturanalyse als Interdiskursanalyse. Am Beispiel des Ursprungs literarischer Symbolik in der Kollektivsymbolik', in Jürgen Fohrmann and Harro Müller (eds.), *Diskurstheorien und Literaturwissenschaft* (Frankfurt am Main: Suhrkamp), 284–307.

Lipsitz, George (1990) *Time Passages: Collective Memory and American Popular Culture* (Minneapolis: University of Minnesota Press).

Loftus, Elizabeth and Katherine Ketcham (1994) *The Myth of Repressed Memory: False Memories and Allegations of Sexual Abuse* (New York: St Martin's Press).

Löschnigg, Martin (1999) '"The Prismatic Hues of Memory...": Autobiographische Modellierung und die Rhetorik der Erinnerung in Dickens' *David Copperfield*', *Poetica*, 31:1–2, 175–200.

Loshitzky, Yosefa (ed.) (1997) *Spielberg's Holocaust: Critical Perspectives on Schindler's List* (Bloomington: Indiana University Press).

Lotman, Jurij M. (1990) *Universe of the Mind: A Semiotic Theory of Culture* (Bloomington: Indiana University Press).

Lotman, Jurij M. and Boris A. Uspensky (1978 [1971]) 'On the Semiotic Mechanism of Culture', trans. George Mihaychuk, *Soviet Semiotics and Criticism: An Anthology*, special issue of *New Literary History* 9:2: 211–32. Originally published as 'O semiotitcheskom mechanizme kul'tury' *Trudy po znakoym sistemam* 5 (1971).

Lowenthal, David (1985) *The Past Is a Foreign Country* (Cambridge: Cambridge University Press).

Lowenthal, David (1996) *Possessed by the Past: The Heritage Crusade and the Spoils of History* (New York: Free Press).

Luhmann, Niklas (1997) 'Gedächtnis' in N.L., *Die Gesellschaft der Gesellschaft* (Frankfurt am Main: Suhrkamp), 576–94.

Luhmann, Niklas (2000a) *Art as a Social System*, transl. Eva M. Knodt (Stanford, CA: Stanford University Press).

Luhmann, Niklas (2000b) *The Reality of the Mass Media* (Stanford, CA: Stanford University Press) Cultural Memory in the Present.

Macdonald, Sharon (2009) *Difficult Heritage: Negotiating the Nazi Past in Nuremberg and Beyond*. (Milton Park, Abingdon, Oxon: Routledge).

Mack, Arien and William Hirst, (eds.) (2008) *Collective Memory and Collective Identity*, special issue of *Social Research: An International Quarterly of the Social Sciences*, 75:1.

Mageo, Jeannette Marie (2001) *Cultural Memory: Reconfiguring History and Identity in the Postcolonial Pacific* (Honolulu: University of Hawai'i Press).

Manier, David and William Hirst (2008) 'A Cognitive Taxonomy of Collective Memories', in Astrid Erll, Ansgar Nünning (eds.) and Sara B. Young (coll.), *Cultural Memory Studies: An International and Interdisciplinary Handbook* (Berlin/New York: de Gruyter), 253–62.

Mannheim, Karl (1952) 'The Sociological Problem of Generations [1928/9]' in Paul Kecskemeti (ed.) *Karl Mannheim: Essays on the Sociology of Knowledge* (London: Routledge), 276–320.

Marcel, Jean-Christophe and Laurent Mucchielli (2008) 'Maurice Halbwachs' *mémoire collective*', in Astrid Erll, Ansgar Nünning (eds.) and Sara B. Young (coll.), *Cultural Memory Studies: An International and Interdisciplinary Handbook* (Berlin/New York: de Gruyter), 141–50.

Margalit, Avishai (2002) *The Ethics of Memory* (Cambridge, MA: Harvard University Press).

Markowitsch, Hans J. (2002) *Dem Gedächtnis auf der Spur: Vom Erinnern und Vergessen* (Darmstadt: Primus).

Markowitsch, Hans J. (2008) 'Cultural Memory and the Neurosciences', in Astrid Erll, Ansgar Nünning (eds.) and Sara B. Young (coll.), *Cultural Memory Studies: An International and Interdisciplinary Handbook* (Berlin/New York: de Gruyter), 275–83.

Markowitsch, Hans J. and Lars-Göran Nilsson (1999) *Cognitive Neuroscience of Memory* (Seattle: Hogrefe & Huber).

Matsuda, Matt K. (1996) *The Memory of the Modern* (New York: Oxford University Press).

Maturana, Humberto R., and Francisco J. Varela (1992) *The Tree of Knowledge: The Biological Roots of Human Understanding* (Boston: Shambhala).

McClelland, James I. (2000) 'Connectionist Models of Memory', in Endel Tulving and Fergus I.M. Craik (eds.), *The Oxford Handbook of Memory* (New York: Oxford University Press), 583–96.

McKee, Robert (1997) *Story: Substance, Structure, Style and the Principles of Screenwriting* (New York: Regan Books).

McLuhan, Marshall (1964) *Understanding Media: The Extensions of Man* (London: Routledge & K. Paul).

Megill, Allan (1998) 'History, Memory, Identity', *History of the Human Sciences*, 11:3, 37–62.

Michaud, Philippe-Alain (2004) *Aby Warburg and the Image in Motion* (New York: Zone Books).

Middleton, David and Steven D. Brown (2005) *The Social Psychology of Experience: Studies in Remembering and Forgetting* (London: Sage).

Middleton, David and Derek Edwards (eds.) (1990) *Collective Remembering* (London: Sage).

Middleton, Peter and Tim Woods (2000) *Literatures of Memory: History, Time, and Space in Postwar Writing* (Manchester: Manchester University Press).

Mihkelev, Anneli and Benedikts Kalnačs (eds.) (2007) *We Have Something in Common: the Baltic Memory* (Tallinn: Under and Tuglas Literature Centre of the Estonian Academy of Sciences).

Misztal, Barbara A. (2003) *Theories of Social Remembering* (Maidenhead: Open University Press).

Morris-Suzuki, Tessa (2005) *The Past Within Us: Media, Memory, History* (London: Verso).

Mosse, George L. (1990) *Fallen Soldiers: Reshaping the Memory of the World Wars* (New York: Oxford University Press).

Nalbantian, Suzanne (2003) *Memory in Literature: From Rousseau to Neuroscience* (Basingstoke: Palgrave Macmillan).

Namer, Gérard (2000) *Halbwachs et la mémoire sociale* (Paris: L'Harmattan).

Neisser, Ulric and E. Winograd (1989) *Remembering Reconsidered: Ecological and Traditional Approaches to the Study of Memory* (Cambridge: Cambridge University Press).

Neisser, Ulric (ed.) (1982) *Memory Observed: Remembering in Natural Contexts* (New York: Freeman).

Neisser, Ulric (1967) *Cognitive Psychology* (New York: Appleton-Century-Crofts).

Neubauer, John and Helga Geyer-Ryan (eds.) (2000) *Gendered Memories* (Amsterdam: Rodopi) Literature as Cultural Memory 4.

Neumann, Birgit (2008) 'The Literary Representation of Memory', in Astrid Erll, Ansgar Nünning (eds.) and Sara B. Young (coll.), *Cultural Memory Studies: An International and Interdisciplinary Handbook* (Berlin/New York: de Gruyter), 333–44.

Niethammer, Lutz (1995) 'Diesseits des "Floating Gap": Das kollektive Gedächtnis und die Konstruktion von Identität im wissenschaftlichen Diskurs', in Kristin Platt and Mihran Dabag (eds.), *Generation und Gedächtnis: Erinnerungen und kollektive Identitäten* (Opladen: Leske und Budrich), 25–50.

Niethammer, Lutz (2000) *Kollektive Identität: Heimliche Quellen einer unheimlichen Konjunktur* (Reinbek: Rowohlt).

Nora, Pierre (1978) 'Mémoire collective', in Jacques Le Goff, Roger Chartier and Jacques Revel (eds.), *La nouvelle histoire* (Paris: Retz), 398–401.

Nora, Pierre (ed.) (1984–1992) *Les lieux de mémoire I. La République* (Paris: Gallimard, 1984); *Les lieux de mémoire II. La Nation* (Paris: Gallimard, 1986); *Les lieux de mémoire III. Les France* (Paris: Gallimard, 1992).

Nora, Pierre (ed.) (1996–1998) *Realms of Memory*, rev. and abr. trans. of *Les lieux de mémoire* by Arthur Goldhammer, ed. by Lawrence D. Kritzman, Conflicts and Divisions 1 (New York: Columbia University Press).

Nora, Pierre (2001) 'Memoirs of Men of State. From Commynes to de Gaulle', in P.N. (ed.), *Rethinking France. Vol. 1: Les Lieux De Mémoire: The State* (Chicago: University of Chicago Press), 401–51.

Nora, Pierre (1989) 'Between Memory and History: Les Lieux de Mémoire' trans. by Marc Roudebush, *Representations*, 26, 7–25.

Nora, Pierre (1996) 'General Introduction: Between Memory and History' in *Realms of Memory: Rethinking the French Past*, rev. and abr. trans. of *Les lieux de mémoire* by Arthur Goldhammer, ed. by Lawrence D. Kritzman, Conflicts and Divisions 1 (New York: Columbia University Press), 1–20.

Nora, Pierre (2001–2010) *Rethinking France. Les Lieux De Memoire*, 4 vols, trans. by David P. Jordan (Chicago: University of Chicago Press).

Nora, Pierre (2006) 'La France est malade de sa mémoire', interview by Jacques Buob and Alain Franchon, *Le Monde 2* (105): 6–9.

Nünning, Ansgar (1997) 'Crossing Borders and Blurring Genres: Towards a Typology and Poetics of Postmodernist Historical Fiction in England since the 1960s', *European Journal of English Studies*, 1:2, 217–38.

Nünning, Ansgar (2002) 'Metaphors the British Thought, Felt and Ruled by, or: Modest Proposals for Historicizing Cognitive Metaphor Theory and for Exploring Metaphors of Empire as a Cultural Phenomenon', in Marion Gymnich, Ansgar Nünning and Vera Nünning (eds.), *Literature and Linguistics: Approaches, Models, and Applications. Studies in Honour of Jon Erickson* (Trier: WVT), 101–27.

Nünning, Ansgar, Marion Gymnich and Roy Sommer (eds.) (2006) *Literature and Memory: Theoretical Paradigms—Genres—Functions* (Tübingen: Narr).

Nuttall, Sarah (2009) *Entanglement: Literary and Cultural Reflections on Post Apartheid* (Johannesburg: Wits University Press).

Nuttall, Sarah and Carli Coetzee (eds.) (1998) *Negotiating the Past: The Making of Memory in South Africa* (Cape Town: Oxford University Press).

Oexle, Otto Gerhard (1994) 'Memoria in der Gesellschaft und in der Kultur des Mittelalters', in Joachim Heinzle (ed.), *Modernes Mittelalter: Neue Bilder einer populären Epoche* (Frankfurt am Main: Insel-Verlag), 297–323.

Oexle, Otto Gerhard (ed.) (1995) *Memoria als Kultur* (Göttingen: Vandenhoeck & Ruprecht).

Olick, Jeffrey K. (1999a) 'Collective Memory. The Two Cultures', *Sociological Theory*, 17:3, 333–48.

Olick, Jeffrey K. (1999b) 'Genre Memories and Memory Genres: A Dialogical Analysis of May 8, 1945 Commemorations in the Federal Republic of Germany', *American Sociological Review*, 64:3, 381–402.

Olick, Jeffrey K. (ed.) (2003) *States of Memory: Continuities, Conflicts, and Transformations in National Retrospection* (Durham: Duke University Press) Politics, History, and Culture.

Olick, Jeffrey K. (2005) *In the House of the Hangman: The Agonies of German Defeat, 1943–1949* (Chicago: University of Chicago Press).

Olick, Jeffrey K. (2007) *The Politics of Regret: On Collective Memory and Historical Responsibility* (London: Routledge).

Olick, Jeffrey K. (2008) 'From Collective Memory to the Sociology of Mnemonic Practices and Products', in Astrid Erll, Ansgar Nünning (eds.) and Sara B. Young (coll.), *Cultural Memory Studies: An International and Interdisciplinary Handbook* (Berlin/New York: de Gruyter), 151–62.

Olick, Jeffrey K. and Joyce Robbins (1998) 'Social Memory Studies: From "Collective Memory" to the Historical Sociology of Mnemonic Practices', *Annual Review of Sociology*, 24, 105–40.

Olick, Jeffrey K., Vered Vinitzky-Seroussi and Daniel Levy (eds.) (2010) *The Collective Memory Reader* (Oxford: Oxford University Press).

Ong, Walter J. (1982) *Orality and Literacy. The Technologizing of the Word* (London: Methuen).

Parry, Milman (1971) *The Making of Homeric Verse: The Collected Papers of M. Parry* (Oxford: Clarendon Press).

Passerini, Luisa (1987) *Fascism in Popular Memory: The Cultural Experience of the Turin Working Class* (Cambridge: Cambridge University Press).

Passerini, Luisa (ed.) (2005 [1992]) *Memory & Totalitarianism* (New Brunswick: Transaction Publishers) Memory and Narrative.

Passerini, Luisa (2009) *Love and the Idea of Europe* (New York: Berghahn Books).

Peitsch, Helmut, Charles Burdett and Claire Gorrara (1999) *European Memories of the Second World War* (New York: Berghahn Books).

Pennebaker, James W, Darío Páez and Bernard Rimé (eds.) (1997) *Collective Memory of Political Events: Social Psychological Perspectives* (Mahwah, NJ: Lawrence Erlbaum Associates).

Perks, Robert and Alistair Thomson (eds.) (1998) *The Oral History Reader* (London: Routledge).

Pethes, Nicolas and Jens Ruchatz (eds.) (2001) *Gedächtnis und Erinnerung: Ein interdisziplinäres Lexikon* (Reinbek: Rowohlt).

Phillips, Kendall R. (ed.) (2004) *Framing Public Memory* (Tuscaloosa: University of Alabama Press) Rhetoric, Culture, and Social Critique.

Plate, Liedeke (2010) *Transforming Memories in Contemporary Women's Rewriting* (New York: Palgrave Macmillan).

Plate, Liedeke and Anneke Smelik (eds.) (2009) *Technologies of Memory in the Arts* (Houndmills, Basingstoke: Palgrave Macmillan).

Polkinghorne, Donald E. (2005) 'Narrative Psychology and Historical Consciousness: Relationships and Perspectives', in Jürgen Straub (ed.), *Narration, Identity, and Historical Consciousness* (New York: Berghahn Books) Making Sense of History 3, 3–22.

Pollmann, Judith. www.earlymodernmemory.org.

Pollock, Della (2005) *Remembering: Oral History Performance* (New York: Palgrave Macmillan) Palgrave Studies in Oral History.

Portelli, Alessandro (1990) *The Death of Luigi Trastulli, and Other Stories: Form and Meaning in Oral History*, SUNY Series in Oral and Public History (Albany, NY: State University of New York Press).

Posner, Roland and Dagmar Schmauks (2004[1998]) 'Kultursemiotik', in Ansgar Nünning (ed.), *Metzler Lexikon Literatur- und Kulturtheorie: Ansätze – Personen – Grundbegriffe* (Stuttgart: Metzler), 364–5.

Posner, Roland (2004) *Basic Tasks of Cultural Semiotics* (Essen: LAUD).

Prinz, Kirsten (2004) '"Mochte doch keiner was davon hören" – Günter Grass' *Im Krebsgang* und das Feuilleton im Kontext aktueller Erinnerungsverhandlungen', in Astrid Erll and Ansgar Nünning (eds.), *Kulturspezifität Medien des kollektiven Gedächtnisses. Konstruktivität, Historizität* (Berlin/New York: Walter de Gruyter), 179–94.

Radstone, Susannah (ed.) (2000) *Memory and Methodology* (Oxford and New York: Berg).

Radstone, Susannah (2008) 'Memory Studies: For and Against', *Memory Studies*, 1:1, 31–9.

Radstone, Susannah and Kate Hodgkin (eds.) (2003) *Contested Pasts: The Politics of Memory* (London: Routledge).

Radstone, Susannah and Katharine Hodgkin (eds.) (2006) *Memory Cultures: Memory, Subjectivity, and Recognition*. Originally published as *Regimes of Memory* (New Brunswick, NJ: Transaction Publishers, 2003).

Radstone, Susannah and Bill Schwarz (eds.) (2010) *Memory: Histories, Theories, Debates* (New York: Fordham University Press).

Reading, Anna (2002) *The Social Inheritance of the Holocaust: Gender, Culture, and Memory* (New York: Palgrave Macmillan).

Reading, Anna (2009) 'The Globytal: Towards an Understanding of Globalised Memories in the Digital Age', in Anna Maj and Daniel Riha (eds.), *Digital Memories: Exploring Critical Issues* (Oxford: Inter-Disciplinary Press), 31–40.

Reinik, Wesssel and Jeroen Stumpel (eds.) (1999) *Memory and Oblivion: Proceedings of the XXIXth International Congress of the History of Art* (Boston: Kluwer Academic Publishers).

Reulecke, Jürgen (2008) 'Generation/Generationality, Generativity, and Memory', in Astrid Erll, Ansgar Nünning (eds.) and Sara B. Young (coll.), *Cultural Memory Studies: An International and Interdisciplinary Handbook* (Berlin/New York: de Gruyter), 119–26.

Ricoeur, Paul (1984, 1985, 1988) *Time and Narrative*, 3 vols (Chicago and London: University of Chicago Press). Originally published as *Temps et récit*, 3 vols (Paris: Seuil, 1983, 1984, 1985).

Ricoeur, Paul (2004) *Memory, History, Forgetting* (Chicago: University of Chicago Press). Originally published as *La mémoire, l'histoire, l'oubli* (Paris: Seuil, 2000).

Rieger, Stefan (1997) *Speichern, Merken: Die künstlichen Intelligenzen des Barock* (Munich: Fink).

Rigney, Ann (2004) 'Portable Monuments: Literature, Cultural Memory, and the Case of Jeanie Deans', *Poetics Today*, 25:2, 361–96.

Rigney, Ann (2005) 'Plenitude, Scarcity and the Circulation of Cultural Memory', *Journal of European Studies*, 35:1, 11–28.

Rigney, Ann (2008a) 'The Dynamics of Remembrance: Texts between Monumentality and Morphing', in Astrid Erll, Ansgar Nünning (eds.) and Sara B. Young (coll.), *Cultural Memory Studies. An International and Interdisciplinary Handbook* (Berlin/New York: de Gruyter), 345–53.

Rigney, Ann (2008b) 'Divided Pasts: a Premature Memorial and the Dynamics of Cultural Remembrance', *Memory Studies* 1:1, 99–113.

Rigney, Ann (2010) 'The Many Afterlives of Ivanhoe', in Karin, Tilmans, Frank van Vree and J.M. Winter (eds.), *Performing the Past: Memory, History and Identity in Modern Europe* (Amsterdam: Amsterdam University Press), 207–34.

Rigney, Ann (2011) *Portable Monuments: The Afterlives of Walter Scott's Novels* (in press).

Ritchie, Donald A. (ed.) (2010) *The Oxford Handbook of Oral History* (New York: Oxford University Press).

Roediger, Henry L., Yadin Dudai and Susan M. Fitzpatrick (eds.) (2007) *Science of Memory: Concepts* (Oxford: Oxford University Press).

Roesler, Frank, Charan Ranganath, Brigitte Roeder and Rainer H. Klume (eds.) (2009) *Neuroimaging of Human Memory: Linking Cognitive Processes to Neural Systems* (Oxford: Oxford University Press).

Rose, Els (2009) *Ritual Memory: The Apocryphal Acts and Liturgical Commemoration in the Early Medieval West (c. 500–1215)* (Leiden: Brill).

Rosenfeld, Gavriel D. (2009) 'A Looming Crash or a Soft Landing? Forecasting the Future of the Memory "Industry"', *Journal of Modern History*, 81:1, 122–58.

Rosenstone, Robert A. (ed.) (1995) *Visions of the Past: The Challenge of Film to Our Idea of History* (Cambridge, MA: Harvard University Press).

Rossington, Michael, Anne Whitehead and Linda R. Anderson (eds.) (2007) *Theories of Memory: A Reader* (Baltimore: Johns Hopkins University Press).

Roth, Michael S. (1995) *The Ironist's Cage: Memory, Trauma, and the Construction of History* (New York: Columbia University Press).

Rothberg, Michael (2009) *Multidirectional Memory: Remembering the Holocaust in the Age of Decolonization* (Stanford, CA: Stanford University Press) Cultural Memory in the Present.

Rousso, Henry (1991) *The Vichy Syndrome: History and Memory in France Since 1944.* (Cambridge, MA: Harvard University Press). Originally published as *Le Syndrome de Vichy 1944 à nos jours* (Paris: Le Seuil, 1987).

Rubin, David (ed.) (1996) *Remembering our Past: Studies in Autobiographical Memory* (New York: Cambridge University Press).

Ruchatz, Jens (2008) 'The Photograph as Externalization and Trace', in Astrid Erll, Ansgar Nünning (eds.) and Sara B. Young (coll.), *Cultural Memory Studies: An International and Interdisciplinary Handbook* (Berlin/New York: de Gruyter), 367–78.

Rumelhart, David E. (1975) 'Notes on a Schema for Stories', in David LaBerge and Jay Samuels (eds.), *Representation and Understanding: Studies in Cognitive Science* (New York: Academic Press), 211–36.

Rupp, Jan (2010) *Genre and Cultural Memory in Black British Literature* (Trier: WVT).

Rüsen, Jörn (2005) *History: Narration, Interpretation, Orientation* (Oxford: Berghahn Books).

Ryan, Marie-Laure (2004) *Narrative Across Media: The Languages of Storytelling* (Lincoln: University of Nebraska Press).

Saltzman, Lisa (2006) *Making Memory Matter: Strategies of Remembrance in Contemporary Art* (Chicago: University of Chicago Press).

Samuel, Raphael (1994) *Theatres of Memory* (London: Verso).

Samuel, Raphael and Paul R. Thompson (eds.) (1990) *The Myths We Live By*, History Workshop Series (London: Routledge).

Sandl, Marcus (2005) 'Historizität der Erinnerung/Reflexivität des Historischen: Die Herausforderung der Geschichtswissenschaft durch die kulturwissen-schaftliche Gedächtnisforschung', in Günter Oesterle (ed.), *Erinnerung, Gedächtnis, Wissen: Grundzüge einer kulturwissenschaftlichen Gedächtnisforschung* (Göttingen: Vandenhoeck & Ruprecht), 89–119.

Saunders, Max (2008) 'Life-Writing, Cultural Memory, and Literary Studies', in Astrid Erll, Ansgar Nünning (eds.) and Sara B. Young (coll.), *Cultural Memory Studies: An International and Interdisciplinary Handbook* (Berlin and New York: de Gruyter), 321–32.

Schacter, Daniel L. (ed.) (1995) *Memory Distortion: How Minds, Brains, and Societies Reconstruct the Past* (Cambridge, MA: Harvard University Press).

Schacter, Daniel (1996) *Searching for Memory: The Brain, the Mind, and the Past* (New York: Basic Books).

Schacter, Daniel L., Anthony D. Wagner and Randy L. Buckner (2000) 'Memory Systems of 1999', in Endel Tulving and Fergus I.M. Craik (eds.), *The Oxford Handbook of Memory* (New York: Oxford University Press), 627–43.

Schank, Roger C. and Robert P. Abelson (1995) 'Knowledge and Memory: The Real Story', in Robert S. Wyer (ed.), *Knowledge and Memory: Advances in Social Cognition* (Hillsdale, NJ: Erlbaum), 1–85.

Schmidt, Siegfried J. (1992) 'Conventions and Literary Systems', in Mette Hjort (ed.), *Rules and Conventions: Literature, Philosophy, Social Theory* (Baltimore and London: Johns Hopkins University Press), 215–49.

Schmidt, Siegfried J. (2000) *Kalte Faszination: Medien, Kultur, Wissenschaft in der Mediengesellschaft* (Weilerswist: Velbrück).

Schmidt, Siegfried J. (2008) 'Memory and Remembrance. A Constructivist Approach', in Astrid Erll and Ansgar Nünning (eds.) and Sara B. Young (coll.), *Cultural Memory Studies. An International and Interdisciplinary Handbook* (Berlin and New York: de Gruyter), 191–202.

Schönpflug, Wolfgang (2002) 'Grammatik des Erinnerns', *Erwägen, Wissen, Ethik*, 13, 222–5.

Schooler, Jonathan W. and Eric Eich (2000) 'Memory for Emotional Events', in Endel Tulving and Fergus I.M. Craik (eds.), *The Oxford Handbook of Memory* (New York: Oxford University Press), 379–92.

Schudson, Michael (1992) *Watergate in American Memory: How We Remember, Forget, and Reconstruct the Past* (New York: Basic Books).

Schuman, Howard and Jacqueline Scott (1989) 'Generations and Collective Memory', *American Sociological Review*, 54:3, 359–81.

Schwartz, Barry (2008) *Abraham Lincoln in the Post-Heroic Era: History and Memory in Late Twentieth-Century America* (Chicago: University of Chicago Press).

Schwenkel, Christina (2006) 'Recombinant History: Transnational Practices of Memory and Knowledge Production in Contemporary Vietnam', *Cultural Anthropology* 21:1, 3–30.

Seel, Martin (1998) 'Medien der Realität und Realität der Medien' in Sybille Krämer (ed.) *Medien – Computer – Realität. Wirklichkeitsvorstellungen und Neue Medien* (Frankfurt am Main: Suhrkamp), 244–68.

Seixo, Maria Alziro (ed.) (2000) *Travel Writing and Cultural Memory* (Amsterdam: Rodopi).

Semon, Richard (1921) *The Mneme*. Transl. by Richard Wolfgang, Literature as Cultural Memory 9 (London: Allen & Unwin). Originally published as *Die Mneme als erhaltendes Prinzip im Wechsel des organischen Geschehens* (Leipzig: Engelmann, 1904).

Sen, Amartya Kumar (2006) *Identity and Violence: The Illusion of Destiny. Issues of Our Time* (New York: W.W. Norton & Co).

Shandler, Jeffrey (1999) *While America Watches: Televising the Holocaust* (New York: Oxford University Press).

Shannon, Claude Elwood and Warren Weaver (1949) *The Mathematical Theory of Communication* (Urbana: University of Illinois Press).

Shaw, Christopher and Malcolm Chase, (eds.) (1989) *The Imagined Past: History and Nostalgia* (Manchester et al.: Manchester University Press).

Shriver, Donald, Jr. (1995) *An Ethic for Enemies: Forgiveness in Politics* (Oxford: Oxford University Press).

Singh, Amritjit, Joseph T. Skerrett and Robert E. Hogan, (eds.) (1996) *Memory and Cultural Politics: New Approaches to American Ethnic Literatures* (Boston: Northeastern University Press).

Sinz, Rainer (1979) *Neurobiologie und Gedächtnis* (Stuttgart: Gustav Fischer).

Smith, Bruce J. (1985) *Politics & Remembrance: Republican Themes in Machiavelli, Burke, and Tocqueville*, Studies in Moral, Political, and Legal Philosophy (Princeton, NJ: Princeton University Press).

Smith, Grover Cleveland (1996) *T. S. Eliot and the Use of Memory* (Lewisburg: Bucknell University Press).

Smith, Laurajane and Natsuko Akagawa (2009) *Intangible Heritage* (London: Routledge).

Smith, Richard Cándida (ed.) (2006) *Text & Image: Art and the Performance of Memory* (New Brunswick, NJ: Transaction Publishers).

Sobchack, Vivian Carol (ed.) (1996) *The Persistence of History: Cinema, Television, and the Modern Event*, AFI Film Readers (New York: Routledge).

Sollors, Werner (1988) 'First Generation, Second Generation, Third Generation ...: The Cultural Construction of Descent', in *Beyond Ethnicity: Consent and Descent in American Culture* (New York: Oxford University Press), 208–36.

Sommer, Roy (2000) 'Funktionsgeschichten: Überlegungen zur Verwendung des Funktionsbegriffs in der Literaturwissenschaft und Anregungen zu seiner terminologischen Differenzierung', *Literaturwissenschaftliches Jahrbuch*, 41, 319–41.

Sontag, Susan (2004[2003]) *Regarding the Pain of Others* (London: Penguin).

Sørensen, Marie L. S. and John Carman, (eds.) (2009) *Heritage Studies: Methods and Approaches* (London: Routledge).

Stoler, Ann Laura (2008) *Along the Archival Grain: Thinking Through Colonial Ontologies* (Princeton, NJ: Princeton University Press).

Straub, Jürgen (2002) 'Personal and Collective Identity: A Conceptual Analysis', trans. Anthony Nassar, in Heidrun Friese (ed.), *Identities: Time, Difference and Boundaries* (New York: Berghahn), 56–76.

Straub, Jürgen (ed.) (2005) *Narration, Identity, and Historical Consciousness* Making Sense of History 3 (New York: Berghahn Books). Originally published as *Erzählung, Identität und historisches Bewußtsein: Die psychologische Konstruktion von Zeit und Geschichte* (Frankfurt am Main: Suhrkamp, 1998).

Sturken, Marita (1997) *Tangled Memories: The Vietnam War, the AIDS Epidemic, and the Politics of Remembering* (Berkeley: University of California Press).

Sturken, Marita (2007) *Tourists of History: Memory, Kitsch, and Consumerism from Oklahoma City to Ground Zero* (Durham: Duke University Press).

Suleiman, Susan Rubin (2006) *Crises of Memory and the Second World War* (Cambridge, MA: Harvard University Press).

Sutton, David (2001) *Remembrance of Repasts: An Anthropology of Food and Memory* (New York/Oxford: Berg).

Sutton, John (1998) *Philosophy and Memory Traces: Descartes to Connectionism* (Cambridge: Cambridge University Press).

Sutton, John (2006) *Memory, Embodied Cognition, and the Extended Mind* (Abingdon: Routledge).

Tai, Hue-Tam Ho (2001a) 'Remembered Realms. Pierre Nora and French National Memory' *American Historical Review*, 106:3, 906–22.

Tai, Hue-Tam Ho (ed.) (2001b) *The Country of Memory: Remaking the Past in Late Socialist Vietnam* (Berkeley: University of California Press).

Taithe, Bertrand (1999) 'Monuments aux morts? Reading Nora's *Realms of Memory* and Samuel's *Theatres of Memory*', *History of the Human Sciences*, 12:2, 123–39.

Tavuchis, Nicholas (1991) *Mea Culpa: A Sociology of Apology and Reconciliation* (Stanford, CA: Stanford University Press).

Taylor, Diana (2003) *The Archive and the Repertoire: Performing Cultural Memory in the Americas* (Durham: Duke University Press).

Terdiman, Richard (1993) *Present Past: Modernity and the Memory Crisis* (Ithaca, NY: Cornell University Press).

Thompson, E.P. (1963) *The Making of the English Working Class* (London: Victor Gollancz).

Thompson, Paul (1978) *The Voice of the Past* (Oxford: Oxford University Press).

Thrift, Nigel (2004) 'Remembering the Technological Unconscious by Foregrounding Knowledges of Position', *Environment and Planning D: Society and Space*, 22:1, 175–90.

Tollebeek, Jo, Geert Buelens et al. (eds.) (2008) *België, een parcours van herinnering* (Amsterdam: Bakker).

Tomasello, Michael (1999) *The Cultural Origins of Human Cognition* (Cambridge, MA: Harvard University Press).

Tulving, Endel (1983) *Elements of Episodic Memory*, Oxford Psychology Series 2 (Oxford: Oxford University Press).

Tulving, Endel and Fergus I. M. Craik (eds.) (2000) *The Oxford Handbook of Memory* (New York: Oxford University Press).

Tulving, Endel and Hans-J. Markowitsch (1998) 'Episodic and Declarative Memory: Role of the Hippocampus', *Hippocampus*, 8, 198–204.

Tunbridge, J. E. and G. J. Ashworth (1996) *Dissonant Heritage: The Management of the Past As a Resource in Conflict* (Chichester: John Wiley).

Turner, Mark (1996) *The Literary Mind* (New York: Oxford University Press).

van Alphen, Ernst (1999) 'Symptoms of Discursivity: Experience, Memory and Trauma', in Mieke Bal, Jonathan Crewe and Leo Spitzer (eds.), *Acts of Memory: Cultural Recall in the Present* (Hanover, NH and London: University Press of New England), 24–38.

van der Knaap, Ewout (ed.) (2006) *Uncovering the Holocaust: The International Reception of Night and Fog* (London: Wallflower).

van Gorp, Hendrik and Ulla Musarra-Schroeder, (eds.) (2000) *Genres as Repositories of Cultural Memory* (Amsterdam: Rodopi) Literature as Cultural Memory 5.

Vansina, Jan (1985) *Oral Tradition as History* (Madison WI: University of Wisconsin Press).

Vansina, Jan (1965) *Oral Tradition: A Study in Historical Methodology* (London: Routledge & Kegan Paul). Originally published as *De la tradition orale. Essai de méthode historique* (Tervuren: Musée Royal de l'Afrique Centrale, 1961).

Vervliet, Raymond and Annemarie Estor (eds.) (2000) *Methods for the Study of Literature as Cultural Memory* Literature as Cultural Memory 6 (Amsterdam: Rodopi).

Vromen, Suzanne (1975) 'The Sociology of Maurice Halbwachs' (unpublished PhD Thesis, New York University).

Vygotskij, Lev Semenovic (1978) *Mind in Society*, ed. by Michael Cole et al. (Cambridge, MA: Harvard University Press).

Wägenbaur, Thomas (ed.) (1998) *The Poetics of Memory* (Tübingen: Stauffenburg).

Warburg, Aby (1979) *Ausgewählte Schriften und Würdigungen*, ed. by Dieter Wuttke (Baden-Baden: Koerner).

Warburg, Aby (1993) *Bildersammlung zur Geschichte von Sternglaube und Sternkunde im Hamburger Planetarium*, ed. by Uwe Fleckner, Robert Galitz, Claudia Naber and Herwart Nöldeke (Hamburg: Dölling und Galitz).

Warburg, Aby (1998ff) *Gesammelte Schriften: Studienausgabe*, ed. by Horst Bredekamp, Michael Diers, Kurt W. Forster, Nicholas Mann, Salvatore Settis and Martin Warnke (Berlin: Akademie-Verlag).

Warburg, Aby (1999) *The Renewal of Pagan Antiquity: Contributions to the Cultural History of the European Renaissance* (Los Angeles: Getty Research Institute for the History of Art and the Humanities) Texts and Documents.

Warburg, Aby (2000) *Der Bilderatlas Mnemosyne*, ed. by Martin Warnke and Claudia Brink (coll.) (Berlin: Akademie-Verlag).

Wardrip-Fruin, Noah and Nick Montfort (eds.) (2003) *The New Media Reader* (Cambridge, MA: MIT Press).

Weigel, Sigrid (2002) '"Generation" as a Symbolic Form: On the Genealogical Discourse of Memory Since 1945', *The Germanic Review*, 77:4, 264.

Weiner, Brian A. (2005) *Sins of the Parents: The Politics of National Apologies in the United States* (Philadelphia: Temple University Press) Politics, History, and Social Change.

Weinrich, Harald (1964) 'Typen der Gedächtnismetaphorik', *Archiv für Begriffsgeschichte*, 9, 23–6.

Weinrich, Harald (1976) *Sprache in Texten* (Stuttgart: Klett).

Weinrich, Harald (2004) *Lethe: The Art and Critique of Forgetting* (Ithaca: Cornell University Press). Originally published as *Lethe: Kunst und Kritik des Vergessens* (Munich: Beck, 1997).

Welzer, Harald (ed.) (2001) *Das soziale Gedächtnis: Geschichte, Erinnerung, Tradierung* (Hamburg: Hamburger Edition).

Welzer, Harald (ed.) (2007) *Der Krieg der Erinnerung: Holocaust, Kollaboration und Widerstand im europäischen Gedächtnis* (Frankfurt am Main: Fischer).

Welzer, Harald (2010) 'Re-Narrations: How Pasts Change in Conversational Remembering', *Memory Studies*, 3:1, 5–17.

Welzer, Harald (2002) *Das kommunikative Gedächtnis: Eine Theorie der Erinnerung* (Munich: Beck).

Welzer, Harald (2008) 'Communicative Memory', in Astrid Erll, Ansgar Nünning (eds.) and Sara B. Young (coll.), *Cultural Memory Studies: An International and Interdisciplinary Handbook* (Berlin/New York: de Gruyter), 285–98.

Welzer, Harald and Hans J. Markowitsch (2001) 'Umrisse einer interdisziplinären Gedächtnisforschung', *Psychologische Rundschau*, 52, 205–14.

Welzer, Harald, Sabine Moller and Karoline Tschuggnall (2002) *'Opa war kein Nazi': Nationalsozialismus und Holocaust im Familiengedächtnis* (Frankfurt am Main: Fischer).

Wenzel, Jennifer (2009) *Bulletproof: Afterlives of Anticolonial Prophecy in South Africa and Beyond* (Chicago: The University of Chicago Press).

Werbner, Richard (ed.) (1998) *Memory and the Postcolony: African Anthropology and the Critique of Power* (London: Zed Books).

Wertsch, James V. (2002) *Voices of Collective Remembering* (Cambridge: Cambridge University Press).

Wesseling, Henk, (gen. ed.) (2005–06) *Plaatsen van Herinnering*, 4 vols, ed. by Wim Blockmans, Herman Pleij, Maarten Prak, Marita Mathijsen, Jan Bank and Wim van den Doel (Amsterdam: Bakker).

Wettengl, Kurt (ed.) (2000) *Das Gedächtnis der Kunst: Geschichte und Erinnerung in der Kunst der Gegenwart* (Ostfildern-Ruit: Hatje Cantz).

Wheeler, Mark A. (2000) 'Episodic Memory and Autonoetic Awareness', in Endel Tulving and Fergus I.M. Craik (eds.), *The Oxford Handbook of Memory* (New York: Oxford University Press), 597–608.

White, Hayden (1973) *Metahistory: The Historical Imagination in Nineteenth-Century Europe* (Baltimore: Johns Hopkins University Press).

Whitehead, Anne (2009) *Memory*, The New Critical Idiom (London: Routledge).

Williams, Linda M. and Victoria L. Banyard (1999) *Trauma and Memory* (Thousand Oaks, CA: Sage).

Wilson, Janelle L. (2005) *Nostalgia: Sanctuary of Meaning* (Lewisburg: Bucknell University Press).

Winter, Jay (1995) *Sites of Memory, Sites of Mourning: The Great War in European Cultural History* (Cambridge: Cambridge University Press).

Winter, Jay and Emmanuel Sivan (eds.) (1999) *War and Remembrance in the Twentieth Century* (Cambridge: Cambridge University Press).

Wischermann, Clemens (ed.) (1996) *Die Legitimität der Erinnerung und die Geschichtswissenschaft* (Stuttgart: Franz Steiner).

Witz, Leslie (2003) *Apartheid's Festival: Contesting South Africa's National Pasts* (Bloomington, IN: Indiana University Press) African Systems of Thought.

Wohl, Robert (1979) *The Generation of 1914* (Cambridge, MA: Harvard University Press).

Wood, Nancy (1999) *Vectors of Memory: Legacies of Trauma in Postwar Europe* (Oxford: Berg).

Woodfield, Richard (ed.) (2001) *Art History as Cultural History: Warburg's Projects: Critical Voices in Art, Theory and Culture* (Amsterdam: G+B Arts International).

Wright, Patrick (2009 [1985]) *On Living in an Old Country: The National Past in Contemporary Britain* (Oxford/New York: Oxford University Press).

Yates, Frances (1966) *The Art of Memory* (London: Routledge).

Yerushalmi, Yosef Hayim (1996 [1982]) *Zakhor: Jewish Memory and Jewish History* (Seattle: University of Washington Press).

Yoneyama, Lisa (1999) *Hiroshima Traces: Time, Space, and the Dialectics of Memory*, Twentieth-century Japan 10 (Berkeley: University of California Press).

Young, James E. (1988) *Writing and Rewriting the Holocaust: Narrative and Consequences of Interpretation* (Bloomington, IN: Indiana University Press).

Young, James E. (1993) *The Texture of Memory: Holocaust Memorials and Meaning* (New Haven, CT: Yale University Press).

Zelizer, Barbie (1995) 'Reading the Past against the Grain: The Shape of Memory Studies', *Critical Studies in Mass Communication*, 12, 214–39.

Zelizer, Barbie (1998) *Remembering to Forget: Holocaust Memory Through the Camera's Eye* (Chicago: University of Chicago Press).

Zelizer, Barbie (ed.) (2001) *Visual Culture and the Holocaust*, Rutgers Depth of Field Studies (New Brunswick, NJ: Rutgers University Press).

Zemon Davis, Natalie and Randolph Starn (eds.) (1989) *Memory and Counter-Memory*, special issue of *Representations*, 26.

Zerubavel, Eviatar (1996) 'Social Memories: Steps to a Sociology of the Past', *Qualitative Sociology*, 19:2, 283–99.

Zerubavel, Eviatar (2003) *Time Maps: Collective Memory and the Social Shape of the Past* (Chicago: University of Chicago Press).

Index